HOW TO
Cook a Crocodile

a memoir with recipes

Bonnie Lee Black

A PEACE CORPS WRITERS BOOK

An imprint of Peace Corps Worldwide.

FIRST PEACE CORPS WRITERS EDITION, SEPTEMBER 2010.

HOW TO COOK A CROCODILE: A MEMOIR WITH RECIPES.

ISBN: 978-1-935925-00-2

The author gratefully acknowledges the following publications,
in which portions of this book first appeared: "Sans Frigo" (as "The Fridge Factor")
in the anthology *The Great Adventure: Volunteer Stories of Life Overseas*
(U.S. Peace Corps, '97, '99, '02), "Machete Lessons" in the anthology
A Matter of Choice: Twenty-Five People Who Transformed Their Lives (Seal Press, '04),
"The Martha Stewart of Gabon" in *Peace Corps Writers* online ('04), "Pain Americain" in
Alimentum, a culinary literary journal (winter '08), "Dîner" in *globalhuman online journal* ('08),
and "Weather Report" in *Under the Sun* literary magazine ('10).

Also by Bonnie Lee Black: *Somewhere Child,* Viking Press ('81).

Cover photo: Boys in pirogues on the Ogooué River in Lastoursville, Gabon, 1997, by Martha Cooper
Cover design: Kathleen S. Munroe, Starr Design, Littleton, Colorado (www.starrdesign.biz)
Interior page design: Barbara L. Scott, Final Eyes, Taos, New Mexico (www.finaleyes.net)

Type is set in Adobe Garamond, Minion Italic, and Mistral.

For my daughter
and her son and daughter
and their future sons and daughters

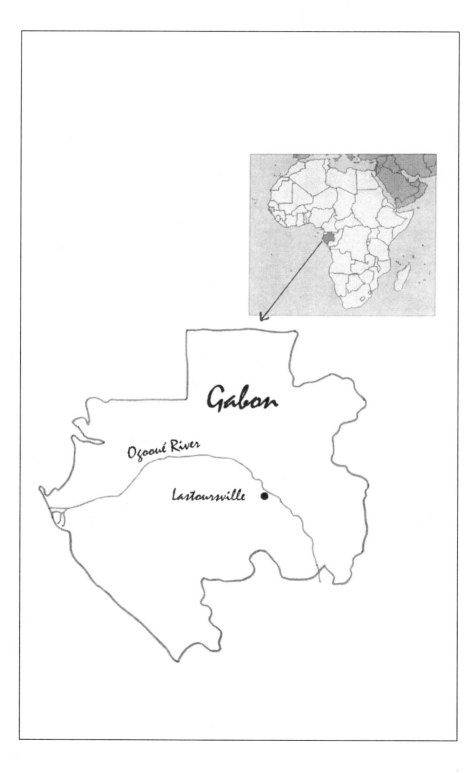

As Lightning to the Children eased
With explanation kind
The Truth must dazzle gradually
Or every man be blind —

— EMILY DICKINSON

Contents

Foreword

One of the many glories of literature is that the author's voice can speak to readers through its pages long after he or she has left this life. In recent years, two audacious women writers in particular have spoken to me again on rereading their classic works, to inspire this memoir in significant ways. In both form and to some extent content, this book is a tribute to these two courageous women: Karen Blixen, who wrote under the pseudonym Isak Dinesen, and Mary Frances Kennedy (known as M.F.K.) Fisher.

Blixen (1885–1962), a Danish baroness, wrote lyrically and lovingly about her life in Africa when she had a farm near Nairobi, Kenya, "at the foot of the Ngong Hills." Her 1938 book, *Out of Africa*, which, in 1985 was made into the Oscar-winning film starring Meryl Streep and Robert Redford, is a collection of true stories drawn from her time there — between 1914 and 1931 — written as her memory later served her, which is to say, not in chronological order. A master storyteller, Blixen leads the reader to believe that her years in Africa were the happiest of her life, and she felt inexplicably more at home there than she did in the European country of her birth.

M.F.K. Fisher (1908–1992), an opinionated, highbrow beauty from California, was the first American woman writer to fearlessly include recipes to illustrate and augment her literary prose. Her 1942 book, *How to Cook a Wolf*, published in the midst of war rationing, when many American households had reason to fear the wolf at the door, was about survival, "about living as decently as possible with the ration cards and blackouts and like miseries of World War II," she said. In this collection of essays, each headed "How to [...]," she eruditely and forthrightly teaches her readers how to survive hard times and do so with style; and her straightforward, step-by-step recipes provide proof that this can be done.

Although I couldn't begin to imitate their writing styles, I do feel that *How to Cook a Crocodile* is directly descended from their books. I think of this book as the wild grandchild of the two grandmothers, *Out of Africa* and *How to Cook a Wolf*. Like *Out of Africa*, it is a collection of true stories drawn from journal notes and memory of my years in Gabon, where I had a home in Lastoursville, on a hill overlooking the Ogooué River. My memories of that time are sweet and vivid, and, like Blixen's, I feel, meaningful enough to share.

Like *How to Cook a Wolf*, my book is also a guide for living healthfully and meaningfully under harsh conditions. Unlike Fisher's *Wolf*, though, my *Crocodile* is more down-to-earth, more adventuresome; less opinionated, high-tone essay; more dramatic, personal narrative. What both books mostly have in common is that the item to be cooked (in their titles) stands purely as a metaphor for survival.

My first memoir, *Somewhere Child*, published by Viking Press in 1981, recounts the loss of my daughter to parental child-snatching. That book found my lost child, as I had fervently hoped, but by then it was too late to reclaim her heart. She had had no choice but to grow up believing the stories her father told her to justify his taking her away from her mother. Her father was her unquestioned hero, and I was the stranger she struggled to forgive.

Everyone in this life suffers heartache and loss; this pain is as universal as the need to eat. What isn't so clear-cut, though, is what to do when you see "the things you gave your life to broken," to use Kipling's words. How do you "stoop and build" your life back up "with worn-out tools"?

In my own case, I changed careers. I'd become a writer in order to find my missing daughter by writing an open letter to her. Written words were the only currency I had in my search for her, and I felt after writing *Somewhere Child* I'd depleted them. I left a writing career and turned to cooking, for its immediacy and concreteness. I became a self-employed chef and caterer in New York City, making memorable dinner parties for others, pretending I was cooking for a family of my own. Cooking, I found, was all-absorbing and healing. Cooking became my life.

Then, in 1995 at the age of fifty — after a breast cancer scare on top of ten years of physically exhausting catering work — I decided to shut down my catering business and return to Africa, where I'd felt, like Karen Blixen, happy and at home when I'd lived there for a time many years before. I needed to go back to Africa, as if it were my motherland.

As a means to this end, I joined the Peace Corps, which sent me to Gabon, where I served as a health and nutrition volunteer for two years in a small town in the middle of the rainforest. Like so many Peace Corps volunteers before me, I emerged from this experience a changed person, having learned much more than I taught. Unlike other Peace Corps authors, though, I tell my tale in a new way: as interconnecting true stories with illustrative recipes.

I have returned to writing, believing now more than ever that writers *must* write. It is our responsibility, our reason for being. It takes courage and audacity, but some truths need to be told and retold in order that the untrue stories don't outlive them. Sometimes written words, carefully crafted and deeply felt, have the power to endure beyond the writer's lifespan. Sometimes a writer's voice lives on.

These stories themselves constitute a recipe, my personal recipe for survival. The main ingredients in this recipe are good food, safe shelter, meaningful work, and unexpected love. *How to Cook a Crocodile* is written not only to share with but also to inspire others to search for their own crocodiles — and cook them too.

PART I

Food and Shelter

Pompano

One of the saving graces of the less-monied people of the world has always been, theoretically, that they were forced to eat more unadulterated, less dishonest food than the rich-bitches.
— M.F.K. FISHER, *How to Cook a Wolf*

Cooking at the James Beard Foundation, NYC, 1991

What I remember most vividly about her place, apart from the fish we served that night for dinner, is the walls. Some of the interior walls of their newly renovated, 18th-floor penthouse apartment on the Upper East Side of Manhattan could *move.* With a push of one finger you could reconfigure rooms: turn a large, well-lit, blond-wood-paneled study into two cozy guest bedrooms, for example. Like magic.

And the walls that didn't move, the walls with windows over-looking what seemed like every inch of the City — the East River, Harlem to the north, Central Park and beyond to the west, all of downtown's dazzling skyline to the south — these walls held works of art the likes of which I'd only seen before in museums, such as Monets, Picassos, and Van Goghs. I expected to see uniformed museum guards keeping watch in the corners of the rooms, but there were none of those.

I'd seen fancy Manhattan homes before, to be sure. Most of my catering clients chose to have parties in their New York apartments precisely *because* they'd just had their places renovated and wanted to show them off to friends, colleagues, business partners, or family.

I had clients on Fifth Avenue, Park Avenue, Central Park West, on the Upper West Side near Columbia University, way downtown, and all over the Upper East Side. All of their apartments were beautiful, breathtaking in their own ways, and reeked of wealth. But none of them were quite like this one, with walls that put on such an opulent and dramatic show.

My clients chose me, I think, because my small business, Bonnie Fare Catering, specialized in at-home parties; I was reasonably priced, honest, dependable, and, above all, I like to think, a good cook. I called my style of cooking "upscale-down home," because I served traditional, homey, "comfort" food, such as chicken potpie or bread pudding in "fancy dress," like art on a plate.

"Everything is fresh and homemade," my advertising copy read, and this was completely true. I made everything myself, for the joy of it really, because I loved to cook. I had changed careers at forty, going from being a well-paid writer/editor in the New York corporate world to being a self-employed caterer in the New York food world, because I was hungry for what a new, culinary career had to offer. I wanted to work with my hands in the realm of the tangible and meaningful. I wanted to immerse myself in the colors, flavors, aromas, and textures of the dishes I created. I needed to pretend my clients were my family and I was cooking for them out of love.

If ice cream was on the dessert menu, I brought my own ice cream machine, which had been my mother's, with me to the client's apartment and made and froze the luscious concoction that very afternoon. For every party, I baked healthy, grainy bread right there in the client's kitchen, to create an old-fashioned, comforting, mamma's-in-the-kitchen-with-her-apron-on aroma to greet their guests as they arrived.

In the almost-ten years I'd been in business, I'd developed a faithful core clientele as well as a slowly growing list of new clients, mainly by word of mouth. A friend once told me she had overheard two uptown ladies talking over lunch in a midtown restaurant: One told the other her daughter wanted to hold her wedding reception in her mother's Manhattan apartment. Her friend told her to call me to do the catering because, she said, I was the best in town for "sweet little home parties and receptions."

Most of my clients treated me with respect, as a professional. Often, they'd call me out of the kitchen as the after-dessert coffee was being served, to take a bow and enjoy their guests' applause. For the most part, though, I remained in the kitchen, leaving my younger, more charming, and more extroverted wait staff to be my emissaries in the front of the house. I felt I had serious, time-sensitive work to do. I was much more comfortable tending my simmering pots and watching what was in the oven than I would have been schmoozing with my clients and their fancy guests over cocktails in the living room.

For me, all the action at these parties took place in the kitchen. Certain scenes stick in my mind: The first time my headwaiter, Michael, an aspiring actor, worked for me; how I'd asked him, just to make small talk as we prepared a tray of hors d'oeuvres together, how catering compared with theater work. "Dahhhling," he said, striking a pose as he hoisted the tray above his shoulder, about to enter the client's living room stage right, "this IS theater!"

Then, later on, Michael's reaction to serving Jane Fonda and Ted Turner at a private dinner party I catered on Central Park West: He returned to the kitchen swooning, "Oh, she's so beautiful! She's so *dreamy!* I've been in love with her all my life! When I was a kid, I had posters of her on my bedroom wall! Now I'm just *this far* away from her! I'm serving her! And she's so thin — such a tiny tushie — she makes you look FAT, Bonnie. By the way, she didn't eat your veal chop. Maybe she's a vegetarian."

"Did Ted eat his dinner?" I asked, more to the point.

"Yes. *Everything.* What an appetite."

At another party, a Christmas fund-raiser for a private grammar school on the Upper East Side, Bill Murray sauntered into my domain as if it was his own and nonchalantly leaned against the kitchen counter next to where I was working.

"Don't I know you from somewhere?" he deadpanned.

"Zabars, perhaps?" I countered, dropping the name of a well-known New York food emporium and going along with the gag.

"No," he said, looking perplexed. "Weren't you in a movie? Wasn't it *Babette's Feast?*"

He leaned into the platter I kept busily preparing for the buffet table — I couldn't, I felt, stop to play audience to his stand-up comedy — and turned his face into mine, giving me one of his impish smiles. "Babette?"

"Yes," I said, caving in. "That's me."

Bill Moyers was on the guest list of a number of parties I did for my clients in the television industry. I had interviewed him years before when I worked as a writer and editor at New York's public television station, WNET, and he remembered me. He never asked, though, what prompted my career change. Maybe he intuited some of my reasoning: Cooking is analogous to writing — in both cases you're creating something nourishing for others to consume — but more people eat than read.

Because of our earlier, professional connection, Moyers always made a point of coming into the kitchen after the meal I'd prepared to greet me with a bear hug and thank me for "the delicious dinner." Once he even apologized for not eating my homemade lemon ice cream. "I wanted to, Bonnie," he said, "but I couldn't. Doctor's orders. Must watch my cholesterol." He had recently suffered a mild heart attack.

At the engagement party for Jill St. John and Robert Wagner, thrown by one of my clients on Park Avenue, the celebrated couple approached me in the kitchen to thank my staff and me personally for "the wonderful party." When they left the room, Michael quipped, alluding to Wagner's first wife, Natalie Wood, who had died in a boating accident many years before, "I hope this one can swim."

And, of course, there were a few unpleasant moments: The times guests would charge into the kitchen demanding something of me immediately — "Gimme a glass of water! NOW!" — in a tone that signified deep disdain for servants. Other guests sheepishly approached me at the stove, speaking to me s-l-o-w-l-y — "Where… is…the… bath…room…?" — as if I were an idiot or someone just off the boat from somewhere far away, yearning for her green card. Without disappointing them, I'd turn and point in the appropriate direction and say, in my best high school French, "*La bah*."

This client, the one with the dancing walls, was a special case.

The first time we met, she gave me a tour of her apartment — the expansive living room with its downtown views, the dining room with its majestic table that easily sat eighteen, the all-white kitchen which alone could contain my entire studio apartment on the Upper West Side, her husband's book-lined study, the maid's quarters…

We sat at a breakfast table in the anteroom of the kitchen. Her words were clipped, her expression rigid, her short dark hair looked immovable, glued. We were, I guessed, about the same age — nearing 50 — but our life paths had obviously taken quite divergent directions. I had been married to wealth once, too, but to me it had seemed like prison. Too young to know what romantic love was, I'd naively believed him when he told me he loved me. Too late, I learned my sole purpose for him — to produce what his money couldn't buy: a blond-haired, blue-eyed child he could call his very own. Sitting across from each other at that table, this client and I were oceans apart.

She told me she'd "been through a number of caterers" and none of them had proved satisfactory. She said she had high standards of excellence, which no caterer she'd tried had been able to meet. She said I'd come highly recommended, so she'd give me a chance.

This one's a challenge, I said to myself. *Good. I like challenges.*

In the next several months, I did a number of parties for her — about one a month — and after each she appeared reluctantly pleased. She seemed to grope for something to criticize but couldn't come up with anything. At last she'd say, "The food was good. Maybe a little less spice next time."

Next time, I thought. *So, there'll be a next time.*

After she'd leave the kitchen, my staff and I would dance around the kitchen floor to celebrate our success. "We pleased the queen!" we'd squeal, *sotto voce,* locking arms and spinning, like a peasant scene from a Bruegel painting. Sometimes Michael and I would do a quick tango, just for laughs. Then we all would pitch in and clean her kitchen until it was back to its original, immaculate, hospital-ward white and every item was returned to its place — the exact place it had been when I'd arrived in the afternoon and taken mental pictures of everything as it was — before we left after midnight from the servants' elevator.

Pompano-en-papillote (fish steamed in a paper case) was the chosen main course for the last dinner party I did for her. Pompano, a small fish, about the length and thickness of my hand, is found only in the Gulf of Mexico and is not always available fresh in Manhattan. My fish market, Citarella's, on the West Side, didn't have it at that time; but my client's fish store, on the East Side, did. I ordered twenty pompano to be delivered directly to the client's apartment.

The afternoon of the party, as I was completing my preparations and packing for this job, the telephone rang.

The client shouted at me, "The fish has just arrived, and it's too much! I'm having a dinner party for eighteen. You ordered twenty fish!"

"Yes," I told her, "I know. I ordered a bit more for the staff. They'll be working at dinnertime. Plus, it's customary for the staff to taste what's on the menu so they can explain it to the guests. We'll be dividing the two extra fish six ways…"

"I'm perfectly capable of explaining to my guests!" she shot back. "I'm not here to feed the help too! They should pick up a slice of pizza before they get here!"

I was tired. Catering is physically demanding work, like professional dancing. I'd begun my catering business at the age of forty, dancing *en point,* on eggs, in effect, for nearly a decade. *Who in her right mind becomes a ballerina at this age?* I often asked myself.

And I hadn't been well. At the age of forty-nine I'd discovered an abnormality in my right breast that pointed directly, I was convinced at the time, to breast cancer. Instead of seeing a doctor right away, however, I chose to wait, to think about it, to listen closely to my heart and body, to keep the sound of this small alarm bell all to myself. The fact was, I was self-employed, self-supporting, and under-insured. I simply couldn't afford to pay for treatment, hospitalization, or surgery out of my own pocket.

So I kept my own counsel and monitored the problem privately. At times I would dismiss it, imagining it would just disappear. At other times, I'd tell myself that breast cancer ran in families; neither my two sisters nor my mother or her mother had had it, so I was in the clear.

In the months that followed, however, as blood continued to seep strangely from my right breast, I thought more about the possibility of death — not in a morbid way, but matter-of-factly. It's a trip we all will take eventually, I felt; and I wanted to calmly, quietly, privately, pack my own bags for it. I thought: *What would I like to accomplish in the time I have left?* Or, put another way: *If I died sooner rather than later, what would I regret not having done?*

Caterers are list-makers by nature. Without countless checklists to guide us, the parties would never take place. So it was natural for me to sit down and methodically write a short list of my five "final" life goals:

- Take dancing lessons
- Write to all my old friends
- Learn to speak French (finally!)
- Return to Africa
- Do some good with my life.

I carried on with my daily routine — my catering business, part-time teaching at the New York Cooking School — but with a slight sense of detachment, as if I were seeing familiar things from a greater distance, as if I were standing on the top deck of an ocean liner about to leave the harbor, waving goodbye, but not sadly. I was excited at the prospect of this new adventure, unafraid of the unknown. I was, in fact, exhausted and greatly in need of a cruise. After almost nine months of this — accepting the bloody discharge from my right breast as destiny, waiting impatiently for the ship to start its engines and set sail for somewhere, anywhere — I learned, by chance, of a free breast cancer clinic in Harlem. I made an appointment and went to it with Michael, my headwaiter.

Walking along 116th Street in Harlem together that afternoon, passing storefronts, burger joints and makeshift churches but not noticing anything except each other, Michael and I spoke of death. I had just revealed to him my secret of possible breast cancer. He shared with me his own life-threatening health concerns.

"Do you think a lot about death?" I asked him.

"Sure," he said, "but I think more about staying healthy."

We were the only white people in the clinic's waiting room; he was the only man. But no one made us feel unwelcome or out of place. Michael held my hand as though we were a couple. To me, he was family.

The doctor who examined me — tall, coffee-colored and elegant — told me that indeed there was a problem "in there" and it would require surgery as soon as possible.

• • •

My breast surgery took place at Harlem Hospital, and the biopsy results came through a few days after: benign. Something had been wrong "in there" and needed to be repaired—the tubing had somehow become knotted, tangled—but cancer wasn't to blame. Cancer wasn't going to be my exit visa either, it appeared, at least in the near future. I had to get back on dry land and go on living. I had to concentrate on being healthy.

But I still had my "final" To Do list in hand, and I became determined to act on it right away, regardless. I immediately enrolled at the Arthur Murray Dance Studio on Broadway to take ballroom and Latin dancing lessons once a week. I began writing long letters to all of my old, far-away friends, telling them how much they meant to me, how much I'd love to see them again.

And then one morning, as I was drinking coffee and reading the *New York Times*, I saw an ad that caught my attention. The ad was an appeal for Peace Corps volunteers to serve in far-off places (*Ah, Africa,* I thought), to learn foreign languages (*including French, certainly*), to do good (*oh, yes*) in the world. The ad's tagline read, "The toughest job you'll ever love."

I clipped the Peace Corps ad from the paper with kitchen scissors and put it in my journal, as if into a large pot of chicken stock, placed on a low flame, on a back burner, to slowly simmer.

My client's shrill voice and scolding, accusatory tone sent shock waves through my body. In my mind, I heard my father's drunken voice: "*You stupid, good-for-nothing…!*" I began to tremble all over. I could hardly hold the phone. My teeth wanted to chatter, so I kept them clenched. *Keep your mouth shut,* I admonished myself, terrified of the regrettable things I could say. Emily Dickinson's wise words, chiseled into the walls of my brain since high school, spoke to me: "*A word is dead, once it is said, some say; I say it just begins to live that day.*"

As I held the phone away from my right ear to distance myself from her rant, my mind surveyed the book-lined walls of my small, orderly studio apartment. For twenty years I'd called this one-room apartment home. Then I thought about the walls of her home, especially the walls of her living room. I'd only seen them that once, the day we met, before I was shown "my place," in her anti-septic kitchen, but they made an indelible impression. *If just one of the works of art on one of those walls were sold at auction,* I thought to myself as she continued to shout at me over the phone, *how many millions would it earn? How many fillets of fish would that amount of money buy? How many hungry people could that fish feed?*

At last, I found some words to say to her. "I'll pay the $14 for the two extra fish," I said. "Don't worry."

I did the dinner party that night, with no further complaints from that client. *Perhaps,* I thought, *she'd just had a bad day; per-haps she and her high-powered husband had had a fight that morning and she had just needed to vent; perhaps she wasn't as heartless as she seemed.* I made the pompano-en-papillote for all eighteen people seated at her elegant dining table, carefully enclosing each seasoned pompano fillet in its paper envelope, folding and pleating each one as though it were a handmade Valentine.

But I never worked for that client again. Something inside me broke that day, as if a china teacup had shattered on my terra-cotta tile kitchen floor. My love affair with catering ended, the way so many love affairs in New York do—abruptly—almost, but not quite, without warning. My need to please well fed people by preparing beautiful food for them evaporated, like steam from a teakettle.

The next morning over coffee, as I was about to share with my long-suffering journal my feelings of physical, mental, and spiritual exhaustion, the Peace Corps ad I'd clipped from the *Times* fell out of my journal's pages. I picked it up and read it this time as if it were a letter from God. "The toughest job you'll ever love," it told me again. *Yes,* I thought. *It's time.*

Pompano (or any fish) en Papillote

Butter a large (about 15 inches in diameter) circle of parchment paper (or aluminum foil). Lay one small (one serving) fish fillet on the paper, right of center. Sprinkle the fish with sliced, blanched vegetables (such as carrots and/or French green beans). Season with salt and pepper, freshly squeezed lemon juice and/or white wine. Fold parchment (or foil) into papillote (paper case), and seal the edges (like a calzone). Place on a cookie sheet and bake for 10 to 15 minutes at 400-425 degrees, or until puffed. Serve each person an individual papillote (unopened), with a small pair of sharp scissors, to open the cases themselves and savor the steamy aroma.

Lemon Ice Cream

   3 tablespoons grated lemon zest
   1 cup freshly squeezed lemon juice
   2 cups sugar
   4 large whole eggs
   4 large egg yolks
   2 cups milk
   2 cups cold heavy cream

In a medium, heavy bottom saucepan, cook (whisking continuously) the zest, lemon juice, sugar, whole eggs, and yolks, until the mixture comes to a simmer (very soft boil). Remove from heat and strain into a bowl. Add the 2 cups of milk to the bowl, then chill. Whip the heavy cream to soft peaks and fold it gently into the chilled lemon-custard mixture. Freeze in an ice cream maker until firm. Makes about 1½ quarts.

Nostalgie d'Afrique

It is hard to leave Africa once she has held you. I'd been
her foster child for three years, and when it came time to go I
had to leave her gently, slowly, by ship. If I had flown
away, the break would have been too sharp, too painful.
— BONNIE LEE BLACK, *Somewhere Child*

An elephant by the side of the road, Rhodesia, 1970

*E*ver since I left Africa — what was then Rhodesia — and returned to the United States in the summer of 1972, I had wanted to go back. Circumstances, however, never allowed it. Due to myriad responsibilities, plus lack of time and lack of money, returning to Africa to live — or even just to visit — was out of the realm of possibility for me, akin to flying to Mars.

But the yearning persisted. For more than twenty years, I longed for Africa's warmth and welcome; her raw, seemingly just-formed beauty and earthiness; the feel of her heartbeat-drumbeat music; the dazzling sight of her huge, star-filled skies; the smell of her floral-scented air, so light and sweet it made breathing a conscious pleasure. I ached for that distant place where time moved gracefully, like a slowly swaying palm tree, and human beings, especially the indigenous people, in my experience, were genuinely generous and humane.

This longing never subsided. It was always there inside, this sense of apartness, wishing I were far away, feeling I just didn't belong where I was. It was the way, I thought, an orphaned child might feel trying to navigate her way in the cold world. Living in

Manhattan, I felt orphaned by the Mother Earth and Father Sky of the Africa I had come to love. The French have a specific expression for this condition. They call it *nostalgie d'Afrique,* homesickness for Africa. Anyone who has lived in Africa — close enough to her earth, long enough for her heartbeat to penetrate — will know what I mean.

I had never in my life felt any kind of homesickness for the place in New Jersey where I grew up, the place I could legitimately call home. That place I'd prefer to forget, but when memories do resurface, against my will, I think of it as the scene of the crime. That was where I learned how to use a rotary phone to dial my first memorized telephone number — the number of the local police — to ask them, "…please come quickly, my father is beating up my mother again! He just knocked her down, and now he's kicking her in the head … *please help us, please hurry!*"

Walking to grammar school in the '50s, passing the neat little houses, shoulder-to-shoulder, all closed up (*and hiding what?*) in our all-white, McCarthyite town, which my mother thought was the entire world, I'd think, *The world is bigger than this.*

In Africa — oddly, inexplicably, mysteriously, much like Karen Blixen — I felt I belonged. Over the years, I've tried to determine why.

My first doll was a larger-than-real-life-baby size, dark-chocolate-color cloth doll named Lulu with a happy, embroidered face and tufts of short, braided wool hair, which my mother hand-made for me in the months before I was born — gambling I'd be a girl. Later, I had a small, chubby-cheeked black baby doll that drank and wet, whom I loved as though she were alive. As an adolescent, when I started attending church with a friend, I watched in awe as the furloughed missionaries showed films of their work in the Congo. When anyone asked me at that time what I planned to be when I grew up, I would answer, "a missionary in Africa." I seemed to know that fate would one day take me there.

When it finally did, though, it wasn't as a missionary of any church. I was on a mission of my own: to bring back my baby. I was twenty-four; it was March 1969, and I'd just learned from the FBI that my ex-husband, who had abducted our 16-month-old, blond-haired, blue-eyed daughter two years before, had been found in Salisbury, Rhodesia, southern Africa. The American authorities could not help me because there was no extradition at that time with renegade Rhodesia, so I flew there myself to be happily reunited with my baby and to bring her back home with me. Once there, however, I learned it would not be that easy. Legal wrangling and major high court cases brought by my ex-husband kept me in the capital, Salisbury, for three years: Long enough to feel embraced by the boundless kindness of strangers, and the warmth, wisdom, and earthiness of Africa herself.

When my ex-husband abducted our daughter again, this time on a court-approved visit with her to Zambia, from which he was extradited, with her, to the United States, I had no choice but to leave Africa and continue my agonizingly long and seemingly futile pursuit. Without any help or resources, writing my book *Somewhere Child*, an open letter to my daughter, was the best that I could do.

When I called the Peace Corps number given in their ad, I went right to the point: I was no longer young — almost fifty: *Was I too old?* I was only interested in serving in Africa, preferably French-speaking Africa: *Would this be possible?* I wanted to do health-and-nutrition work, especially with women and children: *Could they accommodate me?*

Within a year, in July 1996, I was on my way to French-speaking Gabon, in central Africa, to serve as a health and nutrition volunteer at a mother-infant clinic in the rainforest. Before leaving, feeling jubilant about the future, I joked with my best friend and next-door neighbor, Marty, that this time I'd write a happy book about this new experience and I'd call it *Hot Flashes in a Hot*

Country. She and I were about the same age, just past fifty, and the mysteries of menopause for both of us were just around the corner.

Marty, a professional photographer who had served as an English teacher in the Peace Corps in Thailand in the early '60s, shortly after John F. Kennedy's famous "Ask not" entreaty, had learned two important lessons there — that she hated teaching and loved overseas adventures. In the nearly ten years we had been next-door neighbors, we'd become close friends; and, like a loving sister, she supported my decision to join the Peace Corps by agreeing to manage my financial affairs in my two-year absence. She oversaw the sublet of my studio apartment and became the foster mother for my beloved Himalayan cat, Sweet Basil. After twenty-four years of *nostalgie*, I was at last free to return to Africa.

Memba

It is all a question of weeding out what you yourself like
best to do, so that you can live most agreeably in a world full of
an increasing number of disagreeable surprises.
— M.F.K. FISHER, *How to Cook a Wolf*

Village scene, interior of Gabon

Martha Cooper

Germaine Nyangi Mombo sat on a low stool in front of her outdoor cooking pot, which was set on a tripod of three sturdy stones with sticks of wood ablaze beneath it, peeling plantains with a crude knife and then slicing them into the pot.

"*Espions*," she said to me, softly, so that no one else would hear. She didn't look up. Instead, she focused on her work — cutting into and tearing off the green leathery shells, scraping off the tough threads along the sides of the white fruit, slicing each into irregular chunks and dropping them into the pot of boiling water, tossing the peels into the bush. She had a large family to cook for and many plantains lying on the ground beside her left to do.

Her French, like mine, was rudimentary, but I thought I understood what she was telling me. She thought our group of trainees had come to her village, Memba, to spy on them. She thought we were spies.

"*Non, ça n'est pas le cas, Maman.*" I tried to assure her that wasn't true, using the honorific for Mother, since she was the matriarch of this family, and I was her house guest for a week, a temporary member of the family. "*Nous sommes Corps de la Paix. Nous sommes ici en paix.*" The Peace Corps, I tried to point out, is only interested in peace.

From her point of view, though, espionage made sense. Why else would two dozen or so mostly young, white Americans descend on her tiny village deep in the rainforest of Gabon, disperse into individual family compounds, then proceed to go from house to house, clipboards in hand, asking the villagers personal questions? I didn't have the words in French to explain to her the subtleties of our reasons for being there: Our weeklong stay in Memba was part of our ten-week training to become unpaid workers whose two-year-long job would be to help Gabonese villagers and towns-people meet their own long-term needs. How else could we know what those needs were without doing a survey, a "base-line survey," at that — interviewing people in their homes, filling in a state-of-the-art questionnaire? *Frankly, Germaine*, I wanted to tell her, *it doesn't make sense to me, either.*

Germaine's mother, Marie, an elderly woman, bony and frail, approached me where I sat near Germaine by the cooking pot. She had walked, slowly and unsteadily on stick-thin legs, along the winding dirt path, overhung by palms and banana trees, from what I assumed was her hut. She held out her toughened, skeletal hand to me, smiled broadly, bowed her head, and began to chat animatedly in Inzebi, the village's native language. I held her hand in both of mine, as if I were gripping Africa herself, not wanting to let go after all these years. I smiled into her smile and nodded enthusiastically, as if I knew what she was saying.

The drive to Memba from our training site in the capital, Libreville, had taken nine hours, crammed into minivans, over dusty, bumpy, unpaved, often-mountainous roads. This was my first chance to see the interior of Gabon, and what I saw made my heart sink. Unlike the Rhodesia I'd known, whose beauty was preserved, Edenlike, in my memory, what I saw of Gabon from the window of this van looked like a scene from a film of the apocalypse. It was early September, still the dry season, and the people had slashed and burned great swaths of land, in anticipation of a new planting season. What should have been lush and green was black and charred. Charred tree skeletons rose up like desperate, black, stick-hands out of a roiling sea of charred underbrush. It made me think of the life-altering book, *The Fate of the Earth*, by Jonathan Schell, and his riveting imagined descriptions of the aftermath of a nuclear disaster. *Yes, this is what the earth will surely look like, after they drop the bomb*, I thought as I gazed out of the minivan's window, heartsick.

Africa, I had to keep reminding myself, is not one homogeneous country but rather an immense, complicated continent comprised of more than fifty U.S.-state-size, separate nations carved out by self-interested European powers in the late nineteenth century. Britain had grabbed the bulk of southern Africa, including the mostly picturesque, softly rolling high savannah they named Rhodesia, after its "discoverer," Cecil Rhodes. (At its independence from Britain in 1980, Rhodesia was renamed Zimbabwe). The French took most of the bulge of western Africa, including tiny, oil-rich Gabon, on the equator, hugging the Atlantic coast. (Gabon gained its independence from France in 1960.) Zimbabwe boasts a gentle, temperate, agreeable climate, especially at its higher elevations. Gabon, in contrast, is mostly dense rainforest, inhumanly hot and nearly always dripping wet.

But underneath it all, I wanted to think, beneath the wildly disparate surface differences, there was one Mother Earth Africa, with one universal soul, one drumming heartbeat.

My Peace Corps training in Gabon required a number of such mental adjustments. This was not the Africa of my fondest memories, but it was Africa nonetheless. It was a new — to me — Africa, a new challenge, a new mountain to climb. And wasn't life, after all, one long mountain range we were required to hike, mostly alone? I decided to think of this training as another in a series of endurance tests that I was determined to pass.

• • •

My brother had told me, upon returning from Marine Corps boot camp at Parris Island, South Carolina, when he was seventeen and I was eleven, blood-chilling stories of drill instructors' cruelty to the trainees there. The young men, he said, were made to do punishing tasks — hold a rifle out in front of them for hours, do pushups until they collapsed in exhaustion, carry enormous backpacks on endless treks through swampy terrain. One drill instructor, my brother told me, punished a recruit by digging his index finger into the middle of the boy's collarbone and leading him around the parade grounds until the boy almost choked to death.

"*Why?* Tell me!" I begged my brother, my hero, as I sat, worshipfully, at his feet.

"It's a test," my brother said proudly, because he'd made the cut. "They need to weed out the weak ones right away. If you're not strong enough to take it, you can't become a Marine."

Peace Corps training is worlds away from Marine Corps basic training. In the Peace Corps there are no uniforms, no drill instructors, no rifles, no pushups, no physical punishments. The Peace Corps' mission is the antithesis of combat, and its training reflects that fact. Yet, I soon discovered, the ten-week training boiled down to this: a test. The silliness, the inefficiencies, the endless, often pointless classes, the seemingly deliberate withholding of mail from home, the "fascist" (a label given by one of my fellow trainees, the twenty-four-year-old daughter of a Washington diplomat) group leader, and much more, added up to a test of patience and endurance. Several trainees dropped out and returned to the U.S., disillusioned, discouraged, or just plain fed up; but I was determined to stay in Africa.

The best part of my training in Libreville was living in the home of a beautiful young Gabonese woman, Yolande Borobo, and being adopted by her family as one of their own. Yolande (Yo-Yo) became my Gabonese sister (she called me her Vanilla Sister); and if it weren't for her love, encouragement, and humor, I might have given up and gone back too.

But I'd made it this far, to our field trip to Memba, which was the final, acid test. Could I endure life in this "primitive" Gabonese village, without electricity or running water? Could I bathe and wash my hair and do my laundry in the dirty river? Could I live with total strangers who spoke no English and very little French, in a mud-brick house covered only by a thin corrugated aluminum roof? Could I learn to use a privy in the forest, consisting of a large, deep hole in the ground covered by wooden planks and surrounded on only three sides by palm-fronds? Could I endure the battalions of tiny, arbovirus-carrying foo-roo's that bit incessantly at my skin and left red, dime-size itchy welts? *Oh, yes.* I would do it if it killed me.

It is midday, nap time now in Memba — what French-speaking Africans call *repose* or *sieste* — but I prefer to write. The village is quite quiet, except for someone somewhere playing an Afro-pop tape. An old man is dozing off in a doorway of a mud hut across the way; a toddler is in his lap, fast asleep. Chickens are pecking in the yard in front of me, and goats are everywhere, braying. Young mothers, with little children following them like ducklings, are returning from their fieldwork with baskets of manioc leaves and tubers on their backs. When they pass me, they smile and say *"Bonjour!"* Everyone, it seems, knows *"bonjour."*

Yesterday afternoon there was a lively soccer match on the school grounds between the twenty-something-year-old Peace Corps trainees and village teenagers, and all of Memba turned out to watch. I sat on the sidelines, on the dusty ground, with a group of little girls, including Gina and Lilly, two of Germaine's many grandchildren, both about four years old, who clung to me as though I were their own. One of the girls in the group, who must have been school age because she knew a little French, pointed to my khaki pants and said, *"Pantelons sale."*

She was right, of course. My pants, which I hadn't removed,

even at night (fearing bugs in the bed), for several days, were filthy. Nevertheless, I was slightly offended. I pointed to her little feet and said, "*Pieds sale.*" Her eyes widened and a smile crept along her pretty face. She elbowed her younger girlfriends and translated what I'd said into Inzebi, and they all fell over themselves giggling and inspecting the bottoms of their own and each other's feet.

They knew I had to be joking. Of course, their feet were dirty. They walked barefoot on dirt paths and along Memba's one main road; they lived in mud houses with dirt floors. But clothes? Seriously. Clothes had to be *clean.*

Sufficiently shamed, I ran back to my Memba home with Gina and Lilly after the soccer game (score: 2-2), gathered up my laundry, a bucket and soap, changed out of my dirty khakis, and took off down a steep embankment for the river. While I did my washing, knee-high in the muddy water, the two little girls sat side-by-side on the riverbank, hugging their knees, watching over me. It was late afternoon, nearing sunset. They knew if I stayed much longer, I might not find my way home.

September 7, 1996

Dear Marty,

As I write this I'm sitting up in bed in my room in the house where I've been all week. This room is very dark, but I managed to crack open the sealed wooden shutter of the window to let about two inches of sunlight in so I can write.

I have a green plastic bucket three-quarters filled with river water sitting on the dirt floor near my bed, for washing my face and brushing my teeth. Fortunately, I have my own door to the outside, with a lock and key, so I've been able to maintain my safety and privacy.

The little girls of the family just knocked on my door to thank me — in baby French, the same French I speak — for the flip-flops I bought them as gifts. These two little girls, Gina and Lilly, cousins, have badly battered, blistered and infected little feet, so I thought flip-flops were in order.

I also gave the family in my bag of thank-you gifts: a pretty piece of fabric for the mother (wrap-around skirt fabric, called a *pagne*), two big boxes of matches (evidently a luxury item), a big bag of fat round lollipops for the countless kids who may or may not belong to this family, nail clippers, a sewing kit, plus (last but not least) 2,000 CFA — about $4 — a lot of money for people who have none.

The matriarch, Germaine, was very thankful and appreciative when I gave her these things here in my room this morning. She made me take down her full name and promise to visit again the next time I'm in the area. Well, chances are I'll never pass this way again.

Memba, if you want to find it on your Gabon map, is just south of Lebamba in the south-central area. Where I'll be posted, Lastoursville, is way east and north of here, on the train line, so I doubt that I'll have occasion to drive these roads again.

Much love, BB xx

Plantain Chips

Like potatoes, plantains can be baked, boiled, mashed, or fried. To make plantain chips, slice peeled, under-ripe plantains into ¼-inch-thick slices and fry in small batches, one layer deep, in hot oil (such as peanut oil), like potato chips. Drain on paper towels and salt to taste.

The House on the Hill

Now, of all times in our history, we should be
using our minds as well as our hearts in order to survive …
to live gracefully if we live at all.
— M.F.K. FISHER, *How to Cook a Wolf*

Martha Cooper

My house on the hill, near the hospital, Lastoursville

*N*eg-*li*-GENT!" I heard the pediatric nurse shout from the children's ward down the hall as I waited on a wooden bench by her rickety desk to speak with her. From what I could piece together, overhearing her fiery, rapid-fire Gabonese French, she was placing the blame for a four-year-old patient's nearly fatal bout with malaria squarely on the shoulders of the child's poor mother. "You should use bed nets sprayed with insecticide!" the nurse bellowed. "You could have prevented this! You are neglecting your children!"

Her verbal abuse struck me as harsh — blaming the victim. But I kept my head down. I tried to study the notebook in my lap, but my eyes were drawn to the meandering black ants on the dirty, unvarnished, wood-plank floor. From what I had seen and learned so far in Gabon, few people, especially the poorest who lived in remote villages, used bed nets, because — although inexpensive by American measures at about $6 apiece — they couldn't afford them.

Even here in Lastoursville, at this centrally located, relatively sophisticated, government-supported medical center — that looked more like a sprawling, rough-hewn Adirondack boys' camp of the

'50s than any American's image of a hospital — none of the feeble, rusted, metal-frame beds had mosquito netting over them. None of the wide-open windows or doors had any sort of screening. There was absolutely no protection against malaria-carrying mosquitoes — or any other threatening invader, be it insect, snake, animal, or human — in this remote hospital, day or night.

Gabon's President Omar Bongo, one of Africa's last Big Men — who was purported to be the twelfth wealthiest man in the world, thanks to his small country's immense oil, timber, and mineral riches — could easily, according to my calculations, afford to buy bed netting for every one of his slightly more than one million countrymen, especially those most vulnerable to malaria, the youngest children. It seemed to me that he was the one who was being negligent. But my purpose in Gabon was neither political nor religious. It was not my place to express my opinions on such things. No one, I came to observe, *ever*, openly criticized President Bongo, who had maintained a firm grip on power for close to thirty years. I knew I would be wise to keep my thoughts to myself, to keep my lips closed and my eyes wide open. I was still new to Gabon, a guest in this "developing" country, and I knew I had a lot to learn.

The nurse approached like a dissipated storm and sank wearily into her old-and-battered, wooden desk chair, apologizing for keeping me waiting. I had come, she knew, at the hospital director's recommendation that I observe the pediatric unit, which she ran with military skill. She was a short, sturdy woman, dressed in a crisp, white uniform that tightly fitted her compact body. Her round face, with high, full cheekbones, looked youthful; but I could see at her temples, where her head wrap had not quite covered her hair, that she was going gray.

She planted her elbows on the cluttered desktop and rested her turbaned head on her square, brown hands. "Too many of our children die," she sighed in slower French. "I've seen too many children die. From diarrhea, malaria, malnutrition…" Her voice trailed off, and she shook her head. "There are preventions. Why don't people take them? *Why?!* I've been a nurse here for twenty-three years. I've seen enough! I'm tired. I'll be retiring soon. But," she looked up at me hopefully, "I'm glad you've come to help teach them."

She sat straighter in her chair and squared her shoulders. She took a deep breath, became visibly more relaxed, and smiled a childlike smile that made her eyes, even with their corner wrinkle lines, sparkle mischievously. We introduced ourselves. She told me her name was Antoinette; she was forty-eight years old, the mother of five children, now grown up and on their own — *"Dieu merci"* (thank God) — and the grandmother of a one-year-old. She was divorced, she said, in the triumphant tone of a cancer-survivor. Her husband had been a "big drunk" who beat her, so she finally kicked him out. "Just like that," she said, gesturing an energetic two-handed shove, then brushing her flat hands together disgustedly, as if ridding them of caked-on mud. *"Je suis libre!"* she exulted. Free! And, she confided, leaning toward me as if this was still a secret: She was about to embark on a whole new career — as deputy mayor of this town.

Etienne Guy Mouvagha, a senior minister in President Bongo's government and a sometime resident and major real estate investor in Lastoursville, had recently won the local, raucous election for mayor. Because he would be spending most of his time, *comme d'habitude*, in the capital, Libreville, he needed a full-time deputy here in town whom he could depend on, someone who was capable, intelligent, hard working and honest. Fortunately for him, he found all these qualities in the person of the soon-to-retire, long-time pediatric nurse Antoinette.

Mr. Mouvagha, as it turned out, was also the landlord of the small, cement-block "dream house" on the hill, within walking distance of the hospital, which I had my heart set on renting. He'd proven elusive, though, in my efforts to make contact. I was growing anxious and worried about ever finding a decent home for the duration of my two-year service. I knew I needed a solid base camp for what appeared to be a steep mountain climb.

Nothing else was available for rent that wasn't too far away from where I would work at the hospital — too far to walk, or even ride a bike, with all my work-related materials hanging from the handlebars. "Do you think you might put in a word to Mouvagha for me?" I begged Antoinette. "I know I could be happy in that house. I know I could do good work there." She promised, in her new role as deputy mayor, to make a meeting with Mouvagha happen.

The day came. Antoinette arranged for Mouvagha's chauffeur to pick me up at the hospital after my morning lecture and take me to the *grand type*'s (big man's) secluded villa about ten miles away. Tall trees lined the long, paved driveway leading to his large, white-stuccoed mansion. It looked like a scene from an old European storybook, but this was on a mountain ridge in the Central African rainforest. Off on the spreading lawn, under an open, tent-like structure, I saw a group of about twenty, mostly young, African men sitting in a circle on metal folding chairs.

Mr. Mouvagha, I saw, stood up from this meeting when he saw his driver pull into the driveway and me get out of his car. Tall and thin, he walked toward me slowly, reluctantly, like a man older than his fifty-something years, head down, shoulders hunched. He had a once-elegant, world-weariness about him, as if whatever *joie de vivre* he might have had when younger had long since begun to corrode. I had seen him in political posters plastered all over town, but never in person. In his photos, he appeared outgoing, charming; in person, he looked drawn and spent.

He sat in a tall-backed wing chair in his plush living room, like a king on a throne. He gripped the chair's armrests with bony hands and grimaced as he looked at me. ("He does not dislike white people," Antoinette had reassured me beforehand. "He even married one. One of his ex-wives is French.") A gardener was pushing a loud power mower just outside the living room window near my chair, mowing the first such vast green lawn I had seen in Gabon, and the sound of it further garbled Mouvagha's tired, mumbled speech. I strained to understand what he was saying.

Dispensing with the customary social niceties *(Bonjour. Comment allez-vous? Et la famille?...),* Mouvagha shot directly to the bottom line, like a New York loan shark, speaking to me in a mixture of French and English, seemingly annoyed that I wasn't getting his message in either language: He would accept nothing less than 200,000 CFA ($400) per month for the house I was hoping to rent. He didn't seem to hear me when I tried to explain I was a Peace Corps *volunteer* — an unpaid community health worker, who'd come to help the people of his community, *his constituency* — and that the maximum the Peace Corps would pay for our housing was 100,000 CFA ($200). Or maybe he did hear me. He responded with, "I don't care. Nothing less than 200,000 CFA," and then he left the room to return to his palaver outside.

"Your new boss drives a hard bargain," I said to Antoinette in so many French words, the next time I saw her. She looked at me knowingly. *"Il est determiné,"* she said.

Lastoursville, a small town situated on the great Ogooué River — Gabon's equivalent of the mighty Mississippi — ten hours by train from the capital, Libreville, was experiencing a housing shortage at the time I arrived. Day after day, in heat that hovered at or above a hundred degrees, I had walked along the town's unpaved roads, inquiring in my unsteady French about a possible house for rent. When cars and trucks passed by, kicking up billows of dusty dirt that covered me like red snow, I took to pulling a kerchief up over my nose like a cowboy.

Despite its intense heat and detestable dirt, I liked Lastoursville from the start. It reminded me of a town you would see in an old Western movie, and it seemed to bring out the latent fearless-cowgirl in me. There was one wide, dusty main street, no longer than a football field, in the town center; and all of the dozen-or-so, small, one-story whitewashed cement-block buildings that housed the town's shops faced this unnamed unpaved road.

On one side of the main street, only yards away, was the river, where men and boys occasionally fished and boated in long, dugout canoes called *pirogues*, but few dared to swim. *Were they afraid of the ferocious current*, I wondered, *or the even more ominous crocodiles?*

To one side of the main street, along winding dirt roads that climbed the hills overlooking the river and *centreville*, nestled amidst the rain-forested vegetation, were the town's houses, some cement block, most mud-and-wattle, and every one of which, I feared, was occupied.

Except, I discovered in my sweat-drenched quest, for two:

One, on the road that led straight from the main street, had a weatherworn sign in front that read "Jolie Delta Bar" and appeared to have been more than just a bar in its lifetime. Six seedy small bedrooms, each containing nothing more than a rusty bed frame, lined the hallway behind the front room. There was no sink or running water in the kitchen, the sole toilet looked as though it hadn't been flushed in years, and the ceiling had clearly suffered severe seepage during many rainy seasons.

The second unoccupied house, however, was Mouvagha's house on the hill, the house of my dreams. It sat somewhat back from the road — away from the car-dust — at the top of Lastoursville's highest hill, a short walk from the hospital where I would be working. It was a small, solid, and sturdily built one-story cement block structure, with a big mango tree on one side and a huge palm tree in the front. Best of all was the view: facing out, I could see the Ogooué River down below and beyond it the thickly forested mountains that undulated like misty gray and blue waves rolling in from an otherworldly sea. From the moment I first saw this house, sitting alone, abandoned, unloved, and neglected, I knew it had to be mine; and I prayed so loudly, strongly, and incessantly for it, I knew God would have no choice but to give in.

Mouvagha knew there was a severe housing shortage in Lastoursville; he knew how much I longed for that house on the hill near my work at the hospital; and he knew, it seemed, instinctively, I would find a way to pay him the exorbitant amount he was demanding. The house, which was in terrible disrepair, with broken plumbing, no hot water, and no screening, had been the home for countless venomous snakes, scorpions, bats, and cockroaches for far too long (and not a few locals told me privately was *maudit* [cursed]), would never have fetched that much monthly rent in Anytown, U.S.A. Yet Mouvagha was clearly a powerful businessman, accustomed to having his way.

After convincing the Peace Corps that I would transform the little house-on-the-hill into a quasi-"country inn," always open to young Peace Corps travelers and offering them home-away-from-home comforts and homemade meals, the Peace Corps agreed to bend their own rules and pay 150,000 CFA toward my rent. The remaining 50,000 CFA, they said, would have to be deducted from my monthly *mandat* (living allowance). I would squeak by on the equivalent of $200 a month, or three-quarters of the minimum needed to live there.

At the time, Gabon was considered the third most expensive country in the world, after Japan and Switzerland. Even in remote Lastoursville, the prices of everything at the Lebanese grocery stores were higher than prices in Manhattan: $2 for a half-dozen eggs, $4 for a liter of orange juice, $7 for a small bag of dried apricots, $5 for a bottle of bleach. But I knew I'd find a way to make ends meet; I would survive. I would call my "dream house" home, and Mouvagha would get the $400 a month he demanded.

Dear Class

…World Wise Schools, a Peace Corps program, strives to help U.S. schoolchildren better understand and appreciate the diverse cultures and issues of the world. … Since its inception in 1989, World Wise Schools has helped more than 3 million U.S. students communicate directly with Peace Corps Volunteers all over the world.

— PEACE CORPS' WEBSITE

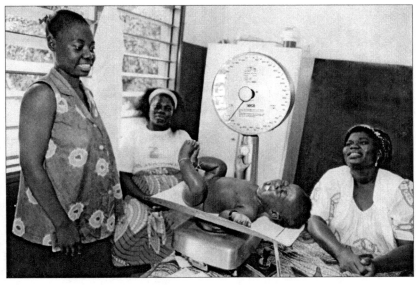

Martha Cooper

Baby-weighing at the mother-infant clinic

Lastoursville, Gabon — October 11, 1996

Dear Class,

Hello again to my favorite fourth-graders! This is the letter I promised to write when the rainy season began. Well, it has begun. Mymymy, how it rains here when it rains! It's like an angel in heaven has turned on a big faucet in the sky and the water just pours straight down. And what a noise it makes! It's very exciting. I love it.

Now the roads that had been so dusty during the dry season are all mud. Walking along them is like walking through an inch or two of snow — only snow is a whole lot cleaner. Of course, everyone's shoes get all mucky and muddy, so people leave their shoes outside when they go indoors. Even at work people walk around barefooted.

I've started working at the hospital a couple of hours every weekday morning, and I like it very much. So far I'm just observing — seeing how they do things, what the needs are, what the problems are, etc. Last week I observed the mommies and babies at the mother-infant clinic; all of these babies were chubby, adorable, and healthy. Their moms were just bringing them in for checkups and to be weighed.

When I was observing in the Pediatrics department, a nurse there explained to me that the biggest problems ("*maladies*," in French) for these children are: malaria (caused by the bite of a certain kind of mosquito), diarrhea (caused by dirty drinking water and poor hygiene in general), anemia (caused by insufficient iron in the diet), and malnutrition (not enough food or not enough of the right kinds of food). Next month, when I begin my work of actually teaching, I hope to teach the mothers how they might *prevent* these illnesses occurring to their children. Like all mothers everywhere in the world, these mothers love their babies very much and don't want them to become sick.

I've been here almost four weeks now, and I am liking it more and more and more. The doctors and nurses at the hospital are extremely intelligent, hard-working, and dedicated; the people I meet in town are kind, warm, generous-of-spirit, and polite. Everyone greets me as I walk down the street with "*Bonjour, madame,*" or "*Bonjour, ma soeur*" (my sister), or, in the case of the tiny little old women with huge heavy baskets on their backs, "*Bonjour, ma petite*" (my little one). This is funny to me, because I am twice as tall as these little old African ladies.

Most of the people are very poor, in terms of material things. But I feel they are rich in their hearts; they seem to understand the most important things in life — family, friends, love, joy, peace. They take care of one another. There are no beggars on the streets.

Out in the villages the people lead even humbler lives than they do here in town. They live in mud huts and cook on open, outdoor fires, balancing their cook pots on three equal-size stones. Two weeks ago I visited some villages with an African friend who has a car, and we actually stopped at a village of pygmies! They all were very short, slightly built people, that's true. But otherwise, they looked and dressed just like everyone else.

Every day is an adventure here. For example, sometimes all of the electric power in town shuts down. No lights. Soooo, we light up the candles. Often, the water shuts down. This is the case right now, as a matter of fact. There is no water coming out of any faucet, or pump or pipe anywhere in Lastoursville. So what do you do? You take a bucket and walk to the nearest stream and scoop some water there to take home.

I just did this about an hour ago. I walked down the muddy slope with a yellow bucket in my hand, and when I got almost to the bottom and hesitated because it was getting treacherous, a little girl about your age took the bucket from me, waded into the stream, filled my bucket with water and carried the heavy thing back up to me. Without being asked to help me, without being paid to help me, she just automatically helped me. That's the way these beautiful people are.

I know you are interested in wild animals, so I've been keeping my eyes open for them. So far, no luck (except for some squished snakes in the street). As I've written to Thomas already, the only animals I see here (so far) are stray dogs and cats, chickens galore (everywhere, even in the shops, walking around), and goats, goats, goats. Sometimes I can't even open the front door because a family of goats is enjoying a comfy nap on the front step. I'm assured there *are* wild animals out there in the forests, but they obviously don't come into town (unless a hunter brings one home for dinner).

I will close now and walk to the Post Office about a mile away and mail this letter to you. I'll write again as soon as I can.

Your Classmate Thomas's
Grandmother, "Nonnie"

Sans Frigo

You can still live with grace and wisdom,
thanks partly to … your own innate sense of what you
must do with the resources you have, to keep the
wolf from snuffing too hungrily through the keyhole.
— M.F.K. FISHER, *How to Cook a Wolf*

Martha Cooper

With my maman *at the* marché

If you live in equatorial Africa and you can't afford a refrigerator, you might as well kiss butter good-bye. And fresh milk and cheese and ice cream and cold drinks and yesterday's leftovers, too, just to name a few.

This was the first lesson I learned at my new post: how to live, as one might put it in the lingua franca of francophone Africa, *sans frigo*, without a fridge.

I can't say I wasn't warned. When my Peace Corps recruiter in New York learned I wanted to trade in my ten-year-old culinary career for a two-year stint teaching community health in Africa, he looked at me long and hard. "You won't be able to cook or eat the same way," he said. The food will be very…ahh…*different*."

No problem, I thought at the time, waving the warning away. "With enough onions and garlic, I can make anything taste good," I told him.

What I didn't consider then, though, was the fridge factor. Such a simple, common, everyday appliance. Every kitchen I'd ever known had had one. A refrigerator — like a sink, stove, and oven — is what makes a kitchen a kitchen, after all. First you cook the food, then serve it, then keep what remains from spoiling by refrigerating or freezing it. Why, a refrigerator is part of the very *definition* of a kitchen. At least that's what I used to think.

My new home in Lastoursville, the house I'd prayed for, lobbied for, almost got down on my knees and begged Mouvagha, the rich owner, to let me rent, didn't have a fridge. And, even if there had been any refrigerators for sale in town, I wouldn't have had enough money to buy one.

I'd spent the first few weeks after my arrival in Lastoursville staying in the spare room of a high school teacher's house in *centreville* by night and house hunting all over town by day. Having a sturdy house, however humble — a home base, or base camp — was a top priority for me. I knew if I could make a secure nest for myself, and a clean, cozy, country-inn-like rest stop to share with younger volunteers passing through Lastoursville in their travels, I could be happy and my community health work could go well. If my house had a kitchen, where I could cook and share healthy meals, I could stay well.

"You kids are damn lucky to have a roof over yer heads an' food in front of you!" my father, drunk or sober, would often say to us at the dinner table. His words implied, if we didn't watch it — if we weren't good, docile, obedient, appreciative, and most of all fearful-of-him kids — we could find ourselves wandering the streets, holding begging bowls, like little African castaways. Thus, I learned early on to place a high value on the fundamentals, food and shelter. And, as a grown woman living on my own, I'd learned the vital importance of providing for these fundamentals for myself.

My house on the hill needed work, to be sure. Inside, it was filthy. It smelled of mold and rodent droppings. The sickly pink interior wall paint was so ugly it hurt my eyes. And the house was infested with all sorts of lowlife requiring eviction: There were cockroaches the size of mice skittering along the kitchen cabinet shelves, spiders and lizards crawling over the walls, noisy bats in the crawl space beneath the roof, flies and bees and mosquitoes in zinging battalions coming and going through the louvered windows, moths that swarmed around bare light bulbs and then littered the floor with their sizzled corpses, and tiny ants marching in determined formations everywhere.

I could handle this, I told myself, blending hope with bravado. I could clean and paint. I could eliminate these unwelcome tenants one way or another. It would take time, and, as my mother would say, "a lot of elbow grease," but I could do it.

What I couldn't do, though, I knew, was keep prepared food from spoiling in hundred-degree heat. Only a refrigerator could do that.

The small kitchen in my house on the hill had a back door that led to what I hoped and dreamed would one day be my first garden. It had a big, enamel sink, with water the color of Coca Cola, straight from the river and decidedly undrinkable, that ran intermittently from the faucet. It had a white-tiled counter for chopping and prepping food, a terra-cotta-tile floor, and a floor-to-ceiling cabinet for storing dishes and dry goods. But it had no space to put a fridge. And even if I could fit one in somehow, on the modest monthly living allowance I received from the Peace Corps, I couldn't afford to buy or even rent one.

I soon began to realize that for most people in the "developing" world, a refrigerator is a luxury item not even near the top of their wish lists. As a volunteer, living at the socioeconomic level of most of the locals, I didn't have a car, although there were some people in Lastoursville — mainly the Lebanese shop owners and the Gabonese *grands types* — who did own cars and pickups. I didn't have a phone or TV either, although I did see and hear signs of such modernity in a few houses as I walked by. But refrigerators? Most people — and that definitely included me — could not afford one.

How does this fact affect the way people shop, cook, and eat, I wondered, after I came face to face with the problem myself. What impact does it have on their overall diet and their health? If you can't keep food from spoiling in the rainforest, where bacteria, as well as all sorts of insect life, thrive, what foods do you choose?

Little by little — or *petit à petit*, as the locals would say — I learned:

Forget leftovers. Some people told me I could leave soups and stews, covered, on the kitchen counter overnight and boil them well the next day. Out of a healthy respect for the dangers of food poisoning, I didn't dare.

Forget wet dairy products. I actually began to appreciate the taste of NIDO, the full-cream, canned powered milk available in Lastoursville's shops, in my morning tea or coffee. Besides, I'd always wanted to cut down on half-and-half, butter, and ice cream anyway.

Forget ice cubes — and cold drinks, or cold anything, for that matter. The sensation of having something cold in my mouth quickly became a memory.

Forget feeding three-course meals to unexpected guests. When a group of hungry young volunteers dropped by at meal-time, as they usually did, empty-handed and expecting to be fed a free, real meal, I could not open a refrigerator door and perform instantaneous culinary magic tricks, like pulling rabbits from a hat. Instead, all I could offer them was homemade soup, still simmering on the stove, and freshly baked bread.

The trick, I soon discovered, was to shop for fresh foods daily and cook only as much as I needed that day, the culinary equivalent of *carpe diem:* Cook for Today. For me, this meant walking every morning, after giving my health lecture at the hospital, the mile down hill from my house to the open-air *marché* in town to see what the women vendors there had to offer.

Midway down the main street, to the left, along a dusty passageway lined with freelance merchants selling pre-cut, two-yard-lengths of colorful African cloth for wrap skirts, or *pagnes*, and cheap Chinese toiletries on unsteady, low wooden tables, was Lastoursville's open-air market, housed in a rickety wooden hangar with a corrugated metal roof.

Just beyond this *marché* was the biggest downtown *boîte de nuit* (nightclub), which seemed to be open for business round the clock, every day of the week. From tinny-sounding speakers, this bar played nonstop tapes of Afro-pop and high-life music — thumping, strumming, plucking, percussion-rich cadences in six-eighths-time, peppered with deep male voices singing longingly, "Oh, mamma, Oh, mamma..." — so loudly that it filled the air of Lastoursville's entire business district like pulsing, wafting nightclub cigarette smoke.

And only a few yards from the bar, to the right, in what once may have been a clearing, was the town dump — an ever-growing mountain of rotting wet refuse baking in the open, equatorial oven called Lastoursville — whose stench made me want to stop breathing.

The *marché* itself, though, drew me in.

"What is this, *maman*? I ask an African woman who has piles of leafy greens in front of her on a rough wooden table. Beneath the table I see her tiny baby sleeping soundly in a *pagne*-lined cardboard box.

"*Epinards,*" she tells me. But it doesn't look at all like the spinach I've always known and loved.

"How much?" I ask her in French.

"*Cent francs,*" she says. I offer her the coin, worth about twenty American cents, and we smile and nod at each other as I struggle to scrunch the leaves into my net shoulder bag.

Then I continue surveying the long rows of rough-hewn wooden tables, considering what else I might want to put into that day's soup. The vendors, all women, call out to me — "*Madame, viens ici!*" (come here!) — to buy their goods. Did I want some manioc (cassava)? *Non, merci.* Fresh tomatoes — bruised and battered from their long, overland haul from far more agricultural Cameroon? *Non, merci.* Plantains? *Pas aujourd'hui* (not today). Small, green, indigenous eggplants? No, thanks; too bitter. Scotch bonnet peppers (*piments*), to give my soup a kick? Why not. Onions? Garlic? *Ah, oui, bien sûr!*

One day early on one of the *marchandes* there, a tiny, wizened woman of about eighty, whose small table sat alone near the entryway to the *marché,* commented on the long, blue denim A-line skirt I was wearing. She said, half-teasingly, in French I could grasp, "You could dance the tango in that skirt."

"Well, then, let's dance!" I said, so she gamely got up from her wooden bench and we danced a little mock-tango — for everyone's enjoyment — right there beside the piles of hot peppers and plantains.

She told me her name was Leora. On a large, round, enameled tray in front of her she sold sandwiches made from chunks of locally made French bread that she slathered with margarine and filled with thick slices of what she called *saucisson* but what looked to me like plain bologna. Every day, after I'd made my rounds, up and down the aisles of skimpy produce offerings, Leora would pat the bench beside her and invite me to "rest my legs."

I sat close to her, close enough to take in the elemental odors of her threadbare clothing and leather-like skin. She smelled to me like fire and earth, wood smoke and loam. She smelled of Africa, and I drank it in.

I sat beside Leora at the *marché* every morning, and over time, in clear, slow, patient French, she shared with me stories about Lastoursville and her life. She told me the town had been named after a young explorer, François de Lastours, from a rich French family, who had died of malaria here in 1885. She pointed toward the road I could take to find a monument built in his honor — now overtaken by jungly bush.

She told me about the arrival by river of missionaries to Lastoursville, when she was a little girl. She mimicked how straight and somberly the missionary wives sat in the dugout canoes — there were no good roads then, she said — and how these rigid white women wore huge white hats covered in netting to their necks, to keep the sun and bugs off their delicate white skin, and how they had to be carried overland in palanquins because they didn't want to muddy their high, buttoned, white leather shoes.

She told me about her married life in the lively coastal city of Port Gentil, where her beloved late husband had been a proud policeman, and she had worked as a cook and seamstress for snooty — she flicked her nose with an arthritic forefinger — French women. Her dream, Leora told me dreamily, was to return to Port Gentil one day, to recapture those happy times and breathe salt air before she died.

When I asked her whether she and her husband had had any children, she shook her head, sadly. *"Non."*

Leora was unusual in this and many other ways. Not only was she truly elderly — decades older than the fifty-two-year life expectancy for Gabon — but she lived alone. She had no family. She had traveled beyond Lastoursville, she was literate, and she spoke fluent French. She was independent: She supported herself entirely by selling her homemade *saucisson* sandwiches; and every morning, regardless of the weather, she walked almost a mile to and from the *marché* in bare feet.

In a strongly matriarchal society, as Gabon has, however, a woman without children is a misfit, almost a pariah. People think there must be something wrong with her. Perhaps she is bewitched. Leora, it seemed to me, was treated like an outcast among the other, much younger, women at the *marché*, and this fact drew me even closer to her.

"Tu vois" (you see), she said to me one morning, indicating with her chin the other vendors there, *"elles sont jalouses de nous."*

"Why should they be jealous of us?" I asked her.

Because, she explained, they saw me as her daughter now.

In fact, in many ways Leora did remind me of my own mother, whose name was Lee and who would have been close to Leora's age if she were still alive. Both women were small, thin, and strong as a sailor's rope; both were a rare blend of spirited and shy, funny and cynical, vulnerable and sinewy. And they both looked at me similarly — with a singular focus, as though I were the most fascinating and baffling creature they had ever seen.

"Where did you *come from?*" my mother would sometimes ask me rhetorically as she washed and I dried dinner dishes in the kitchen when I was too little to reach the sink. "Who *sent* you?" For a time I thought I might have been adopted, and she had forgotten from where. Leora's eyes, whenever I tried to tell her about myself in my halting, groping French, seemed to say the same: *Who sent you to me?*

Leora became my *maman*. We adopted each other, unofficially. Wordlessly, somehow we agreed that she could depend on me. For as long as I lived in Lastoursville, I would care for her if she fell ill, the way I'd cared for my own mother when she was dying of cancer. And Leora, for as long as she could, would be there at the *marché* for me — welcoming me with a smile, patting the space beside her, urging me to rest a while, and looking at me wonderingly, as if to ask, *Where did you come from?*

So every day, after visiting with Leora at the *marché,* as I walked in the late-morning hundred-degree heat up the steep hill to my home, I began to see more and more clearly that not having a fridge was far from the hardship I'd at first imagined. In fact, it was a blessing, which, like so many of life's blessings, had arrived disguised.

Then, when I got home, sweaty but happy, I would empty my net bag on the kitchen counter and proceed to create my "Soup du Jour" — a hearty mélange of familiar and unfamiliar ingredients. Like life in Lastoursville in general, my soup each day was different from the one the day before. But the procedure I followed in making it was, a lot like me, pretty predictable: First, I chopped onions and garlic...

Martha Cooper

Lentil and Couscous Soup

3 tablespoons oil
1 medium onion, peeled and chopped
1 large clove garlic, minced
2 cups chicken stock
   (or 2 cups water with chicken bouillon cube)
1 small *piment* (fresh hot pepper), minced
1 can whole, peeled tomatoes, chopped
1 can cooked lentils
1 cup cooked (or ½ cup uncooked) couscous
1 bunch gumbo leaves (optional), cut in chiffonade

Sauté onion and garlic in oil until soft. Add chicken stock, *piment*, tomatoes, lentils, and couscous and cook until married, about 15 to 20 minutes. Add (optional) gumbo leaves a few minutes before serving. Season with salt and pepper to taste. Makes about 4 servings.

Gabonese Gumbo Soup

3 tablespoons oil
½ onion, chopped
3 cloves garlic, peeled and chopped
1 *piment* (fresh hot pepper), minced
6 gumbo (okra), trimmed and sliced into coins
1 chicken bouillon cube
2½ cups water
½ cup cooked rice
½ cup cooked lentils
½ teaspoon ground gumbo, for flavor and thickening
    (optional)
6 cherry tomatoes, quartered

Sauté onion and garlic in oil until soft. Add *piment*, gumbo, water and bouillon cube and cook until gumbo is soft. Add remaining ingredients and cook 10 to 15 more minutes to marry flavors. Season with salt and pepper to taste. Makes about 2 servings.

Easy Eggplant Soup

2 cups water (or chicken stock)
1 chicken bouillon cube (if using water)
2 cloves garlic, minced
1/3 cup Moussline (or any brand of potato flakes)
2-3 small eggplants, roasted, peeled, and chopped

Combine all and cook until thickened. Season with salt and pepper to taste. Makes about 2 servings.

Potato-Corn Chowder

3 tablespoons oil
1 medium onion, peeled and chopped
2 cloves garlic, minced
½ *piment* (fresh hot pepper), minced
2½ cups water (or chicken stock)
1 chicken bouillon cube (if using water)
2 small potatoes, peeled and diced
1 ear fresh corn kernels (or about 1 cup frozen)
¼ teaspoon dried thyme
2 tablespoons NIDO (or any powdered milk)
2 tablespoons Moussline (or any brand of potato flakes)
1 tablespoon minced fresh parsley

Sauté onion, garlic, and *piment* in oil until soft. Add 2 cups chicken stock (or water and bouillon cube), potatoes, corn and thyme. Cook 10 to 15 minutes. Add NIDO, Moussline, and ½ cup water (or stock), and cook until thickened, about 5 minutes. Add parsley, salt and pepper. Thin with more water if desired. Makes about 2 servings.

How to Cook a Crocodile

*For good food and ambience, head for Chez Madame Nimbe,
which is unmarked but conveniently located in the centre and
one of the most popular places in town. In addition to tables with
tablecloths, there are several sofas and a radio with music, all
giving this place a relaxing home-like feeling. She can prepare all
sorts of bush meat (antelope, porc-pic, etc.) plus regular Gabonese
and Cameroonian dishes, most for CFA 1000. Her poisson
avec sauce for CFA 1000 is truly outstanding, but she may not be
able to offer you that or some of her other more exotic dishes
unless you come in advance and tell her what you want.*
— *Lonely Planet Travel Guide*

My one social outing of the week

Madame Nimba, a short, stocky, no-nonsense Cameroonian woman about my age, seemed unimpressed to see the write-up on her restaurant in my friend Marty's Central Africa guidebook. Marty had come out to Gabon to visit me while traveling more extensively in West Africa, and we'd followed her *Lonely Planet*'s recommendation to eat dinner at Chez Madame Nimba's.

"You're famous!" I said as I showed Madame Nimba the page, listed under Lastoursville, Gabon. "These guides are sold all over the world."

She leaned over the book to take a closer look, then let her eyes roll upward and pursed her lips as if she might whistle. *"Regardez,"* she said formally, pointing a thick forefinger at the paragraph, written in English, a language she neither read nor spoke. Then, in slow, indignant French, she said, "They misspelled my name. *C'est Nimba, avec un 'a,' pas Nimbe.* Besides," she added, "who comes here? This is no tourist town."

"But *we're* here!" I said. "And Marty's a tourist! She came all the way from New York to visit me, and she brought this guidebook. We just *had* to try your restaurant."

Madame Nimba looked knowingly around the small, dimly lit room, with its unpainted, wood-plank walls and empty, rough wooden tables *sans* tablecloths. There was no radio playing, only the distant sound of Afro-pop blasting from the bars in the *marché* downtown — "Oh, mamma! Oh, mamma, mamma!" Marty and I were the only diners at Chez Madame Nimba and would most likely be her only customers that evening.

"You ordered the crocodile?" she asked rhetorically, then turned and walked heavily toward her outdoor kitchen.

I'd sensed, whenever I'd observed Madame Nimba from a distance in town or at church, that she was a prickly, formidable woman. She seemed to be wearing armor that made her already heavy body even heavier. She walked slowly, as though carrying a great weight, even when she carried nothing on her head or in her hands.

But she had a lovely, lilting singing voice. She often sang solos in church and led her church's congregation in singing. It was this singing that drew me to the small brick-and-cinderblock church down the hill from my house, with the roughly carved wooden sign by its entryway, *"L'Eglis Alliance Critienne au Gabon, Paroise de Lastoursville."*

Sunday morning church services became my one big social outing of the week — a chance to dress up and be among the town's people. I didn't know exactly what the dignified, elderly, business-suited Gabonese minister was saying, because he preached his hour-long sermons *en langue* — in the dominant local language, Inzebi. But I had a good idea; I'd heard it all before. His body language — arms reaching up to heaven, then stretched out to embrace the congregation; his warm smile and gentle, wise demeanor — spoke of God's love and the promise of eternal rest for the weary.

Often, I was the only white person there, but I was never made to feel like an outsider. I felt, however fleetingly, a spiritual oneness and sense of belonging with the African congregation. For the dura-

tion of the three-hour service, I thrilled at their lively four-part singing; their rhythmic clapping and swaying; the colorful ensembles the
African women wore; the darling, well-behaved Gabonese children
perched along long wooden benches on one side of the humble sanctuary, wearing their Sunday-best dresses and pants and swinging
their little legs to display their only-worn-on-Sunday shoes.

At times during the long service, my mind wandered. While
sitting in a far back pew one Sunday morning, I counted roughly
one hundred congregants, half of whom were men. These men were
dressed simply, in clean, white, long-sleeved shirts; long, dark trousers; and leather shoes, mostly worn without socks. The women,
on the other hand, regardless of their ages, were dressed colorfully,
like exotic birds, with their turbaned heads held high. From where
I sat at the back, I counted thirty different head-wrap styles, and I
marveled: *How do they do that?*

I knew that most of the turbans were fashioned from *pagne*s,
five-foot-length, wildly colorful cuts of cotton fabric usually used
as wrap skirts, but each woman had found her own way of twisting
and wrapping the fabric high on her head. Some began her wrap
from the front, others began at the back; some pleated their fabric,
others gathered, rolled, or twisted it; some formed pom-pom-like
rosettes at the ends, others ended with something resembling a
starched butterfly.

As the Gabonese minister continued with his interminable sermon, I toyed with one of my own: Shakespeare wrote of "sermons
in stones"; I saw a sermon in these head wraps. They spoke to me
of the women's pride, their timeless beauty, their individualism,
and defiance. Each woman seemed to me to be saying, wordlessly,
"Look at me! Aren't I beautiful? There is no one else on earth like
me! After God made me, He threw away the mold! *Dieu merci!*"

At other times, my eyes — and with them my attention to the
service — wandered out of the little church's open, pane-less window, over the thick, rain-forested mountains in the distance and

the rushing Ogooué River down below, and my mind would flood with memories.

"And what do *you* want to be when you grow up?" Pastor Holbrook's wife's words re-echoed in my mind. She had stopped to make small talk in front of the sanctuary with a small circle of young teens from the church's youth group, of which I was the new president.

"A missionary in Africa," I had answered her earnestly. Having recently seen movies of the church-sponsored missionaries' work in the Congo, my devout, adolescent heart had leapt at the scene. Africa pulled me, called me, like a mother calling her children home from outdoor play at sunset.

"Oh?" Mrs. Holbrook responded. "Well, you know, miles don't make a missionary."

It was time to stand and sing. *Where am I? And what am I doing here?* Fate had not made a missionary of me, to be sure, but it had brought me back to Africa, to this place, at this time. As I gathered up the tattered hymnbook and took a deep breath to begin to join the others in singing, I thought, *Yes, I'm where I should be.*

Madame Nimba was a pillar of this tiny church, and I loved to see her leadership skills in action. Sometimes she would slowly, confidently stride up to the front by the pulpit to lead the congregation in the heart-stirring old hymn, "How Great Thou Art." Like the self-appointed general of this small army of Christian soldiers, she commanded us all to sing the words in our own language, whatever that language might be — Inzebi, Bateki, Banjabi, French, or English.

If my American missionary friend Bev, whose church this was, were in town, she and I would be the only ones singing in English. But Bev was often away visiting her other churches in the region, so I was left to carry the English tune alone, dredging the words up from decades-old memory:

Oh Lord, my God,
when I in awesome wonder
consider all the worlds Thy hands have made —
I see the stars, I hear the rolling thunder;
Thy power throughout the universe displayed —
then sings my soul,
my savior, God, to thee,
How great Thou art! How great Thou art! …

Being a part of this blend of voices using disparate words to express such praise brought tears to my eyes every time.

Occasionally, I would see Madame Nimba in town when I visited the *marché*. One day was particularly memorable because of her intriguing outfit. Along with an emerald green *pagne* with an enormous blue and green peacock printed on it, and a matching head wrap, she was wearing a white T-shirt with a large photo of Bill and Hilary Clinton filling the front.

There they were, the smiling, waving torsos of the then-President and First Lady — with the letters "U.S.A." written boldly below. Although it was not at all unusual to see Africans wearing American T-shirts printed with vivid logos and slogans both commercial and political, it was surprising for me to see the Clintons stretched to such broad dimensions by Madame Nimba's ample breasts. It was like something you'd expect to see in the bizarrely distorting mirror of a carnival's funhouse, rather than in the *marché* of a small town in the middle of the Central African rainforest.

At the time, Bill Clinton was in the throes of the Monica Lewinsky scandal, a scandal most Gabonese seemed to find baffling. Their own president, Omar Bongo, had several wives and countless mistresses; these were the perks of power, the people here believed. Why were Americans making such a fuss? To them, President Clinton, whom they all referred to as "Bill," as though he were everyone's buddy, could do no wrong.

That day, Madame Nimba seemed to be in a good mood. She invited me back to her house to give me some ripe oranges from her tree, and she also let me sample what she called *beignet soufflés* — little, round, golf ball-size, deep-fried gateaux — she'd just cooked to sell in town. When I asked for the recipe for these cloudlike mouthfuls, she answered in fast French, *"Levure, blé, sucre, sel, oeufs, et lait en poudre"* (yeast, flour, sugar, salt, eggs, and powdered milk). As soon as I got home, I experimented with the proportions, and added a ripe banana to the recipe to make it my own.

In time, I worked up the nerve to approach Madame Nimba at her restaurant about a project I had in mind. As this encounter wore on, though, I became increasingly convinced I'd either caught her on an especially bad day or I was possessed of a particularly bad idea.

My thought, I told her in my best, halting, groping French, was to start a cooking school in Lastoursville. I explained that I'd taught at a cooking school in New York City for six years — during the time I had my small catering business there — and since being posted to Lastoursville by the Peace Corps I'd begun giving cooking classes to small groups of women, with some success.

I told her that I taught these local women simple, practical, healthy recipes, made with affordable, available ingredients. My specialties, I said, were a healthful bread recipe, which I called *Pain Americain*, and *Les Trois Groupes Soupe*, a thick, one-pot, soupy meal containing elements of the World Health Organization's three basic food groups. *"Les trois groupes,"* I went on, in my teacherly fashion, "include those that provide bodybuilding protein, such as meat or fish; those that provide ready energy, such as bread or rice; and those that provide vitamins and minerals, such as fruit and vegetables."

I'd thought — I'd hoped, I'd assumed — that as a food professional herself, a veritable colleague, she would be receptive to my idea and she might even want to participate as a teacher. But I could tell from the scowl on her broad, worry-lined face I was quite mistaken.

I attempted humor. "Albert Schweitzer opened the first hospital in Gabon, in Lambaréné," I said, enthusiastically, "so I thought I could go down in history as opening the first cooking school in Gabon, in Lastoursville!"

Madame Nimba was clearly not amused. Throughout my monologue she listened, but darkly. When I ran out of steam and I'd exhausted my French vocabulary on this topic, I waited silently for her response.

Suddenly, in rapid-fire French — which was relatively easy for me to grasp because she wasn't Gabonese, and the accents on her words were more or less where they were supposed to be — she shot from the hip:

"Cooking school?! *Here?!* You must be dreaming! These people don't care about eating well. They only want to eat manioc [cassava]. *Baton de manioc. Feuilles de manioc.* Manioc, manioc! Every day of their lives. *C'est tout!*

"Do you think you'll get any cooperation for this project?" she thundered. "These people are not do-ers. Things don't get *done* here! You cannot depend on anything or anyone. Things break down and stay broken down. People make promises but don't follow through. They're all *paresseux* — indolent. I should know. I'm married to a Gabonese. I've lived in this town with him for thirty years.

"I've been disappointed too many times…," she said, her voice trailing off. The "joy of the Lord" that she sang of in church was clearly eluding her now.

"I think you'd be a wonderful cooking teacher," I persisted. *If she is stubborn and determined,* I thought, *then she's met her match.* "Would you be willing to give me a private cooking lesson?" I asked. "Would you teach me how to make the crocodile dish Marty and I had when she was here visiting me?"

Madame Nimba thought for a moment. Then, to my surprise, she agreed. "*La semaine prochain?*"(next week?) I asked, knowing I was pushing, but she nodded. We set a day and time for the following week, and I returned with a pad and pen.

I sat at her rough, wooden, outdoor-kitchen table and took notes quietly as she worked. She laid out all the ingredients on the table in front of her and began to prep them. She seemed happier than I'd ever seen her. As her thick, able hands worked — chopping, mincing, pushing food aside — she wordlessly explained to me what she was doing. She was in her element, and I understood completely.

She asked me to call her by her first name, Denise.

She took a handful of long lemongrass that grew in her wayward, wild-looking back garden, swished it in a bowl of water, tore it to pieces with her strong hands, then plopped it into a big, black cooking pot. She reached for the baby crocodile, which weighed no more than two kilos, she said, ripped off its baby-soft reptilian skin, as if she were removing a child's flannel ski pajamas, and whacked it into serving-size pieces, leaving the little, clawed feet in tact.

Then she stopped. It was as if the weather abruptly changed and black storm clouds had blown in. She put the knife down and gripped the edge of the table as if to steady herself. Her turbaned head hung heavily, her chin nearly touching her protruding chest, staring at the raw, bluish chunks of crocodile meat in front of her.

"*Qu'est-ce-que se pas?*" I said softly, afraid she might be having a heart attack or stroke.

"*Ma fille,*" she moaned, "my daughter…"

Slowly, she told me. Her daughter, who had been a policewoman in Cameroon, had been murdered the year before. Her body was hacked to pieces. Like this baby crocodile. With a machete. What was left of her was dumped in the forest. Ethnic rivalries. Retribution.

Quickly, she reached a heavy hand for an onion and chopped it. Then with the back of her other hand, she wiped her tearing eyes. *Yes*, I thought, *there is no greater pain for a mother than to lose a child. Yes, I understand.*

She chopped the fresh ginger and garlic without looking up, then added them to the pot.

She'd spent all of her savings to travel to Cameroon for the funeral, she said.

She added a handful of leaves to the pot.

"What are those?" I asked, pointing to the leaves, attempting to change the subject. ("*I measure every Grief I meet,*" Emily Dickinson said, "*With narrow, probing, Eyes — I wonder if It weighs like Mine — Or has an Easier size...*")

Denise's words were too painful for me to hear, to bear. I wanted to weep with her. I, too, had lost a daughter, but not to murder.

Here in Africa, so blissfully far from the past, I seldom let myself think of my painful history, which I'd tried to exorcise in writing *Somewhere Child*; but Madame Nimba's grief tore the bandages off of my own. *No!* I admonished myself, *You mustn't cry anymore. What good would that do? You've cried for decades. You've cried enough. No, it is better now to cook. Cooking is healing. Cooking is life.*

"Madadoomba," Denise said in Banjabi, holding up one of the mysterious leaves. I didn't press her for an explanation, but I took an extra leaf to examine at home.

All of the ingredients went into the pot, along with chopped canned tomatoes, fresh hot peppers, and a healthy dollop of salt. Denise covered all of the ingredients with water and put the covered pot on the open, outdoor fire.

While the crocodile cooked, we talked about other things. She told me about her life in Lastoursville, how alone and far from home she felt as a Cameroonian woman still treated like an interloper by the locals after thirty years. She felt marooned on an inhospitable island, with a husband who was oblivious to her needs. Her heart, it was clear to me, was broken. Now few people came to her restaurant, because, as she rightly stated, this was not a tourist town. Other than cooking, singing was her only outlet. She loved to cook and to sing.

Crocodile, as one might guess, tastes like a cross between chicken and fish. This dish was tender and delicious, with its piquant sauce made more mysterious by the slightly bitter flavor of the *madadoomba* leaves.

"I'd love to make this myself," I told her as we shared the finished meal together. "Where could I find a baby crocodile?"

Madame Denise Nimba let her eyes roll upward and pursed her lips as if she was about to whistle. She didn't answer me. She still kept some secrets.

Singing in church

Banana Beignets

½ teaspoon dried yeast
1/3 cup water
1 tablespoon NIDO (or any powdered milk)
2 tablespoons sugar
1 pinch of salt
1 large egg
1 teaspoon pure vanilla extract
1 ripe banana
1 cup all-purpose flour
(peanut oil for frying)

Blend all ingredients (up to and including flour). Allow to rise to double. Drop by tablespoons into hot peanut oil. Drain. Sprinkle with sugar and cinnamon. Makes about a dozen.

Crocodile Stew
(*Chez Madame Nimba*, Lastoursville, Gabon)

1 baby crocodile (about 2 kilos), cleaned, skinned,
   and cut into large chunks
1 bunch lemongrass (about 12 stalks), washed and chopped
1 onion, peeled and sliced
1 small head of garlic, all of the cloves peeled and minced
1 large, finger-length piece of fresh ginger, peeled and minced
1 bunch of *feuille* (leaves), washed and chopped [Note: I
   believe Madame Nimba used what is known in English as
   bitterleaf; but spinach or sorrel could be substituted.]
1 *boîte* (can) whole tomatoes, chopped
1-2 whole *piments* (she used Scotch bonnet hot peppers)
1 tablespoon salt

Place lemongrass on the bottom of a *marmite* (Dutch oven). Add crocodile and all remaining ingredients. Add water to almost cover contents. Cover pot and cook about 1 hour or until tender. Serve with rice. Makes 4-6 servings.

Petit à Petit

*Here [in Africa, the black men] differ from the
white men, of whom the majority strive to insure themselves
against the unknown and the assaults of fate. The Negro
is on friendly terms with destiny, having been in her
hands all his time; she is to him, in a way, his home....
He faces any change in life with great calm.*
— ISAK DINESEN, *Out of Africa*

"Main Street" before midday, Lastoursville

Martha Cooper

Some days I got discouraged. The bugs, for example — not to mention the ubiquitous dirt and paralyzing heat — really, really *bugged* me. These bugs were like no other bugs I'd ever known. They were more than brazen pests; they were terrorists and tormentors. They knew the power of their numbers. They knew, despite their diminutive individual size, that they could take down seemingly superior human beings.

Just one hungry mosquito's bite in the night could bring with it potentially deadly malaria. (Fortunately, we volunteers were supplied with costly prophylactics to help prevent such an outcome. Mefloquine, also known as Larium, which plays havoc with the liver if taken long-term and causes fiendish nightmares in the short-term, is almost 100 percent effective in preventing malaria; so we were obliged to take it once a week, faithfully.) One bott fly could lay her eggs in your wet laundry, and those eggs could burrow — like living, breathing, growing, grape-size boils — into your skin. One foo-roo, smaller than a pinhead, could give you a mysterious, debilitating arbovirus. Another, day-biting bug could fell you with dengue fever, for which no treatment exists.

But even beyond the health threats they posed, these ever-present legions of tropical insects were just plain monumentally infuriating to me. When my hands were too busy to swat them, such as when I was kneading bread or digging in my nascent garden, the bugs would take the most advantage. Big, black flies would saunter across the lenses of my prescription sunglasses, blurring my vision. Other, smaller, bugs would crawl up my nose. Still more would fly into my ears, demonically jangling my nerves with their high-pitched whine. Foo-roos ate at my ankles, wrists, neck — wherever some sweet skin was exposed to them — leaving red, itchy welts that I scratched until they bled and then soon became infected.

Because I refused to cover myself from scalp to foot with gooey commercial insect repellants, these "remedies" were useless to me. Like most modern remedial products on the international market, store-bought repellants clearly weren't designed with Africa in mind. Perhaps the Africans were inured to the bugs' annoyance. Or maybe their skin was thicker and tougher than mine. Or, perhaps, they had their own, time-tested, traditional *remedes* that repelled insects fairly successfully. If so, they remained mysteries to me. Consequently, there were days when — and I couldn't even admit this weakness to my *maman* Leora — privately, within the confines of my own solitary existence, the bugs got me down.

And not only that. My inability to communicate with the local people in French was even more disheartening to me. To learn to speak fluent French at last — after nearly thirty-five years (since high school) of false starts and unsuccessful attempts through dry textbooks, tedious cassette tapes, and brief trips to Paris — had been a major motivating factor in my decision to join the Peace Corps and serve in a Francophone African country in the first place.

I had learned to speak culinary French when I changed careers ten years before. After my mother died, I used some of the inheritance she left me to attend a summer course at La Varenne, a well-known cooking school then in Paris, as the first step in becoming a food professional in New York. My mother had been a wonderful cook, and I, as her eldest daughter, her helper and disciple, had learned how to cook at her side. I saw that my cooking always made her happy, especially when I cooked for her during her last two years, when cancer cells slowly destroyed her brain and ultimately took her life. Up until the end, she was able to appreciate the taste of good food — or, at least she seemed to. I knew she would approve of this risky career change, this potentially gratifying use of her gift.

To recover from my mother's cancer — as well as from a broken wedding engagement to a colleague whom I'd mistakenly believed was Mr. Right — I took a leave of absence from my stressful job as a corporate writer-editor in New York and stayed with a friend in Paris that summer. As my heart gradually healed, I fell in love with all things French — especially the French sense of style and timeless beauty, the respectful love and appreciation the French have for true food, and their supremely symphonic language.

I vowed to my Parisian friend, Marie-Laure (with whom I spoke English because she was an English teacher and enjoyed the chance to practice her English with me), I would surprise her by speaking French with her one day. "Learn French!" then became my adamant New Year's resolution every subsequent year, but Marie-Laure would often tease me in letters: "I think you start with Chapter One from the same French grammar book every New Year's Day and give up on it before February arrives."

Nevertheless, I was determined to learn to speak French, one way or the other, if it were the last thing I did — which is why "Learn to speak French well" was near the top of my Things To Do Before I Die list. But here, in Francophone Gabon, on the ground, in the first year at my post, my inability to converse intelligently in French was a daily source of embarrassment and personal disappointment for me. I felt like a small child speaking baby talk. I felt stupid (*and good for nothing*). It made me want to (and I often did), in the privacy of my own home, cry.

I could read and write in French — especially with a fat dictionary nearby. I could speak some French — slowly, painstakingly, word-by-well-accented-word, within a finite vocabulary. I just couldn't carry on real, live, animated, back-and-forth conversations with other human beings in the town where I'd been sent to live and work for two years.

I could ask polite questions, such as, How are you? — *Ça va?* — or inquire cheerily, What's new? — *Quelles nouvelles?* But if the answer I received was longer than short, which it usually was among Africans, for whom the social niceties of elaborate greetings are enormously important, I found, I probably couldn't understand what they were saying.

I would hear sounds that seemed like French coming out of people's mouths in long, fast-moving, seamless streams; but I couldn't discern individual words. To my ear, there were no breaks at all, no telling where one word ended and another began. And the accents — so vital to this musical language — seemed to me to be everywhere but where they belonged. It was, I thought, a little like learning to speak English in Jamaica.

Sometimes I rationalized: Everyone here is at least bilingual. French is a second, if not third, language for all of us. In this town of over twenty different ethnicities, each with its own first language, French — taught only in school, where few people had spent much time — as the common denominator of communication, was bound to suffer.

Centrally located Lastoursville was a crossroads town that attracted people from outlying villages as well as entrepreneurs and adventurers from other African countries. For those Gabonese who dreamed of dressing for success and working in air-conditioned offices, there was nowhere to go but the capital, Libreville, ten hours away by train. But for those with more modest, or realistic, employment goals, Lastoursville and the surrounding area offered some opportunities.

People from local tribes, such as the Banjabi, Baduma, and Bakota, might find work at the hospital, the post office, or the regional high school situated in Lastoursville. People from other Gabonese tribes, from farther away, such as the Bateki, Bapunu, or Fang, might be found working for the railroad or in the forestry camps (*chantiers*) just outside of town.

Refugees and immigrants, both legal and illegal, from other African countries came to sparsely populated Gabon with their trades and specialties as well as their hopes for a better life. Muslim West Africans, from Senegal, Mali, and Chad, for example, set up shop in Lastoursville as small-scale *commerçants*. Nigerians were barbers; Ghanaians, tailors; Congolese, painters; Sao Tomeans, builders; Beninois, auto mechanics; Cameroonians, like Denise Nimba, restaurateurs.

Lebanese men left their wives and children back home in Lebanon to run the largest grocery stores in Lastoursville, where they sold tinned goods that were past their expiration date and other items that were clearly seconds — all at first-rate prices. Frenchmen, who seldom showed their rugged, suntanned faces in town, managed the *chantiers* along the nearby train line. Only two white people lived in Lastoursville — both American women in their fifties — my new friend Bev, the Christian Alliance missionary who was often out of town on church business, and me.

French, then, became the common link among all of Lastoursville's disparate people. It wasn't textbook French or the symphonic French I'd dreamed of speaking one day, but it was serviceable French. It helped keep the peace. It allowed the populace to communicate using commonly understood words instead of with the *swoosh* of a fast-moving machete or the *thud* of a bullet in the chest.

• • •

What the citizenry of Lastoursville lacked in French language accuracy, though, they made up for in speed.

"Lentement, s'il vous plaît" (slowly, please), I would beg, smiling sheepishly to cover up the tears of frustration welling in my eyes and pressing my hand down, as if applying brakes. *Please, please speak more slowly.*

And invariably the African who was speaking to me would say kindly, knowingly, empathetically, *"Ah, oui, 'Petit à petit l'oiseau fait son nid.'"*

Yes, I thought, nodding, *"little by little the bird builds his nest." But for me the clock is ticking; I only have two years here. I'm a New Yorker, which means impatient. I have so much to do, and so little time. How can I teach and learn — or even belong — without words?*

"What are those *words*, Mommy?" I would often ask my mother, pointing to a page I'd opened in a book.

"Ask your teacher when you get to school," my mother, Lee, would tell me sweetly, patting my hand. "I'm busy now, honeybunny."

"But I won't start school for years and *years*," I'd moan. I was only three, and kindergarten seemed like centuries away. I wanted to know the secrets to the mysteries contained in books. Of course I knew the alphabet song — everybody knew that — but I didn't know how all those printed letters — the sharp ones, like N's, that looked like bent knees, and the round ones like O's that were so much like zeroes, like nothings! — fit together to form words.

My young mother, always busy doing something important, like folding laundry, or scrubbing floors, or making a nice dinner, never had the time to explain it to me. "That's what school teachers are for," she'd say to me consolingly.

Sometimes I'd lose my three-year-old temper, in stubborn frustration. I'd pound the book's page with my right index finger. "But I want to know NOW!"

"Be a good bunny," she'd calmly answer me, "and help me with the baby."

Time and again, when I tried to have an exchange with someone in Lastoursville and he or she could see my difficulties finding *le mot juste* or following their half of the conversation, the person would try to soothe and comfort me. It was as if he or she were saying in English, *There, there. It'll be all right. You'll get it. You'll do fine....* Instead, what they said in French was, *"Ah, oui, 'petit à petit'..."*

And I'd jump in and complete the saying, to let the person know I knew it. But did I? This maxim was repeated so often to me it became like a tinselly advertising slogan: empty words.

Apart from my walks to the *marché* every morning and my visits there with *maman* Leora — who spoke French to me slowly and clearly, like a mother to a young child — I didn't do much socializing. How could I socialize without words?

Instead, I spent my first months transforming my dream house into a homey nest that would be clean and welcoming and safe from intruders — specifically, the hateful bugs. Alone, with a bucket and brushes, I scrubbed and painted. By hand, I sewed curtains and covered cheap foam pillows with bright African fabrics. I designed an L-shaped sofa for the living room that a local carpenter built for me for the equivalent of $40. I made a coffee table from a flat, discarded door, supported by empty five-gallon paint tins, and spread delicious-looking issues of *Gourmet* magazine on the top of it.

My missionary friend Bev, with whom I could speak English, loaned me a folding table and plastic chairs for my dining room. I bought a small stove-oven combination, made in Eastern Europe, from one of the local Lebanese merchants with some of my Peace Corps allowance, so I could bake bread. I arranged for window screens to be installed, to keep the loathsome bugs forever out of my house.

• • •

One morning, sitting at the makeshift desk I'd set up in the front bed-room, on the small, portable Smith-Corona typewriter I'd brought with me from New York, I prepared a two-page, single-spaced, type-written memorandum in French outlining the community health projects I had in mind and the subjects I hoped to teach at the hospital's mother-infant clinic. The memo was addressed to the hospital's director, Dr. Christophe Djimet, *Medecin Chef, Centre Medical de Lastoursville;* from me, *Agent de Santé, Corps de la Paix.* The lecture subjects I listed included nutrition, breast-feeding, weaning, family planning, hygiene, diarrheal diseases, insect-borne diseases, vaccinations, STD/AIDS, cooking, gardening, composting, recycling, and more. I had high hopes and big dreams. All I needed to do was learn how to communicate in French.

It had become my morning ritual, since moving into this house on the hill, to rise before dawn. I made a tea tray and brought it into this front room, where I would pray for strength for the day, write in my journal, write letters to friends, study French, watch the sun yawningly rise from behind the mist-shrouded mountains in the distance, and listen to the nearby birds sing. The songbirds in the big palm tree outside this front window — yellow birds, called Village Weavers, because they were bold enough to live in towns — seemed to me to be the happiest creatures alive. For them, every day was a feast day, because of the abundance of bugs. The bugs that I detested made these birds fat and happy and gave them their joyous songs to sing. How could I, then, go on wishing the insects' extinction? Where would my mornings be without the birdsong?

As I sat at my Smith-Corona by the window, typing the memo to Dr. Djimet and worrying about how I would achieve all my lofty goals, I looked out for inspiration at the yellow birds, glee-fully singing and seemingly dancing in the air as they worked in the palm tree. I took the time to watch them.

For the first time in my life, it seemed, I had time to sit back and observe birds. In my twenty years living and working in New

York City I was always in a rush, always stressed. The only birds I ever noticed there were the citified, opportunistic pigeons, who never sang. Or if they did, they never sang to me.

I watched one Village Weaver use her beak to tear thin palm fronds into thinner strips and then weave them, patiently, methodically, painstakingly into her elongated, capsule-like nest. How did she know to tie her nest so firmly to the tree and make the nest's opening at the bottom? How could she be so ingenious and indefatigable? She didn't quit. And she seemed so happy in her work — singing full-heartedly the whole time, as though it were pure joy.

Dozens of nests just like hers hung from that palm tree like Christmas ornaments. These nests, with their openings underneath, I'd noticed, miraculously, stayed put — despite the lashing rains and gale-like winds of the rainy season that had just begun. These nests were built to last. What little architectural wonders, I thought. And what skill and tenacity it took to weave them.

Ah, oui! "Petit à petit l'oiseau fait son nid" indeed! I told myself: *You must learn from these patient, observant, resilient Africans how to take a lesson from the birds.*

Machete Lessons

It is true that, when the wolf first proves he is actually there, you feel a sense of panic. "…In heaven's name!"
— M.F.K. FISHER, *How to Cook a Wolf*

Women carry machetes when they harvest their crops

There I was, standing at my kitchen sink, dripping with perspiration from the heat and humidity, washing the morning's dishes as if I were anywhere in the world, when, out of the corner of my eye, I noticed something long and thin and pale green, wiggling.

Without looking up, my first thought was, *Clothes line? No,* I remembered, the cord I picked up the other day in town when I bought these dishes was white, not green. I washed and rinsed my plastic coffee mug, set it in the plastic dish drainer and, at last, lifted my head. What I saw was a snake, a young green mamba snake, no more than two feet away from my face.

Ohmygod, ohmygod, I thought without thinking. Then, instinctively, to shoo the snake away, I splashed it with dishwater. A foolish move indeed.

Whereas the snake may have been merely uncomfortable before — stuck somehow in the window's screening — it was now truly angry at me. I could see the anger it its eyes.

In my haste, I'd forgotten the warning: Whatever you do, Africans say, don't make a snake angry; snakes don't like to feel trapped or cornered, or god-forbid, attacked. They're all right as long as they're free to slither away: You go your way, they go theirs, *no problème*. It's when they feel threatened and caught in a bind that they fight for their freedom, show their venom. That's when you're in danger.

This snake had somehow gotten caught in an undetected tear in the newly installed screening in my kitchen window — screening designed to keep malaria-carrying mosquitoes, as well as countless other equatorial insects OUT, and a sense of much-needed homey-security IN — and he was now writhing in anger. Clearly, I was in danger.

My mind raced. My body froze, hands dripping with soapsuds levitating above the dish pan.

Scream? *Why?* No one would hear me or come to my aid. In my studio apartment in New York City, neighbors could hear each other sneeze during the day and snore at night; but here in the African rainforest, my new neighbors were either too far away or out at midday. My house stood alone near the top of a hill, surrounded by thick, muffling vegetation. And, besides, I'd often been told that the long-abandoned house I'd rented was *maudit* — cursed, haunted. The locals kept their distance. I was quite alone.

Run? *Where?* This house was my home now — at least for the duration of my two-years' service — and I had no intention of relinquishing it to wild and deadly intruders, even if they considered themselves the rightful tenants. I stood my ground.

The snake hissed at me hideously, its eyes bulging. I knew I must do something. *It's you or me, buddy,* I said to myself, affecting my best, tough-girl New York accent. I knew if this snake bit me, there'd be no Poison Control Center to call for self-help guidance; and, besides, I didn't have a phone. Instead, I reached into the kitchen cupboard where I kept my machete.

Fortunately, I'd invested in this sharp, two-foot-long machete just a few days before. Machetes, I'd observed, are the all-purpose tool in Gabon. Men carry them when they go into the forest hunting. Women carry them into the fields when they harvest their crops. Kids carry them to school to help with the yard work there. Once I saw a whole elementary school's worth of kids running down the hill, alarmingly in my direction, waving their machetes playfully on their way home. I immediately thought, *I should get one of those too.*

During my catering days in New York, I'd become comfortable wielding a 12-inch chef's knife. But this machete was twice as long, at least twice as wide, and many times heavier than my favorite Henckels. I had to lift the machete with both hands to swing at the snake, coming down on its head like a guillotine.

It must have been the adrenaline that got to me, because I kept whacking, until there were pieces of snake, like chopped-up *saucisson*, all over my kitchen floor.

I stopped, bent down, and studied the bloody mess. This was the first time, I realized, I'd ever killed anything bigger than a fly — something with a face, a silenced wide-open mouth. Eyes.

Albert Schweitzer came to mind again. This doctor, humanitarian, and theologian, the first European to bring Western medicine to Gabon, believed it wrong to kill even a fly. Should I feel ashamed of what I'd just done? Frankly, I didn't. I felt relieved, empowered, reborn. The Peace Corps promised adventure, and I was getting it.

The next day, when I walked in the midday heat from the top of my hill to the center of town, I had to tell some locals what had happened. Africans, it was clear to me even in the short time since my posting, are impressively strong and courageous human beings. They have to be, to withstand the crushing physical obstacles they encounter every day of their lives: debilitating weather, incessant insects, ever-present bacteria, intestinal worms, unspeakable germs... Those who make it past five years of age, I thought, are sturdy specimens indeed. My primary job as a health volunteer was to teach young mothers how to keep their babies alive past the age of five. But I soon felt, as a thin-skinned, middle-aged white woman far from home, they had more to teach me.

To keep snakes away, one shopkeeper counseled me, you must take precautions: Cut all the grass around your house, then pour *petrol* all around it. Snakes hide in grass. And they hate the smell of *petrol*.

I crossed the dusty main road and approached the town's only gas station to buy a *bidon* of *petrol* to carry up the hill to my house.

The burly owner listened to my story silently, nodding his head, his strong black arms crossed at his massive chest.

"I killed a snake yesterday," I told him in my still-halting French. "In my kitchen. With my machete. All by myself..."

The man looked me up and down. As a Peace Corps volunteer, living at the socioeconomic level of the townsfolk — that is, without a car, without servants, without any money to speak of — I knew I was something of a curio. All white people were assumed to be rich. I didn't fit that profile. What the gas station owner saw was a thin, middle-aged woman, self-cut short blond hair gone wild with the humidity, T-shirt sticking to her chest from perspiration, well-worn missionary-style skirt modestly drooping to her ankles, sensible walking sandals (that no female French ex-pat would be caught dead in). I was getting used to being ogled.

But when this man finally spoke to me he said something that struck me as the kindest compliment an outsider could ever receive.

"Vraiment," he said, still nodding his head, as if I'd been through some sort of initiation and had passed the test, "you are an African now."

Carrying the heavy *bidon* filled with petrol the one mile uphill, I felt tall and strong and proud. I felt I'd finally arrived.

The Martha Stewart of Gabon

But anyone in the world, with intelligence and spirit and the knowledge that it must be done, can live with her inspired oblivion to the ugliness of poverty.
— M.F.K. Fisher, *How to Cook a Wolf*

My living room in Lastoursville—"like a real home"

My cohorts called me "the Martha Stewart of Gabon." It was meant to be funny — young Peace Corps volunteers' inclination to make light of everything around them in order to survive the harsh realities of life at their remote posts — but like most jokes and cartoons, it derived its humor precisely from its proximity to raw truth. In fact, although the real Martha Stewart and I lived in totally different worlds, we actually had a lot in common.

We are about the same age (she's four years older), about the same height and coloring. We were both the eldest daughters of working-class families from suburban New Jersey. We were both scholarship students at college on 116th Street and Broadway in Manhattan — she, at Barnard; I, across the street, at Columbia. We were both, briefly, fashion models. We are both divorced and mothers of one child, both daughters who were born the same year, 1965. And, significantly, we were both food-obsessed professional caterers for a time and passionate homemakers for all time.

In the realms of wealth, power, and fame, however, the real Martha Stewart and I were at opposite ends of the spectrum, and that was fine with me. As an essentially shy person with simple tastes, I had never wanted to become famous or rich or, god forbid, wield power over others. Somehow, I'd always only seen the down-side of these great American ambitions — such as the loss of both privacy and solitude, plus exposure to public scrutiny and judgment.

"How dreary," Emily Dickinson said, "to be Somebody! How public — like a Frog — To tell your name — the livelong June — To an admiring Bog!" From the moment I first read these words in high school English class and wrote them on the walls of my mind, I knew it would never be my life's goal to be a Somebody in the Bog.

The real Martha Stewart, on the other hand, rose from her humble beginnings to reach empress status; and she, unlike me, had the self-confidence to carry it off. Referred to in the press as "the diva of domesticity," "the paragon of domestic virtue" and "the queen of all things house and home," Martha Stewart became famous all over the media-watching world.

During my catering years in New York — at a time when Martha was the food professional most food professionals loved to hate — I used her recipes with impunity because they were both dependable and glamorous. One in particular stands out in my mind: On a lightly floured board, roll one sheet of (purchased) puff pastry into a large square; place a whole wheel of brie in the center; gently pull up the sides of the pastry and tie the ends with kitchen string, like a beggar's purse; paint the surface with egg wash and bake until golden. This simple hors d'oeuvre, which emerged from the oven like a gift for a queen, was more than glorious to look at. With its molten cheese and delicate-crust counterpoint, it was the perfect cocktail accompaniment.

My short-lived fame among a small band of young Peace Corps volunteers as "the Martha Stewart of Gabon" would not have threatened the real Martha. Little Gabon — the size of Colorado — would surely be one country in the world where, if she knew of it at all, Martha truly wouldn't care about being famous.

The label stuck for me there, though, when it went into print. In a write-up for the December '96 issue of the monthly newsletter, *Peace Corps-Gabon Health Notes*, Cindy, the volunteer posted in Koula Moutou, told of the Thanksgiving dinner eighteen of us new volunteers had had at her house:

> …With Bonnie leading the way in the kitchen, we had a feast that was incredible. … turkey…stuffing…mashed potatoes, gravy, green beans…carrots, *feuilles de manioc* (okay, that isn't really traditional, but we are in Gabon!), pumpkin pie, apple tart and bread pudding! Bonnie was the true Martha Stewart of Gabon. She made sure that everything came out perfect — right down to the flowers and napkins on the harvest table. It felt like a real Thanksgiving.

From then on, my nickname among my fellow PCVs became "Martha"; and frankly, I was a little flattered by it. It inspired me to become a role model for these young people, most of whom were at least half my age. I wanted to show them, through my own lifestyle there, that although we all were living in the back of beyond, in the middle of a hot, wet rainforest as dense as a head of broccoli; although we all lived on a meager allowance in towns and villages where there was really nothing to buy anyway, we could rise above!

We didn't have to live (as many of them were doing) in the kind of squalor that would shock their middle-class American parents, or subsist on tinned sardines and stale cookies. We could learn to make decent-enough meals with available ingredients, as well as herbs and spices sent from home. We could get the knack of gracious entertaining by candlelight (since the power lines were nearly always down). We could decorate the interiors of our mud-wattle huts or cement-block houses in such a way that they would be cheerful and welcoming. It's amazing what one coat of paint and some brightly colored African fabric can do!

It became my mission to teach my fellow PCVs, by example. My house in Lastoursville, one degree south of the equator, was on the train line. There is one train in Gabon, which reaches from Libreville, the country's cosmopolitan capital, on the Atlantic coast, to Franceville in the southeast. Lastoursville sits near the middle of that line, a ten-hour train trip to the capital, so volunteers often stopped at my house in their travels. They knew I had room for them, clean sheets and dry towels, screened windows, thick homemade soup, fresh home-baked bread, just-washed floors, and current issues of the *New Yorker* and *Gourmet* magazines neatly arranged on my living room coffee table.

"This is like a real *home*," some would say, with more than a tinge of homesickness in their voices, as they gripped like a lover the issue of *Gourmet* that featured a thickly frosted chocolate layer cake on its cover.

"But you can do it, too!" I'd tell them, launching into Martha mode. I'd show them how I built my own bed, using NIDO tins for the legs; how I'd hammered together a wooden loom for weaving doormats out of discarded plastic bags; how I used the tiny, ubiquitous, red, tomato-paste cans (washed, with both ends removed) as napkin rings; how I made tie-back curtains for the living room, without the benefit of a sewing machine; how I made flowers out of dried corn husks for the dining room centerpiece bouquet; how I planted pineapple tops and forced avocado pits (in time, I had thirty little avocado trees growing in separate small containers on my front porch). So Martha.

At one point, I even went a bit crazy with Peace Corps-issue Magic Markers. In the bedroom that my postmate Morgan used when she came into town for mail and supplies once a week from her village, Mana-Mana, I painted a huge, rattan headboard on the wall at the head of her bed. On the wall to the right, I painted a low bedside table, with an immense vase on it filled with colorful flowers. Not content with that, I surprised her by drawing a large-screen TV on the wall across from her bed. She was thrilled when she saw it — none of us had TV's at our posts — but she chided me for hiding the remote.

The decorating touch that I think the real Martha Stewart would have appreciated most was in my bathroom in Gabon. I took green markers and drew tall, wild grass from the baseboard up. I painted a clear, rain-free, baby blue sky, dotted with cotton-ball clouds on the ceiling. At head-height, I drew a drooping, black telephone line from one corner of the room to the other, then the other, and the other, and painted colorful birds perched on each line in happy clusters. And then, to express my soaring sentiments in that exuberant moment, I wrote in loopy, two-inch-high script along the drawing of the longest telephone line: "Like a bird on a wire, like a drunk in a midnight choir, I have found my own way to be free."

Brie en Croute
(from Martha Stewart's *Hors D'Oeuvres*)

1 pound puff pastry [available frozen, by Pepperidge Farm]
1 wheel of brie cheese (60 percent butterfat), about 2.8 pounds
1 egg yolk
4 tablespoons heavy cream

Roll out the puff pastry into a circle approximately 24 inches in diameter. Place the wheel of brie in the center and gather up the edges of the dough, as evenly as possible, to encase the cheese completely. You should have a bundle of dough at the top. Tie this with a 12-inch strand of cotton twine to hold it together. Using scissors, trim off excess dough and chill the cheese and dough on a parchment-lined baking sheet for at least 1 hour.

Preheat the oven to 400 degrees. Combine the egg yolk and the cream and brush the mixture on top of the pastry, covering as much as possible. Bake for 35 to 40 minutes, or until pastry is puffed and golden brown. (You may need to reduce the oven temperature during cooking to keep the pastry from browning too quickly.)

Cool the brie en croute on a rack and serve warm or at room temperature. Serves 38.

NOTE: This can be made several hours before serving; it will be fine at room temperature. The cheese can be enclosed in the dough the day before serving, then chilled until it is baked the next day.

Weather Report

But when the earth answered like a sounding-board
in a deep fertile roar, and the world sang round you in all
dimensions, all above and below — that was the rain.
It was like coming back to the Sea, when you have been a
long time away from it, like a lover's embrace.
— Isak Dinesen, *Out of Africa*

"Hazy, hot, and humid" — Lastoursville, on the equator

Martha Cooper

Sometimes I imagined that if I had a television set in Lastoursville, and if there were a local news program on it, its weather-forecast segment would be the same every day: "hazy, hot, and humid" — not unlike the sweltering dog days of August I remembered from my childhood in New Jersey. This imaginary TV station would not even need a real person, a meteorologist, to make this forecast; they could use a tape recording and play it over again each day: "Today you can expect white-grey, overcast skies; thick, wet air; and insufferable heat." In fact, there would have been no need to report this as news; such weather was a given, a constant fact of life in Gabon.

As a small African country straddling the equator, Gabon has a tropical climate, with year-round high temperatures, close to 100 percent humidity, and an average annual rainfall of more than 120 inches. The driest months are June, July, August, and early September. The rest of the year is muggy and scorching, with heavy rains from evening until morning.

Author Thurston Clarke, who served in the Peace Corps in Tunisia in the late '60s, spent three years traveling the earth at its midsection — a grueling 25,000-mile odyssey that spanned three continents — to write his fascinating book *Equator*. During his stay in Libreville, Gabon, he reports he "felt like a small roast in a large microwave, cooked to the bone." When he visits the Schweitzer hospital in Lambaréné, which is within 50 miles of the equator (on the same latitude as Lastoursville), he tells Maria Lagendijk, the only surviving member of Schweitzer's European staff, he "had never been anywhere as uncomfortably hot as Lambaréné." She responds, "Le Grand Docteur [Schweitzer] always told us you must have great spiritual activity to fight the heat."

Belgian writer Georges Simenon (best known for his Maigret novels), in his book *Coup de Lune,* described the climate of Gabon as "unhealthful." It is "the kind of heat," he said, "you associate with fever and hospitals." It is an inhumane heat, immobilizing, demoralizing, deadening.

Human beings, I often thought living there, are no more suited to life on the equator than they are to life on the North or South poles. This may help explain why Gabon's population of slightly more than one million people is the lowest in all of Africa, and it has one of the highest infant-mortality rates in the world.

The midday heat, I saw and felt in Lastoursville, is so paralyzing everything stops: Children go home from school, and offices and shops close from noon until three. All you can do is lie, immobile, spread-eagle on a bed beneath mosquito netting (if you're lucky enough to have mosquito netting) and sweat yourself into a *sieste* (nap) after eating lunch.

The rain, when it arrives, is something of a relief. It sweetens the air and lowers the mercury a few degrees. Some Peace Corps volunteers were known to put on their swimsuits — or not even that — and go outside and dance wildly in the welcomed rain as if they'd gone berserk. I often placed large plastic buckets on my front lawn to collect the rain when the tap water in my house was cut.

This was rain unlike rain I'd ever known. It was preceded by lightning that electrocuted the sky and thunder like cosmic cannon fire. The universe, I felt sure, was at war, with bellicose planets clashing and clubbing one another, making the earth growl in self-defense.

"What rains we had last night!" I wrote in my journal on December 12, 1996. "So dramatic. It was a veritable sound and light show right here, *sur la colline"* (on the hill):

> At one point, after 10, after I'd closed everything and turned off the lights and was trying to fall asleep, there was an enormous burst of lightning and a huge crack of thunder, and I thought, *That's it, I'm dead; the house was just struck by lightning.* So I reached for my flashlight to inspect the damage: The wind had blown the door to my bedroom down flat on the floor. And I lived to tell the tale.

The wind that followed the lightning and thunder arrived with the force and swoosh of a samurai's sword. It shook the trees with a fearsome ferocity. It picked up the rickety tin roofs on mud huts and tossed them into the forest like Frisbees. The rain then fell like a vertical river, not like rain at all. This was an assault, a free-fall from the heavens, sent, seemingly, with angry vengeance, to leach the soil of nutrients, trample fragile seedlings, and drown all hope of advancement.

People blame Africa's glacially slow progress on many things — the legacy of colonialism, corrupt governments, internecine wars, deadly illnesses like AIDS and malaria, to say nothing of poverty — and all of these reasons are surely true to some extent; but I would add to this list, at least as it applies to Gabon: the climate. Human beings simply cannot function efficiently under these climatic conditions. In Gabon, I observed, health, sanitation, transportation, communication, education, employment — all were significantly crippled by the debilitating weather.

Modern industrial and technological devices, made in and designed for more temperate climates, don't operate long under these conditions either. In the equatorial rainforest, with all its humidity, dust, heat, and rain, these modern devices soon break down and are left like animal carcasses on the side of the road to rust and rot in the mist-shrouded equatorial sun. No well-meaning development worker from the northern hemisphere, passing through the interior of Gabon in an air-conditioned SUV — even slowly — could begin to empathize with the daily Sisyphean challenge the local people face just to survive in this climate.

In this hot-wet atmosphere, disease-carrying insects and bacteria thrive, and everyone — especially the youngest and frailest — is perpetually vulnerable because these vectors are omnipresent. Bloodthirsty, malaria-carrying mosquitoes, which flourish in tropical zones, account for more than two million deaths worldwide each year, mostly in sub-Saharan Africa. Most of these deaths occur to children under five who have not yet developed immunity. In Gabon, malaria remains the leading cause of death among preschool children and the second leading cause of death, after AIDS, among people of all ages. Part of my job as a public health worker was to teach the possible precautions against such diseases. But the people knew, and I did too, that nothing could be done about the weather.

When it rained, people didn't venture out to work or to school or to the market. Everything came to a halt. How, I wondered, can a country and a people — most of whom, outside of Libreville, have no electricity much less air conditioning in their homes and workplaces — living in these conditions compete in the world? My answer was, they can't.

Living in this climate I found that matches didn't light because they'd gotten too moist, envelopes sealed themselves before I put anything in them, leather shoes and belts developed a uniform moldy fuzz, and my hand-washed laundry (I didn't have a washing machine), hung indoors in a screened-in room, took three full days to dry. Laundry could not be hung outdoors due to bott flies that lay their eggs in wet laundry; those eggs then burrow into the clothes-wearer's skin and fester like boils.

On the plus side, the sky-high humidity curled my short hair, which masked my amateur, self-imposed efforts at haircutting. And, forced to choose between the extreme heat of the equator or the extreme cold of the arctic, I would opt for the heat. I've always loved summer and have had a high tolerance for heat. To me, life in Lastoursville became like an endless northeast-U.S. August, a particularly wet and sweltering one at that.

I found it curious, too, to learn that the French word "*temps*" means both weather and time. I thought this combination especially apropos in Gabon because one directly and irrevocably affected the other. There, the weather controls everything. Nature rules. When there's a big rainstorm, scheduled meetings and appointments don't take place, phone lines go down, logging trucks get stuck on muddy roads and block traffic, sometimes for days.

What then becomes of time? It becomes irrelevant, immaterial, shapeless, and formless. It goes up in smoke. The appointed time for the meeting? Well, forget it. That telephone call from the one pay phone in town? Maybe tomorrow. The destination you had to reach by road at a certain hour? *Tant pis.*

The French *temps* in both senses represents a difficult adjustment for an English-speaking American in Gabon, I found. Living in New York for twenty years, I observed that Nature was made subordinate to Man, and the clock was king. In the rainforest of Gabon, I saw that Nature is the ruling monarch, and the clock just doesn't count.

Stretches of triple-digit temperatures in the United States make top-story news. People suddenly die of heat stroke. "A searing heat wave nearly two weeks old is responsible for more than 100 deaths across California, the authorities said," reported the *New York Times* a few years ago. In equatorial Gabon, such weather isn't news. It's a way of life.

Gabon Gourmet

*I was much interested in cookery myself, and on my
first visit back to Europe, I took lessons from a French chef at
a celebrated restaurant, because I thought it would be an
amusing thing to be able to make good food in Africa.*
— Isak Dinesen, *Out of Africa*

Teaching "Survival Cooking" to Peace Corps trainees in Libreville

Whenever fellow Peace Corps volunteers visited my house in their travels — arriving hungry, tired, and, invariably, sweaty and dirty from a long drive on their motorcycles or hours spent in the back of an open bush taxi careening along dusty roads — they were drawn to the *Gourmet* magazines on my living room coffee table.

"Ooooooh," some would swoon, glimpsing the seductive cover from afar, then walk past me toward the topmost issue as if it were a long-lost lover, "FOOD, beautiful food! I'm so sick of canned sardines and *feuilles de manioc!*" Sometimes one of them went so far as to kiss the cover photo the way Old World old timers bend to kiss dropped bread. "And look at this!" a sharp-eyed volunteer might say, studying the fine print on the cover. "It's the latest issue! My mail from home takes *months* to get to my post. What's your secret?"

"My friend Gail mails them to me — *par avion.*"

"Oh, really? Who's Gail?"

"The Editor in Chief at *Gourmet.*"

"Well, whoo-hoo! Lucky you."

I did feel lucky. My friends in the New York food world were supportive of my Peace Corps decision and generous in their gifts to me. Many sent the seed packets I begged for. Some sent care packages containing such welcomed items as dried Italian herbs, Indian and Moroccan spices, lemon curd, raspberry jam, aged balsamic vinegar, and extra virgin olive oil imported from Tuscany. Others, such as cookbook author Barbara Kafka and nutrition writer and professor Marion Nestle, sent valuable information I'd requested that would aid in my work, especially on methods of food preservation in the tropics. My friend Gail Zweigenthal, Ruth Reichl's predecessor at *Gourmet*, had her secretary, Robin, airmail me their latest issue every month.

The moment a new *Gourmet* arrived in my hands, I shelved everything else. First, I took perverse pleasure in ripping out whole pages that had ads on both sides:

Ha! Who really needs this diamond-studded Cartier bracelet? RIP. Yes, I'd love some Haagen-Dazs caramel swirl right now, but that's just not possible. RIP. "Life takes VISA." Well, not here in the rainforest! RIP. Oh, and look at this woman who's about my age, with her perfectly coiffed, short blond hair and designer outfit, holding a glass of glistening white wine and straining a smile, standing beside her gray-haired, gold-wedding-banded hubby, looking out over the railing of their Princess Cruise ship at the lovely, languid, blue Mediterranean. I cannot relate. RIP.

With no TV in my life, no billboards on any of the roadways, no print ads anywhere (because so little was printed at all), and only commercial-free Radio France and Voice of America available on shortwave radio in Lastoursville, I was reveling in my advertisement-free life. Nothing and no one was ordering me to "buy this Olay moisturizer and look years younger," "drive this BMW and be the envy of your neighbors," "wear this Rolex and impress prospective clients," or "drink this London Dry Gin and you'll be 'in.'" From this blissful distance from the commercial First World, I could see the folly of these empty promises more clearly than ever, and I rebelled against them. I certainly knew, intellectually, that a magazine's advertising revenue supports its editorial department; nevertheless, privately, I enjoyed stripping my life of aggressive ads, one issue of *Gourmet* at a time.

From every issue I tore close to thirty pages of advertising, but I didn't throw these pages away. I kept a thickening file of this richly colorful, glossy paper to use for crafts projects as well as possible cutouts for posters for my health lectures at the hospital. The clipped ads never went to waste.

What was left in each issue, then, were the things that mattered to me: Dazzling food writing, tantalizing food photography, and recipes more beautiful to me than poetry. The articles — about pasta in Puglia, for example, or beekeeping in Tanzania, accompanied by lush photos of the places themselves — took me, as Emily Dickinson would say, "lands away" from Lastoursville, especially on the hottest, buggiest, dustiest days when I was feeling low. And *Gourmet*'s recipes — which I'd long trusted, having built my New York catering business's reputation on their reliability — beckoned to me like sirens.

I studied these recipes with special interest now that the stakes were even higher and the challenges greater. How many of *Gourmet*'s recipes could I make in the interior of Gabon? How adaptable were they? How many substitutions would be required, and at what point would the dish become unrecognizable — or even awful? In every issue there was at least one recipe that appeared promising, one that was simple enough or tropical enough to work, even with the limited ingredients available in Lastoursville. For me these recipes became, in a sense, metaphors for my own ability to adapt to life there.

The larger project that made this inquiry an ongoing challenging pursuit was the revision I undertook of the existing Peace Corps cookbook called *The Gabon Gourmet*. This ¾-inch thick, 8½ x 11, 248-page, photocopied and spiral-bound cookbook was issued to each new volunteer in Gabon, in the hopes that he or she might learn some self-reliance in whatever was to pass for their kitchen at post. Packaged, convenience, and fast foods so familiar to these young volunteers when they were growing up in the States were unheard of in the interior of Gabon.

Even fresh produce was often not available in the *marchés* in Gabon because only 1 percent of the country was agrarian. Dry goods were frequently weevil-ridden and stale. Few of us volunteers had refrigerators. Eating with the locals meant a steady diet of carbohydrate-packed manioc. Young male volunteers often lost so much weight they looked skeletal; young female volunteers, on the other hand, tended to get chubby on countless packets of stale, imported cookies. Learning to cook well from scratch for oneself, perhaps for the first time, therefore, became both a health necessity and a potentially pleasurable pastime at post.

The Gabon Gourmet, whose third edition I revised and expanded by including recipes adapted from *Gourmet* magazine as well as many of my own creation, offered more than 1,000 novice-friendly recipes as well as practical, no-nonsense instructions on food preparation in Gabon. For example, under "Tossed Salad," there was this:

Begin by washing your greens. Whatever type lettuce you use, make sure to wash it carefully, inspecting it well for bugs, grit, and worms. If your lettuce has somewhat 'dubious origins,' you'll probably want to soak it before consumption to kill any bacteria or parasites that might be lurking on the leaves. Choose from the following possibilities:

1) 1 iodine tablet per liter of water; soak for 30 minutes and rinse

2) 3-4 drops chlorine [bleach] per liter of water; soak for 30 minutes and rinse

3) enough potassium permanganate to turn the water a light shade of purple; soak 15 minutes and rinse well.

Bob Courey, an earlier volunteer, left his culinary tracks in the cookbook by teaching his comrades in the interior what to do with a whole chicken: "Most of us," he wrote, "came to Gabon unprepared to deal with a chicken that fights back even though it's dead! Here's how to go about it:

> Cut the head off at the base of the neck.
> Cut off the neck at the shoulders.
> Cut off the feet at the knee joints.
> Cut off the oil gland located on the top side of the tail.
> Cut the skin open under the tail.
> Reach in, trying to keep the back of your hand against the body cavity, and scoop out the guts. This takes a few tries. (Be brave.)
> Throw away the stomach pouch and intestines.
> Throw away the lungs.
> Cut the green gall bladder off the liver, being careful not to puncture the gall bladder. Throw it away.
> Take the gizzard (the largest thing in the guts) and cut it in half. Rinse out the yellow meal; the yellow lining is rubbery and peels off.
> The heart, liver, and gizzard are edible. They can be used in a sauce, soup, or stuffing; or they can be fried. ..."

Slowly, methodically, over a nine-month period, I went through this Peace Corps cookbook, testing questionable recipes; clarifying unclear procedures; making abbreviations and instructions consistent throughout; and adding new recipes that seemed feasible, appealing, and affordable (given our limited monthly allowances). By the time the third edition of *The Gabon Gourmet* was printed and issued to all Peace Corps volunteers in Gabon in July 1997, I felt certain anyone who could follow a recipe could fend for him- or herself, culinarily speaking, at their post. The question remained, though: How many could follow a recipe?

The first person to greet me when I got off the plane in Libreville the day I arrived in Gabon in July 1996 was Peace Corps Country Director Frank Conlon. Tall, slim, and stately, he reached out a welcoming hand to me, smiled genuinely, and said, "We've been waiting for *you*."

Up to that moment, I'd been feeling anxious, disheveled, jet-lagged, sleep-deprived, and older than I'd ever been. Frank's unexpected words made me feel, in addition, flattered, curious, and confused. *"Why?"* I asked him, hoping his response might help to ground me. But there was a long line behind me of younger new recruits for him to greet, and he couldn't linger. Instead, he quickly hinted that "they" had "an idea" for me.

"Oh," I said, reeling from fatigue and the weighty tropical heat. "Okay."

Word had spread in the Peace Corps bureau that I had been both a caterer and a cooking teacher in New York. The latest issue of *Vogue* magazine, which had somehow found its way to Libreville, featured an hors d'oeuvre recipe I'd created for a recent food-lovers gathering in New York, so my culinary "fame" had preceded me. The idea, then, that they had in mind for me was to teach cooking to my group of incoming volunteers during our training period in Libreville. Attendance would be voluntary, and I could teach whatever I wished. *Did I like the idea?* they asked. *Sounds good to me,* I said.

So, during the course of our ten-week training, I offered several three-hour cooking classes, under the banner of what I called "Survival Cooking."

I chose to teach the basics, assuming few had learned to cook at their mother's side growing up and even fewer had ever been to cooking school. I taught them how to shop and stock a kitchen pantry; how to read a recipe; how to prep all ingredients beforehand — what the French call, *mise-en-place*; how to measure, chop, mince, and julienne; how to mix, blend, stir, and fold; how to test for doneness and how to season to taste. I stressed M.F.K. Fisher's philosophy, as she expressed it in *How To Cook a Wolf:* "since we must eat to live, we might as well do it with both grace and gusto."

For my first lesson I chose a simple meal with universal youth-appeal: pizza with tomato sauce topping and a mixed salad with vinaigrette dressing. I set up my demonstration table in the training center's *refectoire* (dining hall) with two huge posters of the pizza dough, tomato sauce, and vinaigrette recipes taped to the wall behind me, and my *mise-en-place* (prepped ingredients) laid out on the table in front of me. I arranged benches for the attendees in a V-shape as close to the front table as possible so all could see well. About twenty-five people attended, including most of the American trainees, a few Gabonese trainers, the Peace Corps nurse, Yemi, and the Senegalese *chef de cuisine* at the training center, whom we all called Mr. Si.

"Good cooking doesn't begin in the kitchen," I told the attentive audience. "It begins at the market. That is true everywhere in the world, but here in Gabon it may be more challenging than elsewhere...."

I gave them a list of generally available staples they should keep on hand: tea, coffee, sugar, NIDO (powered whole milk), white flour, corn meal, dried yeast, chicken bouillon cubes, rice, Mousseline (a French brand of potato flakes), tomato paste, canned tomatoes, oil (olive, if possible; palm, if necessary), canned tuna, canned sardines, dried beans, dried lentils, dried pasta, couscous, black olives, peanut butter, and jam. Among the fresh ingredients they might be able to find (other than the ubiquitous *baton de manioc*) at post were: onions, garlic, hot peppers, sweet bananas, plantains, papayas, pineapples (rarely), lemons, oranges, African spinach, African eggplant, avocados, okra, eggs, and (maybe-maybe-maybe) butter.

"If you plant a garden," I said. "even a small kitchen garden containing fresh herbs such as basil and parsley, as well as some carrots, zucchini, and tomatoes — you'll be able to improve your cooking and your diet enormously."

I asked the group how many had ever made a pizza from scratch, and no hands went up. I stressed that being able to make a delicious pizza at post would not only be empowering but also fun. "A homemade pizza can be healthy, too!" I added, showing them as proof an article-with-recipes I'd just had published in *Self* magazine's "Healthy Plate" section on homemade pizzas.

"And here's how it's done!" I enthused, hoping my love of cooking might be contagious. "First, you gather your ingredients for the dough and measure them out, like this…" I took a clear glass mixing bowl and added one cup of water to it. "In North America, yeast-dough recipes call for 'lukewarm water,' but here in Gabon room-temperature water is already lukewarm!" Then I dissolved one teaspoon of sugar and two teaspoons of dried yeast in the water. "Allow this mixture to rest a little while to see whether the yeast comes alive. It should 'breathe' and start to bubble in the water. If you see signs of yeast-life, then proceed by adding one tablespoon of olive oil plus the dry ingredients…" I measured each and added them to the bowl (after sifting through a fine-meshed strainer, to remove any bugs or debris) — 2 cups white flour, ½ cup corn meal, and 1 teaspoon of salt. "Now combine it all with your hands, like this — yes, I know, it looks like a hopeless mess at first — and turn it out on your flour-dusted table and begin to knead for from eight to ten minutes."

While I kneaded the increasingly soft, pliant dough, I philosophized about recipe-reading to my captive audience. "Printed recipes are like a newfound form of hieroglyphics," I said, "a symbolic, nearly extinct language with layers of sacred meaning, now almost shrouded in mystery. They're like secret codes or like haiku poetry that require some deciphering. They're like directions for traveling in unknown territory. But when you learn how to read the hieroglyphics, break the code, follow the directions, whole new worlds can open up to you! It's creative. It's joyful. It's *delish*."

In subsequent classes, and for each year's incoming trainees, I taught similarly simple, practical dishes — beans and rice, a variety of soups and sauces, whole-grain bread, some African dishes, and a few tropical desserts. Although these dishes may not have met *Gourmet* magazine standards, they did find a permanent place in *The Gabon Gourmet* cookbook — and perhaps in the memories of some of Gabon's volunteers.

Golden, Crispy Pizza Crust
(from "That's Amore," by Bonnie Lee Black,
published in *Self* magazine, August 1996)

1 cup lukewarm water
1 teaspoon sugar
1 tablespoon olive oil
1 envelope dry yeast
½ cup stone-ground cornmeal
1 teaspoon sea salt
2 cup bread flour

Dissolve water, sugar, olive oil and yeast in a mixing bowl or processor bowl. Combine the cornmeal, salt and flour, and add to the yeast mixture. Knead for 8 minutes on a slightly floured work surface or process for 30 seconds. Let rise to double its size, about an hour. Divide risen dough into 5 equal portions. Use immediately, or freeze in individual 4-ounce portions. Makes about 20 ounces of dough, enough for five 9-inch pizzas.

• • •

Pineapple-Papaya Salsa
(adapted from *Gourmet*)

1 tablespoon olive oil
1 red onion, finely chopped
several small *piments* (fresh hot peppers), finely chopped
    (depending on desired heat)
1 cup (about) finely diced fresh ripe pineapple
1 cup (about) finely diced fresh ripe papaya

Combine all in a bowl and mix well. Season to taste with salt and pepper. Serve with grilled chicken, for example. Makes about 2 cups.

Coconut-Lemongrass Rice
(adapted from *Gourmet*)

5 stalks lemongrass (thickly slice lower 6 inches)
4 teaspoons minced fresh ginger
1½ cups raw white rice, washed well and drained
1½ cups water
¾ cup coconut milk
½ teaspoon salt
piments (fresh hot peppers) minced (to taste)
3 scallions (or one small red onion), chopped

Cook all of the above until the rice is tender, then fold in:
3 tablespoons fresh lime (or lemon) juice
¼ cup chopped salted peanuts
½ cup sweetened flaked coconut, lightly toasted and cooled
Makes about 6-8 servings.

Southern Spoon Bread
(adapted from *Gourmet*)

¼ cup melted butter or oil
1 cup white cornmeal
2 teaspoons sugar
1 teaspoon salt
1⅓ cups boiling water

Combine all of the above, stir well, and allow to cool. In a separate bowl, beat together:

3 large eggs
1 tablespoon baking powder
1⅓ cup hot milk

Combine cornmeal and egg mixtures and pour into a buttered baking dish; place dish in larger dish containing boiling water. Bake at 350 degrees until set and golden on top (about 1 hour).

Mexican Spiced Sweet Bread
(adapted from *Gourmet*)

Combine the following in a medium-size bowl, cover, and allow to ferment at room temperature several hours or overnight:

1 cup lukewarm water
1 cup all-purpose flour
2 tablespoons white sugar
1 tablespoon ground cinnamon
½ teaspoon anise seeds, crushed
1 tablespoon dry yeast

Combine the following in a large bowl, then add the above yeast mixture to it:

3 cups flour
¼ cup sugar
¼ cup butter, melted
½ teaspoon salt
2 eggs
¼ cup raisins, if desired

Knead dough 15 minutes. Form into a ball and allow to rise to double in size, about 1 hour (covered loosely with clean kitchen towel). Punch dough down, form into small breads or rolls, and allow to rise on baking sheet to double again (about 45 minutes). Bake at 375 degrees until golden (about 15 minutes for rolls or 30 minutes for bread).

Motorcycle Mamma of Mana-Mana

If you give a man a fish,
he eats for one day.
If you teach the man to fish,
he eats every day.
— CHINESE PROVERB

"*Motorcycle Mamma*" *Morgan and me*

Martha Cooper

The village of Mana-Mana, about 40 kilometers southeast of Lastoursville, was large by Gabonese village standards. It had roughly five hundred inhabitants who lived in traditional houses made of wood-frame walls encased in mud, with roofs of either woven thatch or corrugated metal. The village was bisected by a wide, dirt road; and these squat, mud-wattle houses stood on either side of that road in neat rows, as if their purpose was to greet vehicular travelers like an honor guard as they passed through.

Large families, grouped in clusters or small compounds, occupied most of the houses in Mana-Mana. But Morgan, my pisci-culture postmate, a single, twenty-four-year-old recent college graduate from Michigan, had a spacious house of her own at the far end of the village, a half-hour's walk along the main (well, only) road from where the village began.

Once a week, Morgan made the treacherous, hour-long motorcycle ride from Mana-Mana to Lastoursville along deeply rutted, mountainous dirt roads to pick up her mail at the *boîte postale* we shared, buy provisions at the local Lebanese shops, and visit me. When I heard her approach, her Yamaha buzzing up the hill to my house sounding from a distance like an encroaching bumblebee, I would rush to greet her happily. Although I was twice her age and older than her mother, Morgan and I had become good friends, and I looked forward to our weekly visits. It was a chance to talk, in *English* again, catch up on each other's news, laugh at everything (or at nothing), play a good game of Scrabble (which she usually won), embark on a new crafts project together, and share American meals.

If it wasn't raining, Morgan and her red-white-and-blue motorcycle would arrive covered in a film of brick-red road dust. When she removed her helmet, her long, honey-color hair would be damp from perspiration and flattened to her scalp. When she smiled hello, her white teeth would contrast comically with the road-dust-caked exposed parts of her face. Nevertheless, her Midwestern unspoiled wholesomeness, her calm centeredness, and her total lack of vanity made her a beauty.

Every week I'd greet her with wide arms and tell her what I'd made for our lunch. I often made "mamma food" for us — down-home American dishes like my mother used to make when I was a child. It was food meant to make Morgan feel nourished in more ways than one. At her post in Mana-Mana, I knew, she generally ate with her neighbors outdoors, sitting in a circle on the dry, dusty earth; and manioc in all its limited forms was the standard fare.

"But before we eat, let me show you the latest member of my family," I told her excitedly one day, pulling her into my study, where my hand puppets stood in a motley cluster, held up by tall bottles on my desk.

"You made *another* puppet?" she said, peeling off her dust-covered windbreaker and shaking out her long, matted hair. "I'm starting to worry about you, Bonnie," she teased. "You're alone too much. You behave as if these puppets are *alive*."

"You're going to love this one," I said, picking up the long-faced, bald-headed, bloodshot-beady-eyed puppet whose skin was a faded, old, gray-white gym sock. What little hair he had was a thin fringe of blue yarn at the sides and along the lower back of his head; his sloppy, droopy mustache was made of blue yarn, too; and in his right hand he held a "lit cigarette" made from a piece of lollipop stick painted red at the tip. "His name is Jean Vaurien."

"John Good-for-nothing? That's a hoot! What'll he do?"

"He'll sing a song that says, *'Donne moi l'argent...'* with his hand out, and then the kids will tell him, No! We're not going to give you money! Go get a job!"

"So you're trying to teach them the Protestant work ethic now? That's *really* funny."

One day, over a summertime lunch of tuna-and-macaroni salad, made the way my mother always made it with lots of crisp, chopped celery and creamy Hellman's mayonnaise, Morgan told me, matter-of-factly, about an incident that had occurred near her village the week before. Since there was no local paper nor radio station in Lastoursville, and I wasn't plugged in to the town's word-of-mouth grapevine, I hadn't heard this news. Morgan was my messenger.

A truck driver, speeding on his route through the village next to Mana-Mana, Morgan said, had hit a young mother who was walking by the side of the road, holding her toddler's hand. The young mother was pregnant with her second child. She and her toddler were killed instantly.

The truck driver, a Muslim from Mali, was filled with remorse. He stopped his rig, climbed down from the cab, and tried to make amends. The village elders quickly took charge: They locked the man in an empty hut while they convened an emergency meeting to decide the man's fate.

Meanwhile, the dead woman's husband, father to the dead toddler and unborn baby, as well as other men from the family, enraged and armed with machetes, took matters into their own hands. They climbed onto the roof of the house where the Malian driver was being held, broke through the thatch, and hacked the man to pieces: first an arm, then a leg, then another arm...and lastly, his head.

"Hmmmmm," I said in response, trying to be cool but truly at a loss for words. I felt thankful to be posted in a town, maybe a few rungs up from the possibility of such barbarity. But I didn't want to express any judgment. Morgan always said it's not for us to judge these people; they have their own ways, which remain mysterious to outsiders. Although not a religious person — she felt, for example, that Christian missionaries were among the worst things that ever happened to the continent of Africa, opening the door to imperial exploitation and steering the people away from their own time-honored traditions — Morgan, by nature, followed Christ's clear dictum, "Judge not, lest ye be judged."

"That driver's mistake was, he stopped," Morgan said. "Big, big mistake. They told us in training — you hit something on the road with your bike — a dog, maybe, or a goat or chicken — you just keep on riding. Never stop. Unless, of course, you hit a person. In that case, you ride straight to the nearest police station, and that's where you stop."

At last able to pick up my fork again, I said, "These people live just one village away from you? Doesn't that make you feel a little ...uhmmmm...unsafe?"

Morgan smiled the I-can-handle-it smile often seen on young volunteers. "I'm fine," she said. "Everyone in Mana-Mana is really good to me."

"Have you told your mother this story yet?" I said.

"No, and I'm not going to. And neither will you," she said, still smiling. Her mom back home in Michigan was due to visit Morgan and Mana-Mana soon, and they would certainly come to visit me in Lastoursville.

Although we were posted geographically closer to each other than to any other volunteers in the area, and we shared a post office box in town (hence the term postmate), Morgan's work seemed worlds away from mine.

Whereas I walked all over Lastoursville giving health, nutrition, crafts and cooking classes indoors — in the hospital clinic waiting room, in grammar school and high school classrooms, in church halls, private homes and wherever else I was invited — Morgan traveled by motorcycle to all of the outlying remote villages teaching groups of willing men, outdoors, in the canopied open-air "classroom" of the rainforest, how to farm fish.

And whereas I struggled with schoolbook French, heavily relying on props and songs to help me get my messages across, Morgan ingeniously pieced together a patchwork of rudimentary French and a handful of words from the various local languages to make her points.

At bottom, though, there were parallels in the work we did: We both strove to help improve the nutritive value of the people's diet, thereby confronting a major health problem in the interior of the country: malnutrition. *Baton de manioc* (mashed cassava cooked in banana leaves in the shape of long batons), the Gabonese staple, offers little more than stomach-bulging carbohydrates. Morgan's work was designed to provide a ready source of body-building protein.

As Morgan explained it to me, the purpose of the Peace Corps' pisciculture (fish farming) program was three-pronged: to increase protein in the Gabonese diet, to reduce the villagers' reliance on bush meat, and to provide a means to earn money in the village. To do this, Morgan and her fellow "fish heads," as they affectionately called themselves, taught rural Gabonese how to build and stock ponds for raising fish.

Gabon had rivers, of course, but few people dared to fish them, it seemed to me, due to their treachery. The Ogooué River, Gabon's own Mississippi, rushed past Lastoursville on its long, downhill journey to sea level at the Atlantic; crashing over large, jagged rocks along its bed; slinging errant logs from upriver *chantiers* across its choppy surface; and harboring all kinds of stealthy, hungry crocodiles on its overgrown banks. Building man-made fish ponds in gentle valleys next to streams and springs was a far safer and more benign solution to the challenge of adding fish protein to one's diet. That is, if you were intent on not becoming a crocodile's dinner.

The fish they bred in these ponds, Morgan told me, was tilapia, a hardy, fast-growing fish that can do well in less-than-ideal conditions. According to the historical evidence, she said, tilapia were raised in ponds in Egypt as long as 3,000 years ago; and they not only have a high tolerance for poor water quality and crowding, they also have a high degree of disease resistance. "They're mainly plankton eaters," Morgan added, "so most of their food supply comes from naturally occurring plankton blooms in the water. But we supplement the fish's diet with manioc leaves and termites."

Many of the men, Morgan said, especially those too old or too tired of hunting wild game in the rainforest, were keen to learn the tricks of fish farming and welcomed her instructions. The fact that she was a woman — and young — made no difference to their receptivity. Her lessons were free, easy-to-follow, and practical; so these men attended willingly, hungrily. Using locally available supplies, such as clay, shovels, bamboo pipes, and maybe, if lucky, a wheelbarrow to two, she showed them how to construct their fish ponds. She encouraged them to integrate their fish farming efforts into other agricultural activities, such as mixing mud from the ponds into garden soil as a fertilizer.

If I were the right-brained, artsy puppeteer, Morgan was the left-brained, clear-eyed scientist. She knew the hard-edged, scientific facts, and she generously enlightened me. "The soil here in this rainforested part of the world is among the worst on the planet," she said. "It's totally depleted, barren, infertile, washed out by all the rain. So if the people are going to grow anything, they need all the natural fertilizer they can get."

Progress in pisciculture, as in most other endeavors in the interior of Gabon, with its sweltering equatorial heat and its nearly incessant rains, was *slow*, but, Morgan said optimistically, sure. When she first arrived at her post in September 1996, there was only one fish pond within her territory. By the following year, under her direction, there were three more.

One August day when Morgan came to visit, we went together to lunch at the home of a Frenchwoman we'd recently befriended. Francine lived in Vienne, France, during the school year, where she taught high school English; but she came to Lastourville during summer breaks to be with her French husband, Louis, who was the foreman at a nearby logging company. Morgan and I had met Francine in town not long before — she was easy to spot buying produce at the *marché*, with her curly auburn hair, pale white complexion, and fashionable French summer clothes — and she quickly wrapped her motherly arms around us both and invited us to lunch.

Francine and Louis, with their nine-year-old son Eric, lived in a small but neat bungalow in a middle-class *quartier* called *Cité Iga-Iga*, about a half hour's walk downhill from my house in the opposite direction from *centreville*. The interior of their home was distinctively French, with its plush upholstered chairs with ample arm rests, long white draperies that let in the midday sunlight, heavy wood bookcases and cabinetry varnished to a gleam, plus what seemed to Morgan and me to be ultra-luxurious: air conditioning. Outside, their lush, tropical, flowering plants and vegetable garden, tended by their African gardener, were Francine's pride.

Her clean, white kitchen was tiny but efficient, and her appliances — a large refrigerator with a freezer compartment, a standard-size oven (big enough to roast a twenty-pound turkey) with a four-burner stove-top, a Cuisinart food processor, microwave oven, and hot water heater — immediately gave me kitchen envy. On the counter top I saw bread rising beneath a white kitchen towel. Angelique, Francine's Gabonese maid, had recently attended one of my *Pain Americain* bread-baking classes, and she wanted to prove to me what she'd learned.

Francine, with Angelique's assistance, served us a superb, four-course French meal that day: tomato and lettuce salad with diced beets and vinaigrette, roulade of pork (rolled up with thinly sliced mortadella sausage, crêpes, and herbs) with steamed and buttered broccoli, a selection of French cheeses with home-baked bread, ice cream and yogurt cake.

Louis kept our glasses filled with French Merlot throughout the meal, as if there was no end to their fine wine supply. The French who worked at the logging camps, I learned, had their favorite foods and wines flown in from France on private planes every week. They could bravely suffer the heat, rain, mud, bugs, danger, and high risk of disease in their work felling monstrous Okoume trees deep within Gabon's tropical rainforest; but they could not survive without their weekly supply of genuine French food and wine.

Patting his stomach contentedly, Louis thanked his wife for the delicious meal, and then he and his son drove off in Louis' pickup truck, leaving us three women to talk — in English — at the table.

With wine-loosened tongues, we talked, of course, about our lives. Francine told us she had had two older children, daughters, from a previous marriage; but one of them, Dominique, had died.

"How?" I blurted, unthinkingly, more than a little tipsy.

"It was an accident," Francine said, her face crumpling in sorrow and her pale cheeks reddening with emotion. "Or at least we think it was an accident." She paused to gather herself. "She was at a party with friends in Paris. It was summer. She was sitting on the ledge of an open window. It was a tall apartment building. She fell backward…"

Morgan told of losing her father to cancer just a few years before, when she was still in college. And I spoke, as I seldom did, of losing my only child when her father abducted her as a baby….

There we were, three sturdy women from disparate backgrounds, sitting at a dining room table in a French home on a hot August afternoon in the middle of Africa's equatorial rainforest — eating, talking, laughing, sharing, crying, and getting a little drunk on good wine — finding our common human bond: loss.

At that time, fish heads were the only volunteers who were issued motorcycles. The rest of us got mountain bikes with thick, heavily treaded tires, plus training on how to maintain and repair them. But soon after settling in to my post, I realized that Lastoursville was too hilly for bike riding in over 100-degree heat and 100 percent humidity, and my teaching aids (such as posters, puppets, and pots and pans) were too cumbersome to carry on a bike's handlebars. So I relinquished my bike at the first opportunity. It was easier and safer for me, I thought, to get around town on foot. When it came time to traveling farther afield, however, I had to be both fearless and bold.

The first time I traveled to Mana-Mana to visit Morgan and to give health-related puppet shows to the village children there, I went by bush taxi — in this case, a pickup truck overloaded with African passengers and their belongings. Anxious parents, frightened little children, crying babies, bleating goats, clusters of scrawny chickens (tied at their feet and held upside-down to silence and incapacitate them), huge hands of plantains, baskets of manioc, cheap zippered plastic valises filled to the breaking point — plus me and my big, black backpack and bag of fragile, handmade hand puppets — crammed into the back of the battered pickup in the hope of somehow reaching our distant destinations that day.

The driver, a stocky, middle-aged Gabonese man with a weathered face and bloodshot eyes, motioned to me to sit up front with him, and I didn't resist. In the confines of the cabin, though, sandwiched between the driver and a shy, high school student returning to his village for the weekend, I could tell that the driver had been drinking. I could smell it on his breath, his skin, his clothes. He drove too fast along the rutted mountainous roads. Through the dusty, cracked windshield, I could see steep ravines on both sides. The old pickup bounced and skidded erratically, as if its shocks and brakes were nearly shot.

I felt trapped, the way I'd felt as a child as a passenger in the back seat of my father's Hudson, when he was drunk and weaving his way home after a day spent at his favorite gin mill. "Get me out of here!" I wanted to shout at my father. "Let me out! I'd rather be anywhere in the world but here!" But I said nothing then. I held my feelings in. I knew he wouldn't listen. And even if I'd had the nerve to say something and he did hear me, I knew what his comeback would be: "You want something? I'll give you something — a knuckle sandwich!"

In the bush taxi, I held the dust-covered dashboard with both hands, swallowed hard, and considered my options. There was nothing but thick, mountainous jungle as far as the eye could see. I couldn't ask him to let me out. Mana-Mana was too far to walk.

"*Doucement*" (easy does it), I finally urged him, in as sweet a tone as I could muster, using the internationally recognized sign language of a flat hand, palm down, pumping imaginary brakes. And to my surprise, he slowed. He pulled the truck over to the side of the road, stopped and got out. *Uh-oh*, I thought, *he's about to throw me out*; but then I saw, at the entrance to a small village, some women were selling palm wine from a rickety stand, as if it were lemonade. I watched as the driver flirted with the women, paid for a plastic-mugful of palm wine and downed it like whisky from a shot glass. Then he got back in the truck and we drove off at top speed.

"*Vous voyez?*" (See that?), he said to me, pointing out a dead monkey for sale on the side of the road. Its skinny, unskinned carcass was dangling by a rope from a stick; its mouth wide open, as if frozen in mid-scream. Villagers hunted monkeys for their meat, but eating roasted monkey was forbidden to us volunteers because of the threat of ebola. "That monkey was my uncle!" the driver said, jerking his head in the direction of the monkey, now passed. "HA-HA! *C'est vrai, n'est-ce pas?* All you *blancs* think us Africans are nothing but monkeys."

"*Pas du tout*," I said shaking my head. I quickly changed the subject. "How much further to Mana-Mana?" I was in no mood to argue with him, and I knew from childhood experience that there's no reasoning with a drunk.

"Oh," he said, slowly rubbing his stubbly chin with one hand, while the other rested nonchalantly on the top of the shuddering steering wheel, "about thirty kilometers."

It must have been palm wine season, because at every village we stopped to let a few passengers off, our driver found another palm wine stand waiting to serve him. By the time I got out in Mana-Mana and he drove off, the man had drunk at least six more glasses of palm wine along our route.

Morgan was waiting for me by the village grammar school, and I was never more happy to see her.

"Good trip?" she asked after hugging me hello.

"Exciting," I said, knowing she'd know exactly what I meant. "Truly death-defying." I wiped my sweaty face with the sleeve of my white cotton shirt, brushed road dust from my once-clean khakis, and stomped my Teva-sandaled feet.

"Hungry?" she said. "I made Mexican food for lunch. I even made the tortillas by hand."

"Great. Mexico sounds good. Let's go there!"

"But first, let's say hi to the kids. They've been waiting patiently to meet Chantal."

Chantal Chanson (*chanson* means "song" in French) was the star of my handmade hand puppet theatre troupe. There was something about her that the children adored. Was it her purple yarn bob that swooshed when she sang? Her chipmunky face and wide eyes turned eternally heavenward? Her sweet bow mouth, always open to a song? Her clapping green-felt hands and indefatigable energy? Her lilting singing voice, so different from my own?

Among the little ones of Lastoursville, Chantal was something of a rock star, and her signature song, "*Lavez les Mains*," shot to the top of their charts. Sometimes little children would stop to serenade me with this song when they saw me walking in town.

"*Pour avoir la bonne sante*" (to have good health), Chantal belted out, head bobbing, purple hair flying, green hands clapping manically, "*lavez les mains a l'eau et au savon!*" (wash your hands with water and soap). To avoid intestinal worms, her hit tune continued, wash your hands with water and soap. After using the toilet, she rhapsodized, wash your hands with water and soap. Before preparing a meal, she crooned, and the children jumped in to complete the refrain, "*lavez les mains a l'eau et au savon!!!*"

Morgan and I quickly set up a makeshift theatre in an open shed, and the village children gathered around us in a rapt throng. Within minutes, the children of Mana-Mana, too, were captivated by Chantal's charms. They had obviously never seen anything quite like her before. To them, it seemed, (and not just to me) she was alive. Their wide eyes were so focused on her performance that they didn't notice me or Morgan at all. It was Chantal's voice they heard, not mine. She was the one with charm and charisma, not me.

Little girls in tattered dresses watched her, awestruck, their hands over their mouths. Little boys in threadbare T-shirts and shorts, who were usually on the wild side, Morgan told me, were well behaved, enthralled by the show. Within minutes, everyone knew all of the words, and they were singing and clapping along with sunny Chantal.

Then, after Chantal took a few bows as the kids applauded wildly, I brought out two more puppets who put on a Punch-and-Judy-style show. There was Yvonne Savon (*savon* means "soap"), whose head was carved from a big block of blue soap and her dress made from a hand towel, and her archenemy, Mick Robe (the French pronunciation of *microbe*, or "germ") who was decidedly ugly. Mick's papier-mâché face was birdlike, beaky, green, and mean, with a down-turned mouth and slitty eyes. His green yarn hair was braided in rastas that stuck out all over his head. His robe was made from a brown and beige African print that looked vaguely like microbes under a magnifying glass. He was the puppet the kids loved to hate.

Mick opened his act with an earnest, Pavarotti-style rendition of his theme song, "*Si tu aimes les maladies...*" which, translated, was: "If you love being sick, you love me — Mick Robe! If you love diarrhea, you love me — Mick Robe! If you love filth, you love me — Mick Robe! If you love being sick, then I, Mick Robe, will be happy to make you sick!..." At first, the children were aghast, but when they saw some adults in the audience laughing, their smiles grew too. Yvonne Savon then appeared on the scene and saved the day, overpowering Mick with the magic of her soapsuds.

Our show closed with Renee Repas (*repas* means "meal"), a big-mamma of a puppet with a yellow plastic plate on her head (filled with handmade miniature fruit and vegetables), who gave a Julia Child-like lecture on the importance of eating well every day to keep from falling ill. While Morgan held up a huge poster I'd made, Renee explained dramatically each of the three food groups depicted in the poster's pie chart. "This group, called Protection," she warbled, "with all the nice fruits and veggies in it, provides vitamins and minerals which protect us against illness. This Energy group — which includes such foods as rice, and bread, and manioc — gives us strength to run and jump and work and PLAY! And this one, Construction, includes foods that offer body-building protein, like peanuts, dried beans, eggs, meat, and *fish*."

Fish, everyone in Mana-Mana knew, was the reason for Morgan's being there. Morgan, a little like Chantal, was the star of their village, and everyone seemed to love her. "Fish!" the children repeated at the end of Renee's presentation. "Yay, FISH! Yay, Morgan!" Morgan, along with Renee, took a little bow.

Chantal entertaining the Mana-Mana children

Francine's Yogurt Cake

(For this recipe, use the 8-ounce yogurt container as your measure. Francine referred to this container as the *"pot,"* pronounced *po* in French.)

- 1 pot vanilla yogurt
- ½ pot vegetable oil
- 1 pot white sugar
- 2 large eggs
- 3 pots all-purpose flour
- 1 teaspoon pure vanilla extract
- 2 teaspoons baking powder

Preheat oven to 350 degrees. Grease and flour a 9-inch round cake pan. Blend all ingredients well and pour into cake pan. Bake 25-30 minutes or until tester (wooden toothpick) comes out clean.

Spicy Blackened Tilapia
(adapted from *Gourmet*)

1 tablespoon sweet paprika
1 teaspoon dried oregano, crumbled
1 teaspoon dried thyme, crumbled
½ teaspoon cayenne (or more, to taste)
1 teaspoon garlic powder
1 teaspoon sugar
1 teaspoon salt
¼ teaspoon freshly ground black pepper
4 tilapia fillets, skinned
2 tablespoon olive oil
2 tablespoon unsalted butter
lemon wedges, as accompaniment

Combine spices and seasonings in a small bowl. Pat tilapia fillets dry, then sprinkle spice mixture on both sides of fish, coating well. Heat oil in a 12-inch skillet over moderately high heat until hot but not smoking. Add 1 tablespoon of butter to skillet and heat until foam subsides. Add two fish fillets and cook, turning once, until cooked through, about 8 minutes total. Transfer fillets to plates and keep warm. Add remaining 1 tablespoon butter to pan and cook remaining two fillets in same manner. Serve with lemon wedges. Makes 4 servings.

Exposés

Anyone who wants to do good under our African conditions must fight any tendency in himself to let his nerves and temper be upset by all the big and little difficulties of daily life, and must retain his full joy in his work.
— DR. ALBERT SCHWEITZER, *The Primeval Forest*

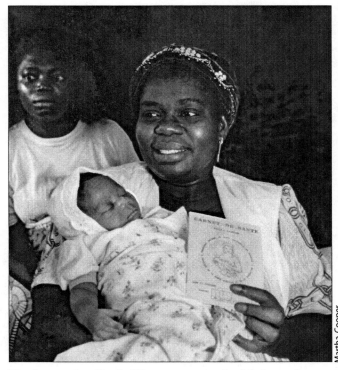

Head nurse Caroline holding a young mother's baby and carnet

W hat if you needed a blood transfusion," Caroline, the large, commanding head nurse at the mother-infant clinic shouted in angry Gabonese French at the room full of young mothers in the clinic's waiting room, "and *she*"—she pointed a forceful forefinger at me, sitting off to the side, wishing I could hide — "was the only one whose blood type matched yours? Would you refuse her blood because her skin is *white*?

All eyes in the room were now focused on me. At first, their stares had been hostile. It was, after all, my fault that they were being berated like misbehaving children, that they had to sit with their babies on their laps in this hot room on these hard wooden benches instead of socializing with each other outside as they had been doing before Caroline ordered them in. But, as they mulled over Caroline's hypothetical question about lifesaving blood, their stares seemed to soften. *Refuse my blood?* They shook their heads.

Caroline paced the length of the front of the room in her tight, white nurse's uniform and white nurse's shoes. Then she stopped and slapped the front table. As the single mother of ten children (each fathered by a different man who'd quickly fled the scene, she'd told me), she obviously knew how to strike fear into her charges. All twenty-or-so mothers in the room sat upright, looking straight ahead at her now.

"Of course you'd take her blood!" Caroline continued, pointing again at me. "She is *human*, just like us Africans! And she has a good heart — that's why she came here."

It touched me that Caroline should say this, because up until this moment I'd felt she saw me only as an unwelcome intrusion. No one in the Peace Corps, I belatedly learned, had forewarned anyone at the hospital — including Dr. Djimet, the chief surgeon and director — that I was coming to town as their first health volunteer to be posted to Lastoursville. I'd simply shown up at his office one day, luminous as a godsend, "the messenger of health," I thought, leaving him and his hospital staff scrambling to accommodate me.

"*C'est vrai*," Caroline continued, nodding her turbaned head in my direction, "her French is not very good" (a fact I couldn't dispute) "but she's *not French!*" — a point in my favor with these people, who still harbored resentment toward their former colonizers. "She comes from the *United States*. She is *American*. Americans don't speak French, they only speak *English!*" The women murmured among themselves, as if I were the first American some had ever seen this close. And they, all at least bilingual, appeared baffled by my linguistic ignorance. *Do you mean there are people who are not forced to learn French in elementary school?* their expressions read.

"She left her family in the United States," Caroline added as a final fillip, "to come all the way to Lastoursville just to teach you mothers about health!" This, Caroline must have known, would hit home with these women because for them, leaving their family and village to help someone else far away would indeed be a great sacrifice.

With that, Caroline turned and looked at me as if to say, "It's all yours now, dearie," then left the waiting room. So I rose from my chair in the corner, smoothed my rumpled skirt, walked behind the front table, and faced the now-attentive audience of young African mothers. This room would be my classroom for two years, and I knew I had to boldly claim it.

"*Ah, bon,*" I began, forcing a smile, trying to exude a whiff of *joie de vivre.* "*Nous sommes ensemble maintenant*" (we're together now), I said.

That was how my "real job" at the hospital began. At first, when I'd invited the mothers, who'd been milling about outside waiting for their names to be called to have their babies weighed or vaccinated, to come in for my health *exposé* (lecture), they ignored me. Some turned their backs on me and continued chatting with their friends. Others eyed me suspiciously, as if to say, "Who are *you?* And what right do you have to tell *us* what to do?" I couldn't coax them to come in.

Caroline's reception too had been cool at first. She compared me unfavorably with the previous volunteer sent from a French nongovernmental organization who had once worked with her. That young French woman was a *real* nurse, Caroline let me know, and she spoke *real* French. How could I, an older American woman who was not a nurse and who spoke atrocious French, even begin to compete?

Undeterred, I asked Caroline to trust me. I explained that I was not sent there as a nurse but rather as a health teacher, whose job it was to emphasize disease *prevention* — something that had the potential to benefit everyone. My French, I assured her, would surely improve because I was determined to learn. Besides, how could it get any worse? My heart, I tried to convey with my limited French as well as my hands and eyes, was in the right place. My assurances must have succeeded in causing her change of heart and eliciting her support. Caroline, in fact, became an ally.

• • •

In Gabon, mothers of infants are required by law to bring their babies in to the nearest health clinic once every month to be officially weighed. The baby's weight is then recorded in a passport-size booklet *(carnet)* which the mother is required to keep for each of her children. If a baby's weight falls below the normal growth range, as indicated on the *"courbe de croissance"* (growth curve) posted on the office wall, it is a clear sign the child requires medical attention, right there at the hospital, that day.

Many of the young mothers who sat on the long, low benches in the clinic's waiting room, holding or nursing their babies while waiting to be called into the nurses' office, had traveled great distances from poor and remote villages at least a full day's journey away to keep their monthly appointments at the Centre Medical de Lastoursville. These mothers were the conscientious ones, and their babies appeared to me to be robust, well loved and cared for. Clearly, mothers with sickly babies, those mothers who were too poor or unwell to make the journey or too uncaring to try, defied the law and came to the hospital only in the case of emergencies.

Like the famous hospital that medical missionary Albert Schweitzer had founded in 1913 in Lambaréné, Gabon, Lastoursville's medical center looked more like a weather-worn summer camp than any kind of hospital. It was a sprawling complex of six tin-roofed, cement-block structures, each painted half brown and half yellow, and each of which was clearly labeled in French: Consultations, Medicine, Surgery, Maternity, Pediatrics, or PMI (mother-infant clinic). Behind these structures were stable-like sheds to accommodate patients' visiting care-giving family members.

Schweitzer had designed a hospital that Africans would find unthreatening and familiar; where relatives could stay to cook and care for their own; where chickens roamed freely, cackling and pecking on the grounds. Lastoursville's hospital followed this practical, if not modern, model. The only place where the word "sanitary" could honestly be applied was in the white-tiled operating room, sole domain of Dr. Christophe Djimet, the hospital's diligent director and only surgeon.

Dr. Djimet, a Chadian in his mid-fifties, was a large, Bunyan-esque man with a kind, round face and tribal scarification on his cheeks. At our first meeting, he told me he had completed his medical training in French-speaking Canada, he'd headed this hospital in Lastoursville for the past ten years, and he was looking forward to his early retirement in a few years, when he and his wife, an anesthesiologist at the hospital, would return to their homeland, Chad. Over time, I observed that Dr. Djimet ran this medical center as a benevolent dictator, and everyone — from his staff of nearly twenty Gabonese nurses to the Lebanese shopkeepers in *centreville* to the entire surrounding populace — was in awe of him. That soon included me.

"Bonjour, tout le monde!" I gaily greet the women in my waiting room-classroom. It is 9 o'clock on a rainy Monday morning, and I have spent the weekend preparing for this moment. The heavy rains may have hampered the travel plans of some mothers, but the dozen-or-so who made the journey, fortunately for me, have come indoors, where they've become my captive audience. I am bare-footed, and so are they. We've left our muddy sandals and flip-flops just outside the front door.

"Je m'appelle Bonnie, *et je suis agent de santé de Corps de la Paix. Je suis très heureuse d'être ici!"* I introduce myself and tell them I'm happy to be there, which is utterly true. I've been up since before dawn drinking Lipton tea and rehearsing my lines, and now the stage is all mine. I hear my former headwaiter Michael's voice in my head, "Dahhhling, this is theater!" and I'm determined to do everything in my power now to get and keep their attention. I figure, *What have I got to lose?*

"I'll begin with a question," I say to the women looking up at me. "Who here likes illness?" I reach my arms out dramatically, palms up, and hunch my shoulders. "Anyone?" The mothers don't know what to make of me. Their eyes ask, *"Could she be serious?"* I walk around the room determinedly, trying to look quizzical.

"No one?" I say. "Ah! GOOD! Neither do I. *Je deteste les maladies!* That's why my life's work now is to teach people how to *prevent* illness. I want to keep sickness *la-bah — loins, loins*" (over there, far, far) — I make a shooing gesture toward the mountains outside, on the other side of the river — "where it won't touch us!" The women seem intrigued by this. *Is this white woman a witch? Does she have magical powers?* As we all know too well, illness and disease here in inhumanly hot, wet, dusty, muddy equatorial Africa lurks everywhere, every day of these women's lives. How could I speak of keeping it away?

"Now," I continue, seeing I have their full attention, "how can we help prevent illnesses from occurring?" I hold up a poster I'd prepared, with pictures depicting each point, to back up my spoken words. "There are many ways: by vaccinating our babies against diseases such as polio, diphtheria, tetanus, and *rougeole* (measles); by eating healthy foods every day to enable our bodies to fight infection; by washing our hands before eating and after elimination to avoid worms; by using a bed net to protect against night-bighting, malaria-carrying mosquitoes; and by avoiding germs..."

I explain to the women that my lectures each month for the duration of my Peace Corps service in Lastoursville will focus on one or another of these preventive measures. Then I make a proposition to them: If, when they come to the clinic to have their babies weighed each month, they attend my lecture, listen well and agree to share what they've learned with a friend in their village ("Each one teach one!" I urge them), I will give them in exchange a small packet of seeds (I show them a sample — a pinch of seeds, such as lettuce, cherry tomatoes, carrots, zucchini or okra — in a recycled Lipton tea envelope) to plant in their own gardens to provide their families with health-giving vegetables.

"Okay?" I ask, in the international language everyone knew. Eyes brighten. Heads nod.

This was shameless bribery, I realized, and it was risky as well. How could I guarantee a steady supply of seeds? Would my urgent requests for seed packets from friends in the U.S. be honored? Would the seeds they sent me get "lost," as so many packages did, in Gabon's kleptomaniacal postal system? I knew I had to take the risk, and I had to believe my bribery would be worth it.

"Today," I say, pointing to my lecture-topics poster again, "I'd like to talk about nutrition and the importance of eating a balanced diet for maintaining good health."

This subject, I knew, might be a hard sell. Changing long-held eating behaviors was difficult for people anywhere in the world, but it would be particularly difficult for these women of limited means. Manioc (cassava), the Gabonese staple, was plentiful and cost virtually nothing. It grew in the hardest soil (I became convinced it could grow in concrete), and it sated hungry stomachs. Why change? In New York, where I had taught a cooking course called Spa Cuisine at the New York Cooking School, comfortably well-off adults would sign up on their doctors' orders after having been diagnosed with dangerously high cholesterol levels. Although these students knew, intellectually, it was empowering to be able to prepare food that is both healthy and tasty, not all of them found the power to break their old, unhealthy eating habits. They found change too hard to do.

I show the women another poster, this one of the World Health Organization's three basic food groupings: "Construction" — protein-rich foods, such as meat, fish, and dried beans; "Energy" — carbohydrate-rich foods, such as bread, rice, and manioc; and "Protection" — vitamin-rich foods, such as fruits and vegetables. I try to make it clear to them that I'm not trying to supplant their staple diet of manioc and plantains but rather add to it the "Protection" foods that provide vitamins and minerals that protect against *maladies*.

I'm relieved that the women are either too shy or too polite to interrupt my lecture, because I'm not at all sure I could understand their Gabonese French if they did ask me questions. Instead, I try to read their faces, their body language, their eyes.

"How can this be done, you ask? Well, one small way might be to make a soup for your family that includes all three groups. Here is my suggested recipe for what I call '*Trois Groupes Soupe*,' and here are the ingredients..."

I tape another poster to the front wall, this one being the soup recipe I'd drawn with Magic Markers, and I pull from a shopping bag on the floor — like a magician from a big, brown hat — the soup ingredients, plus a small soup pot, and place them on the table in front of me with rhythmic thuds. The women seem riveted by these props. *What will this strange white woman do next? How will she cook without a fire?* At this, Caroline, who must have been listening from her office, stopped calling out names and joined the audience, pencil and pad in hand. With ten children to feed, she obviously was keen to learn new ideas.

I go through the motions of making the soup, asking the women to imagine that my soup pot is resting on three large stones with a wood fire beneath it, the way they all cook at home. I pretend to pour a little palm oil (which every family has) into the pot, then pantomime chopping an onion and mincing some garlic cloves and adding them, along with some small, hot red peppers, to the pot, stirring with a wooden spoon. I scoop the air above the pot into my face, as if savoring the resulting aroma, and the women laugh at me. I enjoy the fact that they seem to think I'm a bit crazy. I like the idea of giving them something to talk about when they return to their villages.

The tiny tin of tomato paste, the bouillon cubes, and the small plastic pouches containing lentils and rice that I'd set on the table are familiar to these women because I'd purchased them at the local *marché* for pennies. But cost is an issue for them, I know, so I try to address it. I adapt the adage my mother used throughout my childhood, "I'd rather pay the grocer than the doctor," to their circumstances: "It is better to pay the *marchandeuses* (the women who sell at the market) than the *pharmacie*," I say. "Good food is always less costly than medicine."

As I exaggerate opening the packets of lentils and rice, inspecting the lentils for stones and washing both to remove dirt and bugs, I explain, "These lentils will give your family protein for strength, and the rice will give energy. And the vegetables" — I hold the tomatoes and zucchini aloft in a dramatic display — "that you'll be growing in your kitchen gardens, will provide *beaucoup de vitamines!*"

I walk them through the recipe's procedure and the timing involved. None of the women in the audience are wearing watches, I see, so I tell them what to look for in terms of consistency: "Cook the lentils until almost-soft, then add the rice and cook until the rice is soft, then add the cut-up vegetables and cook until they are soft." I see that some of the women are taking notes in the back of their baby's *carnet*.

True to my word, I give a Lipton tea envelope containing some vegetable seeds to each of the women in attendance as a thank-you gift for listening to my lesson. Then I give them a crash course on gardening in the tropics, a subject, I confess to them I'm just learning myself. I encourage them to care for their fragile seedlings as if they were babies.

The women appear to be taking it all in, but I know I must be realistic. Who knows how many mothers will go home now and make this soup or how many kitchen gardens will actually spring up around town or in the outlying villages in the coming weeks or months? These things are out of my hands. All I can do I know is plant seeds of ideas.

· · ·

Trois Groupes Soupe

1 medium onion, peeled and chopped
2 to 3 garlic cloves, minced
1 teaspoon minced *piment* (fresh hot pepper), or to taste
2 tablespoons olive oil (or other vegetable oil)
½ cup small lentils, washed and picked over
6+ cups water (or chicken stock)
½ cup rice, washed
2 chicken bouillon cubes (if using water)
2 tablespoons tomato paste
2 to 3 fresh tomatoes, cut up
2 to 3 small zucchini (or other green vegetable), cut up
1 teaspoon (or so) curry powder, if desired

Sauté onion, garlic, *piment* in olive oil in a large pot. Add lentils
and 3 cups water (or chicken stock). Cook 20 minutes or so. Add
rice, 3 cups more stock (or water and bouillon cubes) and cook
for 20 more minutes. Add tomato paste, tomatoes, zucchini and
more water if soup is too thick. Cook about 10 more minutes,
until green vegetable is tender. Season with salt and pepper to taste.
Makes about 4-6 servings.

Time Is Money

An Hour is a Sea
Between a few, and me —
With them would Harbor be —
— EMILY DICKINSON

Martha Cooper

With my friend Antoinette, who could stop the rain

*O*ur appointment to see the women of her church, Nazareth, on the banks of the Ogooué and close to the center of town, was at 4 o'clock, and Antoinette and I were running late. It was 3:30 by the time she met me at my house, where she helped me pack and carry the props I needed for my presentation — my rolled-up recipe posters, handmade hand puppets, and ingredients for weaning foods. Her church was at least a half-hour walk into town, and we had to hurry.

"Time is money!" Antoinette announced out-of-the-blue in English, as she scurried ahead of me toward the main road, afraid of being late. I had to laugh. These were the first words I'd ever heard her speak in English, and as far as I knew, the only English expression she knew. Plus, she was perhaps the only Gabonese I'd met in Lastoursville who actually *worried* about being late to anything. As a rule, few people even owned wristwatches, and wall- and desk-calendars, opened to pages years out of date, served merely decorative purposes. Schedules and appointments were generally made on "African time," which meant, in African French, *demain*, or, "sometime in the future, but don't count on it."

Antoinette's "Time is money" pronouncement not only made me laugh out loud, it also made me think about the concept of time. If, by some sorcerer's alchemy, time (as a personal possession) could be converted to money, I thought, then Africans would indeed be rich. Most people in the time-pressed West, on the other hand, would be poor. From my observations in Gabon, most Africans had time to sit and ponder, time to visit friends and care for family, time to sing, dance, create, *live*; they seemed blissfully free of Time's tyranny. The irony for me was that while the monetarily rich West disparages Africans as being uniformly and pathetically "poor," economically "underdeveloped," in terms of their ownership of Time, Africans' secret is that they are enviably and hugely wealthy.

As Antoinette and I walked briskly down the hill, carrying handled shopping bags in both hands, it started to rain. It wasn't a full-blown, all-out rainforest rainfall, the pounding, beating, merciless kind that had become my new definition of "rain." It was more like a Northeastern U.S.–style spring "sprinkle." Nevertheless, Antoinette wouldn't have it.

Both of us were nicely dressed for the presentation, in bright, crisp, freshly pressed cotton skirts and blouses made from colorful African-print fabric. Both of us were wearing cheap-but-pretty, plastic, healed sandals bought at the local *marché*. Neither of us had thought to bring an umbrella, and we wouldn't have had a free hand to hold one anyway. We hadn't prepared for the rain.

Still marching determinedly down the hill, Antoinette looked up to the heavens, allowing the light rain to splash her fully in the face. Suddenly, she took a deep breath and bellowed, "JE-SUS!" — not as an expletive but as an invocation.

"JE-SUS!" she repeated, as the gentle rain continued its patter and a dilapidated taxi sped past us up the hill toward the hospital, kicking road dust in our faces and choking us with filthy exhaust fumes. "Je-sus, Lord, you stop this rain right now! This is your servant Antoinette talking to you! We're going to my church to do your work! We can't let rain spoil our plans! You stop this rain! NOW! Do you hear me?!"

The rain stopped.

A hazy sun sheepishly crept through the veil of pale-gray, overcast sky, tail between his legs, like a scared dog.

We made it to Nazareth on time, our skin perspiring in the equatorial afternoon heat. But our rain-dampened clothes and hair were now dry.

Exhaling, Antoinette smiled at me, her mischievous, little-girl smile, as if to say, "No big deal."

In the large, thatched-roof, open-air sanctuary, within a crocodile's stroll from the wide, forceful river, I gave my presentation to an assembly of about two dozen churchwomen. I spoke in French, relying heavily on the props I'd brought with me — puppets, posters, porridge ingredients — to make up for what my French-speaking skills still lacked. Antoinette stood beside me at the lectern, sometimes prompting my French, but primarily translating what I was saying and doing into the dominant local language, Inzebi. At the appropriate times, she held up my large posters in front of her, which nearly hid her completely from view.

As I'd planned with Antoinette in my home some weeks before, when I'd given her a private cooking lesson she'd requested on how to make Green Papaya Pie, I shared with these churchwomen the kinds of health-related lectures I might offer them at their regular gatherings, if they wished me to do so. The subjects I proposed to them were: family nutrition (including weaning foods), cooking-for-health, bread baking, food preservation, gardening, composting and recycling, puppet theatre (teaching hygiene) for little ones, craft-making-for-profit, and SIDA (AIDS) prevention.

Madeleine, the tall, regal, charismatic leader of the Nazareth women's group, approached me after my presentation to tell me the women were interested in all but two of my proposals. The *marionettes* (puppets) and SIDA lessons were better suited to children's and teens' groups, they felt.

For the remainder of the meeting, the women sang hymns exuberantly and prayed loudly in turn, as the Spirit led. Then, to my amazement, at the end, they held a ferocious faith-healing ceremony for a severely sick baby one mother had been holding in her arms. He was, I could tell from my Peace Corps health training, suffering from kwashiorkor, a form of malnutrition so far gone it is nearly impossible to treat. The name, I had learned, came from the Kwa language of Ghana, meaning "the one who is displaced" — the baby who is weaned too soon because his mother has had another, the baby who fails to get enough nutrients in his meager diet, the baby who fails to thrive.

The naked baby's stomach was grossly distended and his legs bone-thin. His kinky hair was grayish-reddish-yellow, and his face old, dull, and sad. It was hard to guess his age. One? Two? Madeleine and Antoinette, facing each other, held the fragile child between them and prayed at the top of their voices for his healing. Were they speaking in tongues or in Inzebi or a mixture of both? I couldn't tell.

Any other baby would have screamed, terrified to be at the epicenter of this loud drama, but this baby only laid limply and stared blankly at the group of women seated in front of him and staring back at him, as though he didn't care whether he lived or died. Did he notice, I wondered, the expression on the only ghostlike-white face in the pews, an expression that read: "I'm so sorry, but I can't help you"?

Antoinette, though, was not giving up. Her voice became louder and louder as she shouted at God. *How could a pediatric nurse*, I asked myself, *participate in such an unscientific spectacle?* But then I remembered: She could stop the rain.

• • •

Green Papaya Pie

2 eggs
1 cup (or 1 can) sweetened condensed milk
½ teaspoon salt
2 cups cooked, pureed green papaya
   (or pumpkin or acorn squash)
1 tablespoon minced fresh ginger root
1 teaspoon ground cinnamon

Beat all of the ingredients well and pour into a prebaked 9-inch pie shell. Bake 30-35 minutes at 350 degrees.

Pain Americain

It does not cost much. It is pleasant: one of those almost hypnotic businesses, like a dance from some ancient ceremony. It leaves you filled with peace, and the house filled with one of the world's sweetest smells. But it takes a lot of time. If you can find that, the rest is easy. And if you cannot rightly find it, make it, for probably there is no chiropractic treatment, no Yoga exercise, no hour of meditation in a music-throbbing chapel, that will leave you emptier of bad thoughts than this homely ceremony of making bread.
— M.F.K. FISHER, *How to Cook a Wolf*

In my kitchen with freshly baked Bonnie Bread

T his bread," I say in French to the group of African women sitting in front of me in my living room as I hold up a locally made baguette, "is as basic as bread can be. It contains only four ingredients — flour, water, yeast, and salt — the fundamental building blocks of bread. It's good bread," I stress. "But…"

And then I show them my own creation. Round and golden, this loaf resembles the French *pain de compagne*, country-style bread, but only on the outside. I lift it up in two hands like a sacred offering; I show it off like a proud new parent. "But *this* bread," I continue, "is better."

Then I launch into all the reasons why. On the subject of bread I am almost unstoppable. The only thing stopping me now is the fact that I cannot yet speak fluent French.

The twenty-or-so Gabonese and West African women in my living room audience, however, are patient with me and eager to learn. I supplement my halting French with energetic body language and lots of props, which I'd prepared ahead of time, while the women sit politely on my sprawling, L-shaped sofa and the borrowed plastic chairs I've arranged around the room. They're wearing their Sunday-best, vibrantly colorful *pagnes*, with matching tops and head wraps. Most have *cahiers* (notebooks) in their laps and are poised to take notes. Their feet, crossed at the ankles, are bare, because, out of respect, they removed their flip-flops and left them outside on my front porch before entering my home. They look at me expectantly; many mouths forming small O's, like baby birds waiting in a nest to be fed.

"This bread is better because it offers more," I say. "It contains more ingredients with more nutritive value. *C'est plus nourrissant.* It has more flavor, more texture. It's sweeter than French bread — *c'est comme le gateau* (like cake) — so your children will love it. And unlike this dry baguette," I say, tapping my day-old demonstration model on the table to make a clunking sound, which makes the women chuckle, "my bread stays fresh for several days.

"What's more…" I scan the room and look into each woman's eyes. They are poor by American standards but proud, overburdened by large families and little money, but quick to learn and better themselves. Contrary to Madame Nimba's dire warning, these local women have indeed responded to my open invitation and arrived for this class. I feel heartened, vindicated; no, ecstatic. Looking into the faces of these eager women, my heart slowly swells like the rising, demonstration bread dough on the table in front of me.

I want to convey to them a sense of empowerment, suggest the possibility, however slight, of increasing their family's income. They are paying close attention. No one is talking with her neighbor or gazing out of my louvered living room windows at the blazingly sunny day outside. If anyone came to this class out of mere curiosity, to find out what the inside of my house looked like, she isn't showing it now. "What's more," I say slowly, "you can make it *yourself*, like I do here in my home. You could even make more than your family needs and sell it in town…."

So began my cooking classes for *Pain Americain*. Baking bread and teaching others how to do it wasn't new to me. Before I came to Lastoursville, I happily taught bread baking at the New York Cooking School. I had also been baking my own healthy bread, like a religious rite, every week for more than twenty years, ever since I was thirty. And, as a New York caterer, I always made fresh bread in my clients' kitchens for their dinner parties, timing its removal from the oven to coincide with guests' arrival, so the fresh-baked bread's fragrance would embrace them and welcome them in to the clients' home. But teaching bread baking in Africa — in French — *was* new for me. Occasionally, I had to pause and glance down at my lecture outline on the table beside the bag of flour and the mound of dough:

I. *L'introduction*

"Je suis agent de santé, voluntaire de Corps de la Paix," I say — I am a Peace Corps volunteer who is here for two years to teach community health and nutrition. I tell them a little bit about the Peace Corps, since I'm the first health and nutrition volunteer posted to Lastoursville. I tell them I taught cooking and nutrition in New York before becoming a Peace Corps volunteer. At the mention of New York, the women make an "Ahhhh" sound, the African equivalent of "Wow." Still nervous about my ability to communicate effectively, I smile at them, then return my eyes to my outline.

II. *Why Bread?*

"Pourquoi le pain? Because good bread, especially grainy, nutrition-rich bread, offers a sound foundation for a healthy diet. *La bonne nutrition est la meilleure protection contre les MALADIES"* (Good nutrition is the best protection against illness), I stress. And the truth is that here in the equatorial African rainforest, where infectious diseases are rife, one needs all the protection one can get against the myriad, ever-lurking maladies. *"Et aussi, la bonne nourriture est toujours moins chere que les medicaments!"* (Again I stress what was one of my mother's favorite maxims.)

In their slim, grammar school *cahiers* the women copy the recipe for *Pain Americain* that I've written on two poster-size sheets of paper and taped to my living room wall. On the sheets, I drew and colored with bright Magic Markers the measuring utensils, outlining the standard-size teaspoon and tablespoons, readily available at the *marché*, along with a commonly used, one-cup-measure, plastic drinking mug. I drew the procedures too — spoon whirling around in a blue bowl, brown hands kneading the golden dough on a board — so that even those women who couldn't read French could follow.

I tried to make the recipe as easy-to-do as possible, a simple, three-step process, using only affordable, available ingredients: yeast, flour, sugar, salt, corn meal or oatmeal, powdered milk, oil, and maybe an egg. As an added visual aid, I attached to a large piece of chicken wire empty containers — a sugar box, dried yeast packet, kilo-size flour bag, salt container, small plastic mineral water bottle, and so on — and I set this prop prominently against the wall. No one, I've resolved, will leave this class not knowing how to make bread.

By now I'm warmed up; I'm beginning to hit my stride.

"Half the world's population depends on rice for their daily diet," I tell the group. For the Gabonese women who may never have had the benefit of much schooling and who certainly have never traveled farther than Libreville, their own coastal capital city, this information seems to come as news. For them, the staple is manioc, pounded to paste, rolled in banana leaves, and boiled in enormous cauldrons until it becomes a rubbery, tasteless, impervious-to-spoilage mass.

The West African women, though, know the importance of rice. Where they come from — countries such as Mali and Senegal — rice forms the base of every midday meal. In West Africa, rice has been cultivated for centuries.

"For the other half of the world, *wheat* is the dominant grain,"

I go on, now on a roll, "and yeast bread — *which can only be made from wheat* — is the staff of life." To dramatize this point, I walk like a bent-over old person in front of them, using the day-old baguette as my faux cane. The women laugh at my behavior, perhaps because they've never seen a white woman make such a fool of herself. Their laughter spurs me on.

"Bread is *practical,*" I enthuse. "And *portatif* (portable)!" I put down the French bread with a clunk and reverently place my own, round, golden loaf on my head the way these African women carry their baskets. I hold the bread there with two hands and walk again in front of them, this time walking the way they do — head erect, neck straight, tall, and proud.

I return to my demonstration table, a card table on loan from my missionary friend Bev, which I've set up in my living room, at the doorway to the kitchen. Then, with the carefully prepped components spread out in front of me on the table, I glance again at my outline before plunging — literally — into my demonstration.

III. How?

"*Vous voyez*" (you see), I say, as I show them the contents of one bowl, passing it under each woman's eyes and nose. This mixture looks just like a wet, kitchen sponge — puffy and filled with holes." This is the first step — making the "sponge" — combining the yeast with a bit of sugar, plus one cup of *l'eau propre* (clean water) and an equal amount of flour, and then letting the mixture come alive, letting the dried, dormant yeast wake up, eat, and breathe, giving off its signature sharp odor of yeasty life. "You can make *l'éponge* the night before," I say, "and let it sit, covered, until the morning."

The women nod. This mixture looks familiar to them. It's like the soupy, yeasted dough local beignet makers prepare. I often see these women on the side of the road near the *marché* in town, sitting on low stools, beside charcoal-fueled braziers, flicking blobs of their bubbly dough into wok-like pans of hot oil resting on the red coals. The blobs puff and bob on the surface of the oil, as the women stir and flip them. The sight of this makes my breath catch: Exuberant children or teetering toddlers could easily overturn these low-lying, makeshift cooking arrangements, I think, spilling boiling oil on themselves, melting their skin like candle wax, causing unspeakable pain. But I'd never, thankfully, seen this happen to any of them.

The "extras," I tell my still-attentive class — the oil, sugar, powdered milk, egg — *"donnent plus de goût, plus de saveur, et aussi une vie plus longue* (they add extra taste, extra goodness and vitamins, and a longer shelf-life) *que la baguette française.* They make the bread cakier in consistency, more American-style than European," I say. The women seem to like this last idea, since most Francophone Africans hold lingering ill will toward the French and all things European. The fact that I am not a Frenchwoman — proven without doubt by my inability to speak French flowingly, naturally, comfortably — is an ongoing advantage for me.

I measure a scant cup of yellow cornmeal and pour it into a clear bowl. I add a rounded teaspoon of salt, plus more extras: a quarter cup each of sugar and NIDO (powdered whole milk). Then, from a kettle on the stove just inside my kitchen door, I measure a cup of boiling water and pour it on the dry mixture, stirring. I measure a quarter cup of vegetable oil and continue to stir. As the mixture cools, I beat as I speak.

"American children," I tell them, perhaps fibbing a little, "eat a lot of healthy bread, which helps them grow up to be big and strong." Snippets of my mother's voice from long ago rush back to me again, like waves from a distant ocean: *Be good kids and eat all gone. I made you this good food so you'll grow up to be big and strong.*

"When I was a little girl," I say, "like so many other American kids then and now, our mothers made us peanut-butter-and-jelly sandwiches for our school lunches. And I still love peanut-butter-and-jelly sandwiches!"

The women seem intrigued by this combination. They're aware of *confiture* (jellies and jam), and they know *pâte d'arachides* (peanut butter) — in fact, Africans have been pounding roasted peanuts into paste since at least the fifteenth century — but peanut-butter-and-jelly sandwiches? These African women look puzzled. I read their faces: *This must be a crazy American invention.*

When the extras have cooled sufficiently, I crack an egg into the bowl and beat it in. *"L'oeuf n'est pas nécessaire,"* I explain, *"mais, c'est très bon."* The egg is optional.

"Maintenant, l'assemblage!" I combine the "sponge" mixture with the "extras" and begin to incorporate flour. At first this mass is crumbly, seemingly hopeless, as crumbly and hopeless as a lot of things look in Africa, but with rhythmic turning and pushing, over time, the dough becomes soft and smooth. "Like a baby's bottom," I tell the women, the way bread cookbooks traditionally explain the process to neophytes. Most of these students are mothers many times over. They know about babies' bottoms. They find the analogy funny.

"Who would like to take a turn at kneading?" Arms fly up excitedly. I give each volunteer a turn. In this, there are no differences between us. We come from different worlds, we're wrapped in different skin, but our hands are equally capable and strong. We know how to put our back into a job. Kneading bread dough comes naturally to us all. I show them how I turn the mound of dough with the fingers of my right hand, then push it forward with the heel my left palm. Turn, push, turn, push — *"pour dix minutes!"* (for ten minutes) I stress. Each of the women kneads rhythmically, with confidence and strength.

"Now we let this dough take a nap (*un repos*) for an hour," I tell them, as I cover the soft mound with a clean towel, as if pulling covers over a sleepy child. "During this time the dough will double in size, then we'll knead it briefly again, form it into loaves and let it rise again for an hour before baking."

With my previously made and already-risen dough, the women practice making loaves and rolls in different shapes and sizes. By now the group is animated, laughing at each other's efforts, moving as if dancing with the dough, singing just-made-up bread songs about *"le bon pain."* The birds, too, outside my open windows are singing their own happy songs. The whole world, it seems to me, is happy.

Few of the women, I know, own ovens, like the tiny, little-more-than-toaster-oven-size electric oven I have at the doorway to my kitchen. But this needn't be a barrier to their baking bread at home, I tell them. I explain that it's possible to bake small loaves in tightly covered *cocottes* (Dutch ovens) over an open fire: They only need to press pieces of dough into four well-washed and greased aluminum tins (such as tuna fish tins), each to the halfway mark; let rise to double, then place on a "rack" made of five or six small empty tins set in the bottom of a large, dry *cocotte*; cover the *cocotte* tightly and place it over the fire. *Voila!* In about half an hour or so the little breads come out perfectly baked and golden.

IV. En Conclusion

The proof, of course, is always in the eating. When we share the freshly baked bread — an act that literally makes us all "companions," since the word means "those who break bread together" — the women smile and nod and agree among themselves, *"C'est bon! C'est vraiment bon!"* (It's really good!)

News of my bread-baking class quickly circled the town in the time-honored African way, by word-of-mouth. Some responses to it even doubled-back to me. This was the best part, when I learned, indirectly, from the local children, that my bread was being made in some homes in the community. It was not so many homes that they threatened to put the small, local, French baguette bakery out of business; but it was some. And even in the homes where it wasn't being made, I found that my bread had achieved a bit of notoriety.

When a handful of neighborhood grammar school boys came to my door on their way to school one morning and told me they were hungry, they also proved to be choosy. They wanted bread, they said, but not French bread. They wanted my bread. They didn't call it *Pain Americain*; they called it *"pain de maman Bonnie."* And they were bold enough to demand more: They asked me to slather their slices with *confiture* and *pâte d'arachides*, so they could "grow up to be big and strong." How could I refuse?

Bonnie Bread
(aka *Pain Americain*)

1 teaspoon sugar
1 cup water
1 cup white flour (all-purpose or bread flour)
1 teaspoon dried yeast

To make the "sponge," combine all of the above ingredients in a bowl, mix until blended, cover and allow to ferment at room temperature overnight.

1 cup boiling water
1 rounded teaspoon salt
¼ cup sugar (or honey)
½ cup whole-grain meal, such as oatmeal or cornmeal
   (or a combination)
¼ cup NIDO (powdered milk)
¼ cup light vegetable oil (such as canola)
1 egg (optional)

(continued on next page)

In a large bowl, combine the boiling water, salt, sugar (or honey), whole-grain meal, powdered milk, vegetable oil, and (optional) egg. Mix well and allow to cool to room temperature.

5+ cups bread flour

Combine the above mixtures with enough flour to make a pliable dough and knead 8 to 10 minutes. Allow to rise to double in size (about 1 hour at room temperature). Punch down, form into loaves, and allow to rise to double again. Bake in preheated (400-degree) oven until golden, about 30-40 minutes. Makes two large loaves.

A Thank-You to Paul

Michael and Paul of Bonnie Fare Catering, NYC

April 14, 1997

Dearest Paul,

If I am doing something good with my life by living and working here in the Back of Beyond for two years (and there are days when I think this could be true), then you are definitely doing something good every time you write to me. Your letters sustain me, comfort me, hug and kiss me, *and* your generous enclosures reduce my economic worries enormously. Thank you, dearest Paul, for your immense generosity of heart, mind, and wallet. Just when I'm feeling abandoned (there's been NO MAIL in my p.o. box for nearly three weeks), unloved (there's NO MALE here who tells me he loves me), and broke (I'm getting SO tired of sardines), along comes a letter from you that lifts me up, wraps its arms around me, and puts three fives and a ten in my empty pocket.

I, too, think of you every day that I'm here, Paul, darling. In the ways that you and I are alike, such as liking things clean, tidy, and organized, you would find life here to be as difficult as I do to deal with. Clean is a feeling I can only feel nostalgic about most of the time. It's hard to stay clean when you're sweating all the time, your only transportation is your feet on dirt roads, town is a mile away downhill (which means home-again is *up*hill), and there's NO WATER coming out of the taps in your house for days and weeks on end. This afternoon, for example, I was awakened from my after-lunch nap (a new-for-me daily custom; what else can one do during the killer midday heat?) by loud cracks of thunder. So I quickly got up and raced around the house gathering plastic buckets to put outside on my front porch to catch the raindrops rolling off the roof. The rain, unfortunately, didn't last long; but I was able to collect *some* water, which is more than I had before.

The other thing you'd hate as much as I do is the BUGS. As I type this at the table I rigged up in the spare bedroom (which I call my study), I have to stop every so often to scratch my forearms and legs because I'm being bitten by little (so small you can't see them, so they get in through the screens with no prob.) bugs called foo-roos. They leave red, itchy welts that drive me *crazy*. I scratch sometimes until I start to bleed, and then of course other bugs come along, as if on cue, to suck the blood. The one bug I don't have to worry about as much as others have to here is the malaria-carrying mosquito. They're around, of course, but the medication the Peace Corps makes us take, called Mefloquine, effectively prevents this disease.

On the plus side, though, the work that I'm doing here is *needed* (and I like to feel needed), and from time to time I even get the sense that it's appreciated. The kids love my puppet shows (now when they see me in town they rush up to me with open arms and delighted, bright, adorable faces to greet me excitedly), the women love my cooking classes and seem to value my health lectures, and the high school kids seem very attentive to my AIDS presentations. What more could a community health worker ask for?

My house (forgetting for a moment the water problem) is really nice. I finished painting it myself (the professional painter got sick, borrowed some money from me for medication, and never came back; I figure he either skipped town or died), so now it's all clean and fresh-looking. I have a maid come every Monday a.m. for three hours (whom you are helping to pay for, by the way) to clean the bathrooms and floors, so the spider-and-scorpion population is now down to near-zero (thank GOD). My little garden in the back gives me such joy. Every day that I pick a handful of perfect little cherry tomatoes my heart practically bursts. I bake healthy, grainy bread for myself about three times a week in my little oven; and every day for lunch I make a healthy, some-sort-of-veg-melange soup to go along with my sardine (or tuna — those are the choices) sandwich on Bonnie Bread. So I'm trying my best to stay healthy and live happily. It's a challenge, but so far — thank God again — I've been able to meet it.

When I say "thank God" I'm not referring to some puffy, cloudlike guy floating somewhere blithely in the sky. I'm talking about the Faceless, Formless, Genderless FORCE FOR GOOD that prompts you, for example, to write to me and say exactly the things that I need to hear to keep me going. So when I say "thank God," I really mean "thank you" — for listening to that Force and allowing it to guide your thoughts and words and actions (ie, fingers tapping computer keys). I believe in that Force, and I know you do too.

Lots and lots of love,
BB xx

Love Letters

This is my letter to the World
That never wrote to Me —
The simple News that Nature told —
With tender Majesty …
— EMILY DICKINSON

I filed his letters under "History"

*L*ove letters began arriving in early 1997 from a man I'd known only platonically years before when he was married. But since his divorce, since his three children had grown and moved away, since he'd retired from his business and had had a brush with cancer, he'd remembered me, tracked me down, and decided to write to me, almost daily, of his love for me and his dreams of our future together.

His letters began to arrive at a low point in my time in Gabon, when the hot-humid weather made my joints ache, and I began to walk up the hill to my home with a slight limp. I was feeling old, alone, and unlovable. His letters, like a sleight of hand, changed that for a time. They swept me off my sore, aching feet.

He wrote long, heartfelt, eloquent letters filled with imagination and yearning. These letters were addressed to my name, in Lastoursville, Gabon; but the more I read them — and reread them — I was sure they were meant for someone else, a woman who existed only in his mind.

He said that to him I hadn't changed in fifteen years; I was still the "gorgeous" woman he had met in 1981, when I was on a coast-to-coast author tour following the publication of *Somewhere Child*. He was convinced I was still "young and beautiful" — even though he hadn't seen me, nor seen a photo of me, since then.

I looked in the bathroom mirror at my 51-year-old, un-made-up face, my short, self-cropped, wildly uncivilized hairdo, the perspiration rolling down the side of my cheek, the T-shirt sticking to my sweaty flat chest and thought, *Nope, this is not the same woman he saw on national TV*.

I studied the photo of himself he'd enclosed in one of his letters, in which he was wearing only baggy, gray shorts, a bright-red T-shirt and a baseball cap on backward, proudly embracing a man-size mako shark he'd just caught. His big, barrel-like belly reminded me of my father's beer belly, and the baseball cap covered what must have been left of his graying hair. His face wore a victor's smile that seemed to say: "I am the man! The champ! I reeled in this prize-winning fish! Look at me!"

In that letter he told me he was a sportsman now; he bragged about his big, expensive boat, on which he and his buddies went out deep-sea fishing on Long Island Sound every weekend. One day, he wrote wistfully, I could be one in the flock of beautiful, adoring women who waited, with chilled white wine and lovingly packed dinner-picnic baskets, on the dock for their brave men to return from their daylong deep-sea adventures.

As I read such passages, it became more and more clear to me he had no idea who he was writing to.

With each succeeding letter his fantasies became more preposterous and presumptuous. He wrote that he planned to "bathe" me, "worship" me, and love me "forever." He told me in vivid detail what he would do with me when he came to Lastoursville to see me: How he would take me to the bank of the river and make love to me for hours. Like a romance novelist gone wild, he described every move, every lick, every moan.

Perhaps he thought I would find such reading exciting. He

didn't know me well enough to know that romance novels have never been for me. For me, lovemaking always had to be a real-life, hands-on, person-to-person connection; no facsimile on the page, screen, or telephone could ever do.

Or perhaps he simply gave no thought to how his torrid, increasingly self-indulgent love letters might be received. He certainly didn't seem to realize how much I needed to keep that part of me — the part that was sometimes lonely and longing for a man's touch — closed. His letters only made me frustrated for that which was out of my reach, hungry for something I would rather not recall or yearn for. I needed to focus on my work. I needed to file "Sex" under "History."

But writing such love letters must have been pleasurable for him, because he persisted — paragraph after paragraph, page after typewritten page. By July, the file folder in which I kept his letters was an inch thick.

Early on in this correspondence, starving as I was for affection, I couldn't help but feel flattered by his outpouring of "love" and his promises of romance. "Maybe he's Mr. Right!" I wrote excitedly — and delusionally — to Marty in January. As my best friend and next-door neighbor in New York for fifteen years, Marty had certainly been privy to the passing parade of my many Mr. Wrongs. But this initial, fleeting, schoolgirl-giddy feeling soon gave way to dismay, and then disgust.

"Who *are* you writing to?" I finally wrote to him. "You're not considering the realities of my life here. Are you *reading* my letters? Lovemaking on the riverbank would be totally absurd! We'd be eaten alive by bugs — if not by crocodiles."

It took more than seven months of our letters crisscrossing the Atlantic before I finally managed to put a damper on his dreams. Ignoring Emily Dickinson's admonition to "tell all the truth, but tell it slant," I felt I had to set him straight: "I'm not your fantasy-woman," I told him. *And you're not my fantasy man*, I wanted to add but didn't. My dream man would never have a beer belly, and he would surely take me fishing *with* him.

"The real me," I told him, "loves the freedom and independence she feels at this stage of her life more than she ever loved her youth and beauty. ... Freedom and independence are giving me fulfillment now. I feel extremely thankful for this and happy to be where I am, doing what I'm doing. Please understand..."

In his last letter, he accused me of breaking his heart. I filed his letters under "History."

There was no shortage of men in Lastoursville; but I kept my distance, coolly, telling myself repeatedly that I was in Lastoursville to work, not to play, and least of all to fall in love. I was in my fifties now, after all, and sometimes limping like an old woman. Lovers were out of the question.

There were Gabonese men around, with disarming smiles and muscular builds. I saw them as I walked home from the *marché*, working shirtless in their fields, harvesting their plantains, and I admired their strength from afar. Anyone who lived to middle age in this part of Africa, I knew, had to be particularly physically strong to survive the punishing physical conditions, the heat and humidity, the dirt and disease. The sight of their masculine, muscular backs and arms at work made my breath catch. I had to look away.

There were, no doubt, countless other men to be found in the town's numerous bars and *boîtes de nuit* (nightclubs), but I never went to them. I had seen enough of bars and drunken men as a child. I stayed home at night.

There were Lebanese shopkeepers who had left their faithful Muslim wives at home in Lebanon and proceeded to be unfaithful in Lastoursville with any available girl or woman of any age, size, color, or creed at every opportunity.

"Would you like me to *come over* tonight?" M'ammed said to

me lecherously in French every time I frequented his shop to buy dry goods. "Aren't you *lonely?*"

"*Pas du tout*" (not at all), I told him blithely, trying to sound convincing.

When he did stop by one evening, I made sure it was strictly business. I sold him a box of Peace Corps-issue condoms (part of my job as a health volunteer) to protect him from the sexually transmitted diseases — especially AIDS — that were rampant in Gabon and that he was sure to contract, given his admittedly indiscriminate sexual behavior, if he failed to take precautions.

There were brazen young men, too, who boldly approached me on the road and asked me for things that might help them make their getaway — a visa to the States, a letter to the U.S. Embassy on their behalf, or, most often, money. "*Donne-moi l'argent*" (give me money) was a request I received almost daily. It always came from well-dressed, well-spoken young and charming Gabonese men, as if they all believed every older white woman was unspeakably rich, with a shoulder bag stuffed with paper money and hands quick to give it all away — in exchange for a sexy smile.

"*Je suis volontaire*" (I am a volunteer), I pointed out politely on my good days, meaning I don't have an income here; you and I are in the same financial boat. On my bad days — when the overwhelming heat, omnipresent dirt, and ubiquitous bugs wore my patience and goodwill thin — I had to bite my lip to keep from snapping, "What do I look like, *a bank?!*"

So the day I met Youssef I was wary.

I was walking up the hill to my house one afternoon in August, and suddenly, like an apparition, he appeared, walking in step beside me. He was dressed in pressed jeans, a clean white T-shirt, and leather sandals. He was tall, several inches taller than I, slim, and nice looking. He walked lopingly, as tall, thin men tend to do. I noticed he had a slight limp.

"Bonjour," he said to me softly, almost shyly. *"Ça va?"*

Even with these few words of greeting, I could tell he was not Gabonese. His accent was from elsewhere.

"Oui, ça va, merci. Et vous?" I couldn't ignore him. I didn't want to be rude.

"Ça va, ça va," he said with a smile so warm and guileless it broke the film of ice in me. *"Je m'appelle Youssef."*

"Youssef?" I said, unused to the name. I asked him how he spelled it so I could see it in my mind and remember it.

He stopped on the road, reached his right hand into his jeans pocket for a Bic ballpoint pen and wrote his name for me in large, blue letters on the broad, pale, nearly white palm of his left hand. Y — O — U...

"YOU!" he said, pointing to me. *"Je parle l'englais un peu!"* (I speak a little English). And we both had to laugh, knowing this may have been one of the few words in English he knew.

As we walked the mile together up the hill, he told me he was on his way to visit a friend at the hospital who had been injured in a logging accident. He told me he himself was Malian, a Muslim, from the Malinke tribe; but he'd grown up in Abidjan, the capital of Ivory Coast. He said he was a professional photographer, or planned to be, as soon as another friend returned from Togo, with the good camera Youssef had paid for with his entire savings, 500,000 CFA (about $1,000). This friend, Youssef told me, had assured him he could find a cheap, good, second-hand camera for him there.

I didn't have the heart to ask what he would do if his friend never returned from Togo with the camera but instead absconded with the money. Youssef seemed to read my mind.

He had faith, he told me. His friend would never let him down. His friend was a Malinke, like himself. He was a man of honor and integrity. *"Dieu est grand"* (God is great), he said.

To change the subject, I asked what brought him to Gabon.

"Je suis aventuriere," he admitted, and I thought, *I'm something of an adventurer myself.*

He spoke his French slowly and clearly enough for me to follow every word. I had been in Lastoursville for nearly a year, yet this felt to me like the first time I had had a real, back-and-forth, mile-length conversation in French with anyone. Uncannily like my tall and slim Scottish grandfather, my father's father, a good man whom I knew too briefly as a child, Youssef had an earnest, quiet, dignified bearing, and I felt safe with him from the start.

When we reached my house at the top of the hill, within a city block's distance from the hospital, Youssef asked whether he might stop by sometime to *"dit bonjour"* (say hello).

"Bien sûr," I said, as though I was sure.

On subsequent visits to my house, Youssef and I talked of many things. He told me about his childhood and his family: He was one of eleven children. His father, 86, whom he only half-jokingly referred to as "the Ayatollah," beat and berated his children to keep them in line, but passed himself off as a fine, upstanding citizen to the neighbors. His 60-year-old mother, on the other hand, was loving and kind; Youssef obviously adored her. He showed me a letter from her he kept with him at all times. "My beloved son," it began in lyrical French and impeccable penmanship, "you are in my thoughts always..."

"Did your mother write this herself?" I asked.

"No," he said. "She dictated it to someone, a professional scribe. My mother cannot read or write. But these are her *sentiments.*" He carefully folded this well worn love letter and tucked it back in his wallet as though it were a million dollar bill. Then he pulled out another folded sheet to show me; it was a map of the world.

"Le monde," he said, smiling, as if this, too, was worth a million to him, and then he patted it and put it away.

He told me he had had to drop out of high school when he became crippled by a faulty injection for malaria. The nurse didn't know what she was doing, he said, and the misplaced needle left him lame for a year. He stayed home with his mother and helped her with whatever work he could do. She nursed him back to health, massaging his bad leg daily, until he was able to walk again, albeit with a limp.

When I asked him, during another of our long conversations, to tell me about Islam, he patiently, quietly explained the five principles of his religion, ticking each one off on the fingers of one hand — belief in one God, daily prayer, alms-giving, fasting during Ramadan, and pilgrimage to Mecca, if possible, during one's lifetime. He told me about the Prophet, Mohammed, and Mohammed's first wife, the widow Khadija, who was fifteen years older than he.

"Because the Prophet was married to a much older woman, there is no stigma in Islam for a younger man to be with an older woman," Youssef said earnestly. "I think young women are *trouble*," he said. "Older women are *wise*." Youssef was thirty-two, twenty years younger than I.

I let his comments drop.

And then one day in August he arrived at my door at noon with a surprise, a bag of fresh beef kidneys from the town's only butcher. *"Rognons!"* he announced with a big grin, *"pour un ragoût!"*

Kidney stew? I hadn't had kidney stew, I realized, since I was a child.

"You are a *carnivorous* animal," my father said to me at the dinner table when I asked for second helpings of meat in lieu of dessert. He had just finished his main course, and my mother was getting up to clear his plate and bring him his dessert. He sat back in his chair at the head of the table to my left, lit a cigarette, took a drag, and blew the smoke in my direction. A small, glass ashtray sat on the table to his right, and the smoke from his cigarette, now cradled by the ashtray, coiled into my face. Still eating, I made a small blowhole out of the left corner of my mouth in an effort to send the smoke back his way without his knowing. Eating his cigarette smoke ruined the taste of my mother's food, but I couldn't complain to him. Head down, I continued to eat my meat.

I loved my mother's food. Her good cooking, I've often thought, was the best thing about my childhood. I knew even then that all of her heroic efforts in the kitchen were designed to please my father, the self-proclaimed gourmand, and to keep him home. Oftentimes she succeeded. "Good dinner, Lee," he'd tell her once in a great while. "You're a pretty good cook." You could see how happy these crumbs of compliments made her. With me — except for rare exceptions, such as brussels sprouts, lima beans, and beets — her cooking never failed to please, and I told her so at every opportunity.

I especially loved what she could do with meat. The fragrance of her Sunday dinner leg of lamb roasts wafting through our house made my heart melt. *This is the aroma of Home,* I thought at the time. *This is the fragrance of Love,* I swooned, hugging my own rib cage. I knew I could never be a vegetarian.

My mother's whole roast chickens were golden, moist, and tender. Her beef braises and stews were richly flavored and melted in my mouth. I even loved her kidney stew, with its softly rounded chunks of meat that tasted actually sweet to me. "How many kids in this world *like* kidney stew?" my father bellowed from his place at the head of the table. "You're a strange one," he said to me, shaking his head.

In the kitchen Youssef and I prepared our kidney stew together. He cleaned and cut up the meat by the sink, while I chopped then sautéed the onions at the stove.

"Did you hear the news?" he said to me as he worked. "Princess Di is dead."

"No," I said and turned to look at him. *Could he be joking? Is this some kind of African humor?* His back was to me, but I could see his hands were wet and bloodied by the kidneys. I knew he hated the sight of blood. His hands worked quickly, as though they were burning. "No, that can't be," I said.

"She was in an automobile accident in Paris yesterday. *Elle est morte*" (She is dead), he said. He told me he'd heard about it on RFI (Radio France International) that morning. He relayed to me all he knew.

We continued to cook in silence. I couldn't find words to say. In my mind, I replayed the televised tape of Diana's wedding. She was a naïve nineteen then — as I was when I married my daughter's father. I saw her shy smile, her downcast eyes, her gentle wave that connected her with commoners like herself. Like me. *Why was she dead now, while I was still alive?* It just wasn't right. It couldn't be.

Youssef and I served our kidney stew over rice — a Malian staple, he told me — then sat together at my dining room table. We held each other's hand, thanked the one God we both believed in that we were alive, and asked God's blessing on our first shared meal.

Our kidney stew was sweet and delicious, I thought. Just like my mother's.

• • •

Kidney Stew

1 pound beef kidneys
1 teaspoon salt
1 medium onion, chopped
1 large clove garlic, minced
4 tablespoons unsalted butter
flour (for dredging)
1/3 cup dry red wine
2 tablespoon tomato paste
2 cups (1 can) beef broth, or 1 beef bouillon cube,
    plus 2 cups water
Salt and freshly ground pepper to taste

Wash kidneys, trim away any fat, membrane, or connective tissue, and place in a bowl. Add 1 teaspoon salt, and water to cover; allow to soak for at least 30 minutes. Drain, rinse, and pat kidneys dry; cut into bite-size chunks. Sauté chopped onion and minced garlic in butter over medium heat until softened. Dredge kidney pieces in flour and cook with onions and garlic until slightly browned. Add wine, tomato paste, and beef broth (or bouillon plus water) and bring to a boil. Lower heat, cover pan, and cook gently for about 10 minutes. Season to taste with salt and freshly ground black pepper. Serve over steamed white rice. Makes 4 servings.

Dîner

Of course, the finest way to know that the egg you plan to eat is a fresh one is to own the hen that makes it.
— M.F.K. FISHER, *How to Cook a Wolf*

Dîner with his Déjeuner and her first egg

*E*verybody around seemed to know I loved to cook. Even the big, red rooster who lived across the way came to my house regularly, looking, I presumed, for a free meal. Little did he know, though, that my number-one meal in the whole world prominently featured roast chicken.

It was something of a joke among my friends that I, the former food professional in New York City, of all culinary capitals, should choose as her favorite meal — the meal she would request as her last if she were to be executed at dawn — a simple, tender, whole roast chicken, served with flavorful risotto and fresh, steamed, buttered broccoli.

This was the meal I fantasized most about at post. Plain, white rice was available in Lastoursville, but Arborio? No. Broccoli? *Malheureusement, non* also. Deep-frozen, often-accidentally-thawed-when-the-town's-power-was-out, then-refrozen chicken parts were available, it's true. But the taste of these and the taste of a whole, trussed, juicy, crispy, golden roast chicken were about as far apart as Lastoursville was from Manhattan.

So when this beautiful rooster started strutting over to my house looking for something to eat — risking his very life by crossing the relatively busy road, where battered taxis whizzed by taking emergency cases to the hospital — I confess at first I had similarly hungry thoughts. I even gave him a nickname, which subsequently stuck. I named him *Dîner* (pronounced DEE-nay), the French word for both "dinner" and "to dine." I thought *I* was looking at a free meal.

"Yooo-hooooo!…cluck-cluck-cluck!…*viens ici, mon petit Dîner!*" I would call to him sweetly (which made the neighborhood children think I'd gone mad), all the while thinking homicidal thoughts. "I have a nice slice of homemade bread here for you to peck at! What you need is a little fattening up…!" But the closer he got, the more my attitude changed. I started to see *Dîner* differently. I experienced a change of heart. Proximity, like timing, I found, can make all the difference in this world.

Funny things happened to Peace Corps volunteers living alone in far-off places tourists seldom see, on the other side of the globe from Fairway on Upper Broadway and Balducci's in the Village. Some volunteers were known to sit and stare at one wall of their hut for hours on end. Others spent whole days deep frying beignets. I seemed to have become emotionally attached to a neighbor's rooster.

When I asked myself how this crazy thing came to be, I could come up with a couple of fairly sane answers. The first was I didn't have any pets in Lastoursville. I'd left my beloved Himalayan cat, Sweet Basil, at home in New York in the care of my friend and next-door neighbor, Marty. I missed him. *Dîner* had begun to fill Basil's shoes, so to speak. Another reason was that *Dîner* was a first for me, and the novelty of our relationship was oddly appealing. He was the first living, crowing rooster I'd ever gotten that close to in the feathered flesh. Since I didn't grow up on a farm, poultry for me had always been something only encountered in a cold, plucked, gutted, raw, lifeless, cut-up, or whole and ready-to-roast form in a grocer's or butcher's refrigerated meat case.

Eat this rooster, *Dîner?* I soon realized I couldn't think of it. He was too beautiful, too elegant, too utterly regal. Below his bright-red crown, his widening body was covered by a feather-cape the color of the polished copper pots hanging on the kitchen wall of my New York apartment. His haughty, black tail feathers reminded me of my favorite, shiny black silk pants (now in storage), the pants I wore only to posh New York cocktail parties, and I knew I'd have no use for in the rainforest.

Dîner was dignified, too, and proud. I loved the way he strutted around my house — kingly head held high, copper chest puffed way out — like he owned the place. And what a voice! Vibrant, piercing — ear splitting, in fact, at close range. When he hopped up on my front porch and serenaded me at dawn every day, I found the sound of his commanding cock-a-doodle-doos strangely comforting.

So, instead of eating *Dîner,* I decided to feed him and make him happy. For selfish reasons, I guess: I wanted him to keep coming back to me.

One afternoon when I spotted him strutting away, crossing the road again, going back to his real home, I was crestfallen. *Was he angry? Disappointed? Still hungry? Didn't he like my bread? What could I do to win him back?* I wondered. *What do chickens eat, anyway?*

Someone told me that chickens like to eat rice. *Of course! Chicken-and-rice! Why hadn't I thought of that?* So, then, every morning, when I heard his distinctive, expectant, close-up cry, I would quietly unlock, unbolt, and unchain my front door and toss a handful of raw rice onto the porch for him. The first time I did this he was startled, almost insulted at having food thrown at him. He turned his back on me, walked off, and toured the grounds. Then he began to expect his breakfast. He didn't even flinch as the kernels bounced and scattered at his feet. *Soon,* I thought, *I'll have him eating out of my hand.*

And then I had an even better idea: I'd find him a wife.

One day Youssef arrived with a cardboard box containing a young, shy, blond hen. I name her *Déjeuner* (lunch), and *Dîner* fell in love with her instantly. They became inseparable, strolling around my house side-by-side, pecking and cooing to each other. Youssef said he'd never seen anything like it.

I designed and Youssef built a henhouse for *Déjeuner* out of bamboo and chicken wire. She grew fat and happy and began to lay eggs. I called her eggs my *Petits Déjeuners* (breakfast). And, yes, I used *them* for cooking.

Classic Roast Chicken

1 whole roasting chicken, about 3½ pounds
2 to 3 tablespoons olive oil
salt and pepper

Preheat oven to 425 degrees. Set a roasting rack inside a 9 x 13-inch baking or roasting pan. Remove the innards from the chicken and rinse the chicken, inside and out, under cold running water. Pat dry with paper towels.

Liberally season the inside of the chicken with salt and pepper. Rub the outside well with oil. Tuck the wings under the back, tie the legs together at the ends with kitchen twine, and set the chicken, breast-side-up on the roasting rack.

Tent the chicken loosely with foil and roast 30 minutes. Remove foil and roast 30 more minutes. Remove chicken from oven and test for doneness: Prick the thigh with the tip of a paring knife; if the juices run clear, the chicken is done. If the juice is pink, return to oven to roast for up to 15 more minutes. Allow chicken to sit for 5 to 10 minutes before carving. Serves 4.

Easy, Low-Fat Risotto
(adapted from Barbara Kafka's
Microwave Gourmet Healthstyle Cookbook)

½ cup finely chopped onion
3 tablespoons butter
1 cup Arborio (Italian short-grain) rice
3 cups homemade chicken stock
  or canned chicken broth
¼ cup grated Parmesan cheese
¼ cup chopped fresh herbs (optional)

In a 3-quart microwaveable casserole, combine the chopped onion and butter. Cover loosely and cook on high 2 to 3 minutes, until the onions are tender. Add rice and stir well.

Stir in broth. Cook, uncovered, for 9 minutes. Stir and cook for 9 to 11 minutes more, or until rice is al dente. Remove from oven. Add cheese and herbs, if desired.

Cover with a kitchen towel and let stand for 5 minutes, or until rice absorbs excess liquid. Season to taste with salt and pepper. Serves 4 as a first course, 6 as a side dish.

A Simple Omelet

2 eggs
1 tablespoon water
¼ teaspoon salt
1/8 teaspoon pepper
1 tablespoon butter
Filling, if desired: ¼ cup of any of the following: chopped ham; grated cheese; crumbled, cooked bacon; cooked, sliced mushrooms; or 2 tablespoons minced, fresh herbs

• • •

Combine the eggs, water, salt, and pepper in a bowl and beat with a fork to blend well.

Set an 8-inch nonstick skillet over medium-high heat until hot. Add the butter and tilt the pan, swirling the butter to coat the bottom and sides of pan.

When the butter foams, pour in the beaten eggs, and let rest, un--disturbed, for about 5 seconds, to set. Using a wooden spatula, gently lift the cooked part of the egg away from the edge of the pan in four places, allowing the liquid egg to run under and toward the rim.

After about 30 seconds, spread the (optional) filling in a line just to one side of the center of the omelet, then slip the spatula under the egg mass on the other side of the pan and flip that half of the omelet over onto the other half to enclose the filling. (If no filling is used, simply flip one half of the omelet over onto the other half.)

Carefully tilt the pan over a plate so the omelet falls out bottom-side-up. Serve immediately. Makes one serving.

Jeanne d'Arc

*With swamp fever, or tropical malaria, I have,
unfortunately, like every other doctor in the tropics, plenty to do.*
— ALBERT SCHWEITZER, *The Primeval Forest*

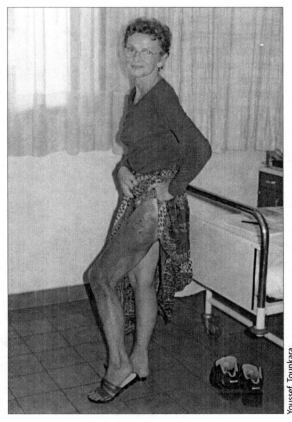

My last day at the clinic in Libreville

Youssef Tounkara

Youssef had malaria — *le palu*, as the Africans called it — when he arrived at my house, unexpectedly, the day before Thanksgiving. So I led him to the spare room I called my study, with the makeshift desk — a wide wooden plank laid over empty, freshly painted oil barrels — at the window, overlooking the river and the forested mountains in the distance. I'd made a rudimentary daybed for the room too, from a Peace Corps-hand-me-down, narrow, single mattress resting on boards propped up by NIDO cans and an assortment of colorful pillows against the wall.

"Please lie down here," I told him, and then I covered his shaking body with a blanket. He complained of fever, chills, painful joints, headache, dizziness, weakness. I took his temperature, which confirmed a high fever, gave him some Fansidar from my personal, Peace Corps-issue medical kit (which was against the rules for me to do, but I thought this costly medicine would cure him quickly), and told him I'd make some chicken soup for him for lunch.

Before Youssef's arrival, I'd been busy preparing for the Thanksgiving dinner I was having at my house the next day. I'd invited a handful of people — my Peace Corps postmate, Morgan; my American missionary friend, Bev; my Chadian neighbors Dr. Djimet and his wife; Denise Nimba, the Cameroonian restaurateur, and her husband, a retired Gabonese *fonctionnaire* (beaurocrat); plus Youssef, who was going to take keepsake photographs. For most of the guests, including Youssef, it would be their first traditional American Thanksgiving dinner; and I wanted to make it a memorable event.

Already the poultry stock — made from a combination of chicken carcasses and turkey wings, plus *mirepoix* (chopped onions, carrots, celery and parsley stems) — was gently simmering in a huge stockpot on the front burner of my new, small stovetop and filling my home with its homey fragrance. Chicken stock, I used to tell my cooking school students in New York, is "liquid gold" in the kitchen because it adds a rich flavor to everything made from it, especially soups and sauces.

My menu for the next day's Thanksgiving feast included pumpkin soup as a first course, roast turkey breast (whole turkeys were not available in Lastoursville), mashed potatoes and gravy, canned peas (fresh or even frozen peas were not available either), fresh carrots and salad from my garden, and my homemade Bonnie Bread.

Bev was making her old-fashioned, all-American apple pie and bringing it, she promised, hot-from-the-oven up the hill in her truck, along with her own, homemade vanilla ice cream. I'd told her once, when she'd made these specialties before, that I thought this hot-cold/creamy-tart taste-sensation combination in the mouth was "*orgasmic!*" She bridled at my comment at the time, but she cheerfully agreed to make her sensuous hot-pie-with-cold-ice-cream combination again and again.

I had plenty of stock bubbling on the stove, so I knew I could spare some of it for Youssef's healing soup. It was lunchtime, midday on the equator, unbearably hot and humid, as usual. I was wearing only a tank top and tennis shorts, which I could get away with in the privacy of my own home but not in public in Gabon (where it is culturally inappropriate for a woman to show her legs); and, as always in my house, I was barefoot.

I'd never seen anyone suffering from malaria before. Youssef's long, slender frame beneath the blanket shook like a tree limb in heavy winds. His normally gentle, smiling face looked clenched. His semisweet-chocolate color skin looked ashen.

"Stay here," I told him, smoothing my right hand over his short-cropped hair, "and try to rest. I'll make you some good soup and come right back."

"*D'accord,*" he said, nodding weakly.

I walked down the hallway toward my kitchen at my usual, brisk, Manhattan-pedestrian pace. When I turned the corner hurriedly into the kitchen, I didn't see that something had spilled on the floor. Water? Oil? Whatever it was, it was slippery on the terra cotta tiles. The heel of my right foot skidded on it. I lost my balance. I reached wildly for something to grasp to catch my fall. My left hand fell on the handle of the tall stockpot sitting on the stovetop at the entryway to my kitchen. Without knowing, without thinking, without seeing, I pulled the heavy pot toward me, pouring the boiling liquid down onto my bare left thigh, knee, shin, and foot.

When my mother was dying of cancer, I sat at her bedside and listened to her slow, soft moaning. There are sounds that women make, I thought then, that have a vocabulary all their own. Baby-girl squeals, schoolgirl giggles, lover's sighs, childbirth cries, heart-broken sobs, death's moans — all fall within women's wide, wide range of wordless emotional expression. But the sounds I made that day, as the boiling poultry stock, the burning liquid, molten gold, melted the skin on my left leg as though I were made of candle wax, were unlike anything I had ever heard before. Unlike any sound I had ever heard myself make.

My beloved rooster, *Dîner,* perched beside his beloved *Déjeuner,* just outside my kitchen window, had been a witness to this event. He became so distressed by my cries that he crowed loudly, anxiously, in sympathy.

I was on the kitchen floor, rocking and screaming in pain when Youssef appeared at the kitchen door, wide-eyed, shaken.

"Qu'est-ce-que se pas?!" he said as if he couldn't believe his eyes. Or ears. We had always been so quiet together. He had never heard me raise my voice, much less scream. I myself barely knew who was screaming.

"Get the doctor," I begged him. "Please get Dr. Djimet!"

I thought I could remember, through the exploding pain, that severe burns required water, rehydration, as quickly as possible. So after Youssef left, I hobbled to the shower where I sat with my legs stretched out flat in front of me, letting the cold water pour down on my left leg. The burn wound was huge — the worst part covering the entire front and side of my left thigh — and now blistering grotesquely. "NO!...NO!...NO!" I screamed, as if I could order it to stop blistering, stop knifing me, stop killing me with pain. I felt as if I were about to faint. Was the water helping? I couldn't think. I didn't know. The pain was short-circuiting my brain.

Youssef found Dr. Djimet at his house, further up the hill from mine, directly across from the hospital, having lunch with his wife and teenage son and daughter.

When the two men returned, they lifted me up and carried me gently as if I were a bird with a broken wing. They put me between them in the cab of Dr. Djimet's pickup truck and rushed me to the hospital's surgery room, where Dr. Djimet treated my burn. Youssef stood beside me. He gave me his hand, and I squeezed it with all my strength, to counteract the pain.

"Youssef *a le palu*" (Youssef has malaria), I told Dr. Djimet, gritting my teeth, trying to be brave, as brave as I imagined an

African would be under the same circumstances, as I lay there on the operating table and Dr. Djimet tore the layers of burned and blistered skin from my thigh. But he was concentrating on the task at hand. He ignored my words. The Fansidar, though, must have worked its magic on Youssef. His *palu* seemed to have vanished.

In the days that followed, my condition worsened. I had a violent allergic reaction to the mercurochrome Dr. Djimet had used liberally to dress my wound. I experienced high fevers, cold chills, and gushing sweats for days. I received excellent outpatient attention at the Lastoursville hospital (I chose not to stay there because my home was cleaner), but getting there, on foot, taking baby steps the whole way, was excruciatingly painful; and having the enormous bandages changed there every day, without anesthetic, was like being skinned alive. I couldn't keep from screaming. I tried to be quiet and courageous, to show the African nurses attending me that thin-skinned white people can be brave too, but the screams escaped against my will.

"This whole experience," I wrote to Marty five days after the accident, "has to go to the top of the list of my worst physical nightmares. Another nightmare has been trying to get through to the Peace Corps in Libreville. Would you believe the phones have been under repair at the P.C. Medical Office most of the week? And the lines often don't go through from here to there anyway."

Youssef never left my side. He cared for me, night and day, doing everything he possibly could to comfort me and ease my pain. He fed me, took me to the toilet, changed my drenched shirts and sheets, washed my face, brushed my hair.

One night, when I was delirious with pain and fever, I thought I saw two women — one white and resembling my mother, the other black and unknown to me — reaching out to me from the next life. I wanted to go with them. I wanted so much to go. Wherever these women were, I knew there would be no pain.

"I want to die," I told Youssef, who was sitting beside my bed.

He stretched his long, slim body out next to me on the bed, gently, careful not to disturb my heavily bandaged left leg, and he spoke softly into my ear: "God has sent me to tell you, you cannot go now. *Pas encore* (not yet). This is not your time. You have more work to do, *ici, en Afrique.*"

Yes, I thought, accepting Youssef's words as if from the voice of God, *Africa needs me. And I need Africa even more.*

When Morgan arrived by motorcycle a few days later from her village and saw my worsening condition and Youssef's exhaustion, she swung into action. She found a phone in town that actually worked and eventually got through to the Peace Corps Medical Officer in Libreville, who arranged for my evacuation on the next scheduled flight to Libreville out of Lastoursville. I asked that Youssef fly with me, and the Peace Corps agreed.

"What I *don't* want," I wrote to Marty before Youssef and I flew to Gabon's capital together, "is to be medivac'd back to the U.S. That would break my heart, on top of everything else. ... I want to heal and come back here and pick up where I left off."

Youssef had never flown in a plane before. All of his travel-adventures throughout West Africa, he'd told me, had been by land, in trucks or by bush taxis. This was his first flight.

"Ça va?" I asked him when I saw the knuckles on his large, brown hands nearly turning white gripping the armrest between us.

"Bien sûr," he assured me, masking his fears with pride and dignity.

The Peace Corps doctor, a young Cameroonian man, met us at the airport. He admitted me to an exclusive French clinic, run by the physician-wife of Gabon's president, Omar Bongo. I was given a private room. I begged for, and received, a general anesthetic before they changed my bandages; I could not bear to be skinned alive again. I was hooked up to an intravenous morphine drip. Suddenly, miraculously, my pain almost disappeared. As I wrote in my journal at the time, "It sometimes feels like someone else's pain now, not mine. I know it's there, gnawing at me, but I don't feel directly connected to it. Wonderful stuff, morphine!"

My room was clean, a kind of clean I had almost forgotten, living in always dusty or muddy Lastoursville; and it was air-conditioned. The blindingly white sheets on my hospital bed were clean, sweet smelling, and *dry*. There was not even a hint of the debilitating wet-heat and ever-present bugs that plagued my daily life in Lastoursville. *"Nous sommes au paradis!"* (we're in heaven), I said to Youssef, jubilantly. For a moment I thought I'd indeed died and flown from Lastoursville to paradise.

"Ah, Jeanne d'Arc!" the French doctor said to me when he entered my room on his evening rounds and read my chart.

I told him, in fact, I'd once been to the spot in Rouen, France, where she was burned at the stake, and, yes, I could identify.

"Et j'aime beaucoup le morphine, docteur" (I love morphine), I added playfully, high on the feeling of no longer feeling such pain. He smiled, nodded, and wiggled his eyebrows comically in obvious imitation of Groucho Marx, whom he must have seen on American TV shows growing up in post-World War II France. With that, he left my room.

Youssef stayed with me at the clinic, sleeping in a reclining chair beside my hospital bed at night, attending to my needs all day. As I wrote to Marty from the clinic on December 10:

No one in my life has ever taken care of me the way this man is doing now. I know my mother loved me and did her best, but she had so many other things to do and other people to take care of, she couldn't linger long. Youssef bathes me, feeds me, brings me the bedpan when I need it in the night, changes my wet (from perspiration) sheets, massages my left foot (so it won't stiffen up and make me walk with a limp forevermore), shops for things to make me happy (papaya and mangoes especially), and guards me like his very own life depended on it. He does all this without one grumble or complaint, with a sweet smile, and sweet loving words. ... He behaves as if there's nothing else in the world he'd rather be doing than taking care of me.

Youssef and I shared the food (superb French cuisine, including imported cheeses, fresh baguettes, tender meats, and beautiful salads) on my hospital tray and watched TV movies together (a first for us) in my room at night. Except for his afternoon forays to the *marché* to buy fresh tropical fruit for me while I napped, Youssef never left my bedside.

When I would ask him, "Why are you doing this? Why are you so good to me?" he would answer only, *"C'est normal."*

Normal? I thought. *Normal for whom? For him and other selfless Africans, perhaps, for whom human connectedness, worth more to them than gold, is the rule. But not so much where I come from — where money, more than kindness, too often rules. As one former boyfriend, a financier in New York, used to express this ethos, "He who's got the gold makes the rules."*

News traveled fast among the American expatriate and Peace Corps communities in Libreville, and I began to get visitors. People wanted to see me, the burn victim, now amazingly gregarious, thanks to the morphine, but also Youssef, the hero of the dramatic story they'd heard. This was the man who had risen from his own malarial death bed to get the doctor, just in time; the man who saved the life of a Peace Corps volunteer posted in a remote town in the middle of rain-forested nowhere; the man who'd flown with her to Libreville and never left her side, even to the extent of sleeping in a chair beside her hospital bed.

These visitors showered me with flowers, books, and stationery; and they surprised and embarrassed Youssef with thank-you gifts and praise. Frank Conlon, the Peace Corps director in Gabon, gave

Youssef a black cotton T-shirt with the profile of an African woman's face outlined in white on the front. The T-shirt read in French, "Teach a woman and you teach a country." Youssef accepted the T-shirt humbly and wore it proudly.

Elizabeth Raspolic, the U.S. Ambassador to Gabon, who had months earlier visited my home in Lastoursville and stayed for tea during a tour of the country, came to visit me at the clinic bearing a bouquet of flowers. She asked me what I needed. Still silly from the morphine, I behaved like a ten-year-old and asked for a set of colored felt-tip pens and some paper for drawing. She returned the same day with these gifts to cheer me.

When Amanda Carter, the wife of the U.S. Deputy Ambassador to Gabon, came to visit, she brought several of her own coffee-table-quality quilting books for me to look at and enjoy. Quilting was her passion, she told me, a real comfort to her, living in Gabon, so far away from her true home and extended family in Virginia.

I studied her books in the days that followed, and, in my giddy, drug-induced haze, I could feel myself falling in love with the whole idea of patchwork quilting. I imagined myself returning to my post and sewing pieces of colorful African fabric together; putting torn pieces back together in a new way to create something exciting and original; stitching my leg, my life back together.

There was talk about sending me back to the States for skin grafting, which would mean I would have to be medically terminated from the Peace Corps.

"I don't want it," I told the Peace Corps doctor who visited me and Youssef at the clinic every evening. "I don't want to go." I didn't tell him I could not leave Africa — nor Youssef.

"But this burn wound is likely to leave a big, ugly scar, Bonnie," he told me. "You don't want that, do you? You're a beautiful woman…"

"No," I said, "it doesn't matter. I won't be modeling bathing suits or entering any beauty pageants. I want to return to my post." I dug in my heals. I had to stay in Africa.

"Today, December 18, 1997," I wrote to Marty, "marks my second full week at this clinic, and no one is telling me when they think I'll be released. It all depends on my leg and how quickly it completely heals. Infection is the enemy. I can't return to post until all of the skin is closed and out of danger of infection. And, since Gabon is germ-heaven and every little scratch or pin-prick gets infected, there is always that danger. … Anyway, I'm off the morphine now, cut from my I.V. umbilical cord, hobbling around, trying to make the best of things. Having my sweet angel Youssef here makes all the difference in the world."

Ambassador Raspolic invited Youssef and me to Christmas dinner at her grand residence, so filled with her impressive collection of African folk art that it seemed more like a museum with plush sofas than anyone's home. Dinner was an American-style buffet, turkey with all the trimmings. Since my Thanksgiving dinner in Lastoursville had to be cancelled, this dinner, with Youssef sitting in the place of honor beside the ambassador, became his first American feast. I watched admiringly as Youssef and the ambassador chatted amicably in French. Youssef, so quietly elegant and dignified, looked like royalty to me.

With the Peace Corps' blessing, Youssef and I flew back to Lastoursville together on New Year's Day 1998, and he came to live with me in my house on the hill.

• • •

Chicken Stock — "Liquid Gold"

2 pounds chicken bones — raw and/or left over
   from a roasted chicken
4 medium carrots, scrubbed and chopped into 1-inch pieces
4 medium onions, peeled and chopped into 1-inch pieces
4 stalks celery, chopped into 1-inch pieces
3 medium cloves of garlic, unpeeled and left whole
10 whole, black peppercorns
1 bay leaf
1 small bunch of parsley stems
Cold water

Place all ingredients in a tall stockpot large enough to hold everything comfortably. Cover with cold water, and bring to a boil over
high heat. Reduce heat to a simmer, and skim off any foam or fat that
rises to the surface. Cook at a simmer for at least 2 hours, uncovered.
Strain and cool quickly. Refrigerate or pour into plastic containers
and freeze.

PART II

Work and Love

Youssef

*…[W]hen you share [a meal] with another …
it becomes dignified. Suddenly it takes on part of the ancient
religious solemnity of the Breaking of Bread, the Sharing
of Salt. …[T]he fact that you are not alone makes flavors
clearer and a certain philosophic slowness possible.*
— M.F.K. FISHER, *How to Cook a Wolf*

Bonnie Lee Black

Youssef by the Ogooué River in Lastoursville

In the equatorial heat, in the closeness of the thick rainforest that blocked the night sky, in the solitude of my ovenlike cinder block house on the hill in Lastoursville, our differences melted away. Alone together there, Youssef and I were reduced to our essences.

The externals evaporated: We became virtually age-less, color-less, nation-less, language-less. The fact that Youssef was Malian and had never been beyond Francophone Africa; that he was born five days after I gave birth to my daughter, my only child, when I was twenty; that he spoke barely one word of English with a confident smile ("yes!"); and that he'd had to drop out of school at twenty due to crippling illness, was background, not barrier. We connected at the core, and at that core, we were two solitary human beings, with like hearts, souls, and minds.

Despite the fact that we came from different worlds, we found ourselves standing on the same patch of earth, far from our families and countries of origin. Despite our diametrically different back-grounds, we held harmonious values and worldviews. We both believed in one Great God, one human family, one beckoning globe filled with potential adventure. We both retained — despite some measure of adult disillusion and world-wisdom — a childlike sense of wonder. And we both were sufficiently brave to embrace the unknown.

Youssef never asked me for anything. We shared everything. We shared clothes; we wore the same size jeans and baggy T-shirts. We shared house and garden chores. We shared a bed and made love, uncomplicatedly, as though we were cooking and eating a good meal together.

Yes, lovemaking for us was like good food — healthy, necessary, delicious. And it was deliciously free of encumbrances, such as guilt; or accoutrements, such as sexy lingerie; or perversions, such as pornography — none of which had ever held any appeal for me, or him. Our lovemaking was as natural as breathing.

"A tu jouer?" he would always whisper. *Are you satisfied?*

How could I not be?

Every morning I would rise before dawn, before Youssef woke, to have tea alone in my study. I would sit at my makeshift desk facing the front louvered windows and watch the sun rise hazily over the distant, forested mountains on the other side of the river. I would pray, think, write, study French, and count my blessings. In this solitude, for an hour or two, I would listen to the myriad birds in the enormous palm tree off to the left sing their morning songs, and my heart would soar. *How could I be so lucky?*

My happily married cousin, comfortably ensconced in New Jersey, would write me laudatory letters, telling me I was "so courageous" to be there in Africa, so selfless to give up "all the comforts of American life" to work among the poor and needy. How could I tell her I had never felt so rich, never been more happy?

I had lived alone in a small studio apartment in New York for twenty years before returning to the Africa for which I had long felt homesick. Men had come and gone in my life during that time, never staying long enough to sincerely say, "I love you." Straight men in Manhattan then knew that heterosexual women outnumbered them by roughly fifty to one; they knew there was another attractive-enough available woman around every corner.

I had not come to Africa to find a house big enough to share, nor to find a good man to love me. But I was, nevertheless, deeply thankful for these newly found, unanticipated blessings.

When Youssef knocked softly on my study door at about seven each morning and I let him in, he was already showered, shaved, sweet smelling, and crisply dressed in freshly pressed khakis and a clean, ironed T-shirt, tucked in. Every day, his first words as he reached out to me were, *"Je t'aime beaucoup, cherie"* (I love you very much, darling).

"Et moi aussi," I said to him from the shelter of his arms, as if in a dream from which I never wanted to wake. I wanted to stop time, freeze the frame, as we stood there, in my cinder-block home in the middle of absolutely nowhere. But my time in the Peace Corps had an expiration date stamped on the bottom: September 1998, only nine months away, and I could hear time's moon-faced clock ticking. *How could I leave this?* I wondered as he held me to his lean, sinewy body. *How could I leave his love?*

One day, as Youssef and I were walking up the hill together on our way home from the *marché*, he asked me to marry him. He said I was the only woman he'd ever asked, the first woman other than his mother he'd ever loved; he wanted to spend his life with me.

"Quoi?" I said, not sure I'd heard him correctly. He repeated his proposal.

"Are you just looking for a passport to the States," I asked him laughingly, trying to make light of the moment, "like all the others who want to marry Peace Corps volunteers?"

"I would never want to live in the USA," he said somberly, seemingly hurt by my glib response. "I could never be happy living in a place where I would be treated like a second-class citizen." My mind flew back to something my English boyfriend, Mel, had said in Rhodesia in the early '70s when we were contemplating marriage: "I'd never live in the States," he said. "It's full of bloody Americans."

"That's true," I told Youssef. "You're right. The U.S. is indeed racist, still. That's the ugly truth."

Youssef lifted his head and raised his chin. He often spoke of dignity, which in his spoken French sounded to me like "DEEN," something he prized more than money. Dignity and pride were his treasured possessions, which no one could take from him. He would not stoop to second-class status for anyone.

We walked silently for a while, both of us carrying bags of produce from the *marché*, both of us sweating in the late-morning heat. My burn scar still hurt — it was as if a large sheet of leather in the shape of Idaho had been Superglued to my left thigh, and every step I took pulled the newly knitted skin tissue nearly to the breaking point — so I walked slowly, like a much older woman. Youssef, ever patient, slowed his pace to keep pace with me.

"I am much too old for you," I said matter-of-factly. "I'm old enough to be your mother. We can never get married. One day you'll wake up and decide you want to have a family; you'll want a younger wife who can bear you children."

"Africa has enough children," he said.

"Yes, but you might change your mind someday. I don't want to stand in the way of that. I think we must be together *jour par jour*, on a day-to-day basis, as if we had no future, only the present. Our lives are intersecting now, but we may well go in different directions in the future. Please don't speak of marriage again."

Saying these words to him made me feel, fleetingly, noble and selfless. The truth was, the very human me wished we could be together forever.

"The heart once broken," Edna St. Vincent Millay wrote, "is a heart no more, and is absolved from all a heart must be..." My heart, though awash in newfound love, had trouble trusting, due to all the heartbreaks of the past. My mind, too, demanded answers to unanswerable questions: *Why him? Why here? Why now?*

There were times when I overanalyzed what Youssef and I had and why it came to be. One reason, I thought, may have been that Youssef had a surprising fear of blood, and after my burn accident I no longer bled. The sight of human blood, the metallic smell of it, any close contact with it, made Youssef feel ill. I never asked him why, but I sometimes imagined. Had he witnessed a bloody, deadly bush-taxi accident in his African travels? Or was his fear older: Had he seen his beloved mother hemorrhaging on the ground from a miscarriage? Did he feel helpless, as a little boy, to help her? As it was, he avoided all possibility of encountering it.

I'd expected menopause to creep up on me over a span of months or even years. In fact, I'd jokingly told my girlfriends in New York before leaving for Gabon at age fifty that I was going to equatorial Africa for two years to write a book entitled *Hot Flashes in a Hot Country*. As it happened, I hadn't felt any hot flashes, perhaps because Gabon is so constantly hot a hot flash wouldn't register. Instead, my burn accident had so traumatized my body that my periods simply stopped for good. Menopause for me was anticlimactic. For Youssef, who feared not only blood but also any unwanted pregnancy, this was indeed a good thing.

The fact that I had small breasts was also a plus. "You have the body of a teenager," Youssef told me the first time we slept together, which he meant as a compliment. For African men, who are generously breast-fed throughout their infancy and exposed throughout their lives to the sight of mothers openly breast-feeding their babies, a woman's breasts seem to hold little to no erotic appeal. They're seen instead as sources of an infant's sustenance, not playthings for grown men's pleasure.

"You'd be perfect if you had big boobs," one ex-boyfriend in New York had said to me in parting. *And you'll be perfect when you grow up*, I wanted to say to him but didn't. For Youssef, it seemed, large breasts would have been superfluous.

Another fact was that Youssef genuinely revered older women, all older women. He told me this was an important aspect of his culture: In Mali older women are honored for their wisdom, centeredness, and rich life experience. Young women, in contrast, are considered silly, flighty, "green." Youssef even went so far as to swoon at the mention of the name Madeleine Albright, who was then making news by becoming the first female U.S. Secretary of State. "Madda-LANE All-*BRIGHT!*" he would say, hands crossed over his chest. I would laugh, thinking he was kidding. But he wasn't kidding. He truly felt she was a beautiful, strong, capable woman who would use her considerable powers to do good in the world. "*Elle est for-mi-dable!*" he would say.

Sometimes, though, I just had to approach him directly. I didn't have to ask, "Do you love me?" as I'd often foolishly done with previous men who'd flitted through my life. (Mel's response always was, "Well, I come to dinner here every night, don't I?") This time, I needed to know *Why*. When I asked what it was about me he loved, his answer was, "I admire your character and stability." After having been appreciated only for my outward appearance in the past, when I was young and considered beautiful, I'd finally met a man who saw beneath my thin white skin.

One morning in my study I wrote a poem to express this phenomenon, called "Beauty," which ended with the lines: "It seems I am for him a calm and solid island set in a tumultuous sea./This, for him, for now at least, is Beauty."

In Abidjan, the capital of Ivory Coast, where Youssef grew up and lived until his mid-twenties, he'd worked as a chef for a while at an upscale African café. He knew how to cook and cook well. So one of the many things we shared was a love of good food, carefully prepared.

We took turns making lunch, our main meal of the day. He would prepare his favorite dishes, mostly traditional Malian fare, such as gumbo, saka-saka, or West African peanut stew — always served with rice. ("Malians must eat rice every day," he informed me, smiling broadly. "We are like the Chinese.") And I would make American, French, Italian, or Moroccan dishes that were new to him.

When it was his turn to cook, I sat quietly in one of my white plastic armchairs brought into the kitchen so I could watch him in action.

For saka-saka, the thick, scrumptious, saucy stew he made from *feuilles de manioc*, or cassava leaves, Youssef picked the tenderest leaves from the manioc growing like weeds in our back yard, washed them repeatedly, chopped them finely, then boiled the chopped *feuilles* in salted water for at least ten minutes to remove the potentially lethal cyanide contained in the plant's tubers and leaves. Like me, Youssef was hyper-methodical in his cooking methods and near-fanatical in his standards for food safety. "Manioc can be dangerously poisonous," he lectured me. "But when it's prepared correctly, it's delicious."

He added the mass of well-drained, cooked manioc leaves to a large saucepan containing sautéed onion, chopped canned sardines, a chicken bouillon cube, minced *piments* (hot peppers), and lots of minced garlic.

"Let me show you a better way to chop garlic," I said, jumping from my chair to reclaim my familiar leadership role of catering chef and cooking instructor. "First, you place the whole garlic clove on the cutting board, like this, and then you smash it with the flat of the knife, like this, and then —"

"Non, merci," he said softly, shaking his head and shooting me a look that said it all: *You have your ways of doing things, and I have mine. You are you, and I am me. You and I are NOT in competition.*

"D'accord," I agreed, as I sat back down in the plastic chair and continued watching his demonstration.

For his birthday I made a special American menu, made up of things Youssef had never before eaten: grilled hamburgers, from a chunk of beef I laboriously chopped by hand, on buns I baked myself, with macaroni salad, tomato-and-avocado salad, and chocolate birthday cake, that I also baked from scratch. Youssef was flattered by and grateful for my efforts to give him the first such birthday party of his life, but he missed not having his requisite rice with the main course, and he found the chocolate cake too rich for his digestive system. He later told me shyly it had made him sick to his stomach, so I never made another rich American dessert for us again.

My official workday at the hospital's mother-infant clinic was over before eleven every weekday morning, after I'd given my health presentation of the day to the captive audience of young mothers sitting in the waiting room. I had always walked directly from the clinic to the *marché* in *centreville* to do my daily food shopping, but now I no longer walked that downhill mile alone. Youssef joined me.

No one in town seemed the least bit shocked or even surprised to see me with a steady companion who was an African man significantly younger than I. Being part of a couple — of any ethnicity and any age, it seemed — was far more "normal" to them than the way I had been living: alone. "It is not good for a woman to live alone like this; it is not safe," some locals had cluck-clucked at me before my burn accident, before that traumatic turning point in my life in Lastoursville. Now, seeing Youssef and me together, they seemed to smile approvingly and breathe a sigh of relief.

Oddly enough, Youssef and I did look like a matching pair — both tall and slim, reserved, benign foreigners who had somehow found each other in this remote rainforest — walking in step down the town's steepest hill. And perhaps because most had seen so few white women in their lives, the townspeople had no way of gauging my age. Was I old — and bent like a dried twig by time? No. Was I young — still energetic enough to walk miles in the midday sun?

Yes. But…? Maybe they concluded that white women are not only lacking in color, as albinos are, they're also ageless, frozen in time, like bugs trapped in amber.

This became our daily routine: After shopping for the fresh ingredients we needed for that day's meal and visiting with *maman* Leora at the *marché*, Youssef and I would walk home and prepare a nice lunch. Then we would spend at least an hour at the dining room table — carefully laid with a colorful African cloth, matching napkins rolled into napkin rings, a bouquet centerpiece I'd made from cornhusks, a whole loaf of homemade bread, a French Bordeaux bottle refilled with cheap, locally bought Spanish red wine — savoring our meal. We took turns asking the blessing before eating, holding hands and praying to the same God (whom, we both believed, sanctioned red wine with savory meals). We ate slowly and talked animatedly. Or, I should say, Youssef did most of the talking, while I listened.

Normally a shy, quiet man who kept his own counsel, at our table over lunch Youssef liked to expound. Perhaps having been a middle child in a family of eleven who had grown up to be a lone traveler, he wasn't accustomed to being focused on and listened to like this. The novelty of this attention seemed to open a floodgate inside him.

I looked at him, I'm sure, the way my mother had looked at me across the kitchen table when I visited her in later years, when I was in my thirties and she was in her sixties, living alone and able at last to focus on one of her four children. She looked and listened as though every word I uttered was fascinating, even astounding. Her eyes would grow wide, and she'd put her hand to her open mouth and say sincerely, *"Really? I didn't know that!"* which would only spur my storytelling.

Listening to Youssef, I did the same, hanging on his every French word — and trying mightily to grasp each sentence's meaning — as he told me stories about his travels and he shared his knowledge of African politics and history. His true stories were rich and delicious, and I grew to hunger for them even more than for the food we ate at lunch. Over time, he told me the proud history of Mali, his ancestral homeland:

The ancient Empire of Mali, which then encompassed most of western Africa — Youssef said with a sweep of his hand — dated from the early thirteenth to the late fifteenth centuries. This empire rose to greatness under the leadership of the legendary king Sundiata Keita, known as "the Lion King," who was a Malinke — like Youssef himself. During this period, the city of Timbuktu in the north of the kingdom was a commercial, cultural, and intellectual capital, equal in historical importance to Athens or Rome. Great mosques, schools, libraries, and universities were built at this time; and extant manuscripts from that period show the subjects taught: theology, philosophy, law, history, mathematics, politics, medicine, and astronomy. All this, in Africa, during the Middle Ages.

Youssef told me about the European takeover of Africa in the late nineteenth century, when the then maritime powers, informed by bold explorers of Africa's enormous natural resources, cut the continent up like a huge cake into rough-hewn chunks, greedily expropriating its riches for themselves. With the stroke of a pen, at the Berlin Conference of 1884, Africa was divided and conquered by the major European nations, with no regard for the cultural and linguistic boundaries that had existed there for centuries. "They broke Africa's heart into pieces," Youssef said, "and she still hasn't recovered, despite most African countries' independence from colonial rule." He told me about Africa's "Big Men" dictators, many of them puppets of the West, their cruelty and corruption.

And he told me about his uncle, his father's brother, who as a young man had served in the French army during World War II. "On the way back to Africa, right after the war ended," Youssef said with no trace of bitterness or rancor in his voice, "the ship my uncle was on, filled with African war veterans, was deliberately sunk by the French. They all were drowned."

"Pourquoi?" I asked him in horror. "Why would they do that?"

"To avoid having to pay the veterans' pensions," Youssef claimed and truly believed. *"C'est la guerre. C'est la vie en Afrique."*

Listening to Youssef so intently, I improved my French comprehension, I learned more about Africa than I had ever dreamed, and I discovered as though for the first time in my life that listening like this — without questioning, debating, or interrupting — is indeed an act of love.

After we finished eating, we put our dishes in the kitchen sink, rinsed them quickly to evade the ever-present opportunistic ants, and then took a *sieste*. Despite the oppressive midday equatorial heat, we slept together soundly until three.

• • •

Youssef's West African Beef Stew

1 pound stewing beef, cubed
2 to 3 tablespoons all-purpose flour
½ teaspoon salt
¼ teaspoon pepper
a pinch of cayenne
3 tablespoons oil
2 medium onions, chopped
3 large garlic cloves, minced
1 tablespoon minced fresh ginger root
1 teaspoon minced fresh *piment* (hot pepper)
3 to 4 cups water (or canned beef broth)
2 beef bouillon cubes (if using water)
1 tablespoon soy sauce
¼ cup tomato paste
½-¾ cup smooth peanut butter
(Optional: chopped vegetables, such as butternut squash, eggplant, and/or zucchini)

In a bowl, toss the beef cubes with the flour and seasonings. In a large, flameproof casserole, brown the meat in the oil on all sides. Add the onions, garlic, ginger, and hot pepper and cook, stirring, until onions are soft.

Add bouillon cubes, tomato paste, and 3 cups water (or broth). Stir in peanut butter until dissolved and simmer, covered, over low flame for 30 minutes.

Add chopped vegetables of choice, if desired, and more water, if necessary, and continue cooking until vegetables are tender, about 10 minutes. Serve over cooked white rice.

Makes about 4 servings.

Discovering Beans

*Paradox though it seems, it is nowhere easier
to starve than amid the luxurious vegetation of the
game-haunted forests of Equatorial Africa!*
— ALBERT SCHWEITZER, *The Primeval Forest*

In my garden, planting an avocado tree I'd grown from a pit

ardening was new to me. All my life I'd wanted a garden of my own. The thought of opening a back door, taking a few steps, and picking truly garden-fresh fruit and vegetables for that day's meals had been a deep yearning inside me for as long as I could remember.

The problem had been, though, that for most of my adult life I'd lived in a studio apartment on Riverside Drive on the Upper West Side of Manhattan. For twenty years I had an enviable, fifth-floor view of the Hudson River and sometimes spectacular, Technicolor sunsets that bathed the interior of my small apartment in pure gold. But, alas, no back door, no backyard, no kitchen garden.

Until Gabon. In my house on the hill overlooking the Ogooué, surrounded by mountains blanketed by forests, I had a sweet, small kitchen — with a back door — and, just a few steps beyond that back door, my first garden.

The list of things I tried, and failed, to grow from seed packets sent from home was long. The list of things I tried to grow, and succeeded at growing, from the pits and seeds of fruits and vegetables consumed there was shorter: avocado and papaya trees, one mango tree, indigenous pumpkins, and gumbo (okra) plants galore. And the ways I tried, organically, and heroically, to improve the adobe-red, pottery-hard, dead-tired soil could be summed up in one mantra: compost, compost, compost. But the biggest gardening lesson I learned at the time had to do with beans.

I'd read in one of my many vegetable gardening books that Native Americans planted their bean and corn seeds together so the beans could climb up the corn stalks as a natural support. *Aha*, I thought, when I saw seed corn for sale spread out on a wooden table at the *marché* in town one morning: *Corn! Maïs! I'll try growing African maïs now, Native American style.*

But let me back up...

Before I moved into my house on the hill, it had been empty for a long time. It was not only uninhabited, it was, even for quite a while after I gingerly called the place home, uninhabitable. Too close to the forest for comfort, the house had harbored all sorts of slithering, crawling, ominous, venomous creatures that I, I immodestly brag, bravely slew single-handedly, with my ever-ready machete. Grand totals: eleven scorpions; three poisonous snakes; and countless huge, black, furry, deadly spiders.

The solution? *Debrousse.* That is to say, clear the land surrounding the house of all wild vegetation; create a space, like a firebreak, between the house and the forest so the unwelcome, evil, little creatures would keep a safe distance. And the answer to the question, What to do with all that naked, exposed earth? Plant, of course: an orderly, civilized, nourishment-providing garden.

Nourishment is the key word here, because Nutrition was an integral part of my job, my *raison d'être*, there. As a health volunteer, a teacher of Community Health and Nutrition, creating "model gardens" for others in the community to emulate was part of my mission. In the forested interior, at least, the Gabonese people are, not surprisingly, hunters by nature, not farmers. Vegetable gardening — working the difficult, infertile soil to produce healthy additions to what is often an imbalanced diet — was, I found, a hard sell.

So gardening became more than a beautiful dream-come-true in my new life in Gabon, it also became an exercise in, among other things, self-defense, self-preservation, education, determination, and research. This is how I justified all the time I spent in my garden: It wasn't just play, it was "work." It wasn't just a religious experience, it was "science." Often, when I was outside gardening, I lost all track of time, the way my artistic mother always told me she lost track of time when she was painting. The heat, the bugs, the mud, the perspiration dripping into and stinging my eyes — none of these stopped me. I was transported. I felt transcendent.

At times, when I was down or discouraged *(Will I ever learn the French language? Will what I'm doing here make any kind of difference at all?)*, the garden lifted me up. "Patience," it whispered to me in a wordless, universal language, "you must have more patience.... Everything takes time.... Just keep planting seeds...."

"Seeds!" I begged shamelessly in letters to friends back home. "You want to know what you can send me? Send me seeds, please! Not just for my own home garden — I've fallen in love with gardening, to tell you the truth — but also for my classes. 'Gardening for Nutrition' is one of the subjects I teach at the clinic; and I like to give small envelopes (recycled Lipton Tea-bag envelopes) containing vegetable seeds to each mother, as a little thank-you-for-listening gift, at the end of my lectures...."

Whenever seed packets arrived in the mail, I quickly incorporated them into my "work," with mixed results. In this hot-wet climate, the broccoli, cauliflower, spinach, and onions, for example, didn't stand a chance. But the parsley, basil, lettuce, eggplant, and tomato seeds, on the other hand, thrived.

My biggest lesson, though, came from beans. One day, quite unscientifically, I dumped all of the corn seeds I had ("True Gold," and "Quickie F-1 Hybrid" sent by friends, plus the indigenous local kernels I'd recently bought at the *marché*) and just as many beans (the "Kentucky Wonders" I'd received in the mail from my sister, as well as a fistful of dried red and white beans from the *marché)* into a bowl, added some water, and let them soak for a couple of days, until they began to sprout.

Then, rather too hurriedly, I admit, I planted them all in one afternoon — maybe too deeply, maybe too close together, both corn and bean seeds in each hole — in advance of the rainy season. I waited and watered and watched. Days and days went by. Nothing. *Gardening teaches patience,* I counseled myself, *and gardening in Africa teaches patience squared.*

After a few weeks there was some sign of life here and there — either a corn or a bean plant was struggling to emerge from its *enterrement* — but not as many as one would expect from all those seeds, all that work. *Chalk it up to the soil,* I thought. *It's no wonder the Gabonese are hunters.*

In December when my burn accident had taken me to Libreville, I had not had time to make gardening arrangements. *Malheureusement,* I was gone a month, and when I returned my nascent garden was unrecognizable. On first cursory inspection, I wasn't even sure my garden was still there. In my absence, it appeared, there'd been a war between the civilized and the *sauvage;* and wild had won. What had been my neatly planted, lovingly tended, full-of-promise (if not produce) garden had become, thanks to generous rains, a jungle of overwhelming weeds.

For the first week after my return from Libreville, I didn't leave the house. I couldn't go out of my back door. Not only was it physically difficult to walk after my accident, but I couldn't bring myself to face my obliterated garden. I focused what energy I had on getting the interior of my house back in order.

In Gabon it's easy to let things get you down. The heat and sweat, rain and mud, the ever-present, always aggravating insects; the poverty, disease, and apathy; the Sisyphean feeling that despite your best intentions, the force of gravity is against you. It's easy to question your purpose, doubt the efficacy of your efforts. *Why*, I wondered, *should the people in this town learn to toil in this poor-quality earth under the fierce equatorial sun to grow vegetables that will be destroyed by bugs, when they can tiptoe off in the cool of night into the forest they know so well, shine a flashlight into the sleepy eyes of a gazelle, raise a rifle and confidently shoot tomorrow's entrée? Who should be teaching whom here?*

Finally, when *tristesse* turned back to stubbornness, I grabbed my machete and marched (well, hobbled) out the kitchen door. The closer I got to my jungle, the easier it was to distinguish friend from foe: Insects don't seem to eat the leaves of weeds. It was easy to locate the corn, too: Their tasseled tops stuck out above the rest. And *something* was climbing up their sorry-looking, spindly stems, appearing to be choking them to death; but it didn't look like bean plants to me. Where were all those beans?

I hacked at the weeds with therapeutic vengeance. I yanked them, roots and all, and threw them in a heap. And in so doing, I discovered the beans. Or what should have been beans. The crinkly, paper-thin leaves of these plants looked more like finely spun spider webs or imported lace than what they were: the aftermath of insects' lunch. Pounded by December rains, these "pole" plants lay flattened, sprawling sadly on the red earth, barely alive. *So much for beans*, I thought.

Dripping with perspiration, yet nowhere near ready to quit, I began to lift the plants up, support them with sticks, give them something to hold on to, give them a fighting chance. And what did I find hiding beneath their lacey leaves? Finger-length, untouched-by-insects, perfectly ripe green beans. Each plant had a secret cache — two or three or four — waiting to be discovered.

Hunting for these wonderful Kentucky Wonders then became a childlike game of hide-and-go-seek. The beans themselves were well camouflaged: They were precisely the same pale-green color of the plants' stems, so it was difficult to tell the two apart. I bent low and parted the rustling leaves with my hands, as if making my way through a miniature jungle. Inevitably, I would find a bean that had escaped capture in the days before, which had grown the length of my forearm and the thickness of my pinkie. "Where have you been, Bean?" I would say to the thing aloud. And the answer I imagined was, "Just waiting for you to find me."

Every day for the following weeks, like a person who was living a dream, I was able to open my back door, take a few steps, and pick a good handful of beautiful fresh beans to add to my *Soup du Jour*.

Soon after, at the clinic, two young mothers approached me to tell me the seeds I'd given them at the end of my "Gardening for Nutrition" lectures several months back had *poussé*'d *bien* (grown well). Their tomato and eggplant plants had provided their families with lots of fresh vegetables, they reported. *"Beaucoup de vitamines!"* one said.

It was moments like these that made it all worthwhile. The fresh Kentucky Wonder beans that I put into my soup, for example, became for me more than just green beans. They were the color, the size, the shape and taste, even the slight squeak, of hope.

• • •

Three-Bean Salad

2 cups canned kidney beans, rinsed well and drained
2 cups canned garbanzo beans, rinsed well and drained
2 cups whole cooked green beans (fresh, canned, or frozen)
1 small red onion, peeled and thinly sliced
1 stalk celery, cut into ¼-inch dice
1 large ripe tomato, cut into smallish chunks
3 tablespoons olive oil
2 tablespoons balsamic vinegar
½ teaspoon salt (or to taste)
¼ teaspoon freshly ground black pepper
(Optional: bean sprouts)

Combine all (up to optional bean sprouts) in a large bowl and toss gently. Cover and allow to marinate several hours or overnight in the refrigerator. Serve on a bed of bean sprouts, if desired. Makes about 4 servings.

Sister Truth

On a revisit to Maine, with my "baby" sister Heather, 1991

Paul Marokus

April 12, 1998

Dearest Heather,

It's a hot, sticky Easter Sunday morning here in the rainforest, and while Youssef sleeps in, I thought I'd spend some of my precious, early morning "quiet time" with you.

Two of your letters reached me this week: one postmarked January 20, and the other postmarked March 12. The envelope of the Jan. letter was already torn open by the time I got it — and, in fact, it was handed to me by my postmate, Morgan, who just happened to see some mail kicking around on the floor near our shared post box. That's the way mail is treated around here.

Anyway, you've been on my mind, sweetheart, and we need to "talk." I was awake for several hours during the night last night, thinking about you. (I also had a severe stomachache.) So I wanted to try to put some of my thoughts on paper asap — before they flew out the window and into the nearest palm tree.

Thank you, as ever, for writing — for telling me about your Christmas travels, sharing your thoughts. You seem, though, to be comparing yourself *unfavorably* to me: I am big and strong and positive, leading a "nirvana experience" life in Central Africa; and you are weak and depressed and filled with self-loathing. This concerns me very much. Let me try to put things in perspective, honey: During our training we are "advised" to keep our letters home positive; after all, mail is opened with impunity in other parts of the world (eg, here), and if, God forbid, we should tell-it-like-it-really-is-at-times and that letter gets opened, we'd find ourselves on the next plane back to the States. I've been trying to avoid that.

The truth is (and I trust this letter isn't intercepted), I try to write letters only when I'm in a positive frame of mind and I'm enjoying my experience here — which is to say, roughly four days out of the week. The other three? *Forgetaboutit.* When it feels like 200 degrees in the shade and the very act of breathing in and out is too much of an exertion; when there are a b'zillion tiny ants *everywhere* — in your toothbrush, bed, clean underwear, fridge, *everywhere*; when there's no water from the taps for days, or the water that does come out is *brown* and smells like you-know-what; when you make appointments with people (school directors, eg) in order to schedule puppet shows for the kids, and time and time and time again the guy isn't there when you get there — well, on such days (3 out of 7) I write only to my journal, never letters home. Heath, this is *not* Nirvana, and I am no better than you (just a little taller and five years older). We're both little human beings trying to make sense of and get by in this crazy world.

The biggest difference between us at the moment is that we're in different *places*. Here, it's difficult to remain *physically* healthy; in the States (in my view), it's difficult to remain *mentally, emotionally, and spiritually* healthy.

Here, with the HEAT, *humidity*, RAIN, *bugsssssss*, dirty water, and germs galore, lethal infectious diseases seem to be lurking at every turn. In the sanitary States, again, in my view, the problems are psychological and spiritual: pressure, pace, pointlessness. Everything is moving so fast and no one has the time to ask, *WHY? Where are we headed?* I'm not sure people were meant to live on the equator (which accounts for the fact that Gabon is underpopulated by African standards — only about one million people in the *whole country*) — but I'm sure people were not meant to live in pressure cookers either (which accounts for the millions of Americans living on Prozac). ...

I think life is very difficult, a constant struggle — not a struggle to be "happy" but a struggle to stay on your own footpath and keep hiking. The people who trip us up and impede our travels should be avoided, and the people who lend a hand when we trip and fall should be cherished. But basically we're on our own, and the road (if we live long lives) is long and mountainous, with lots of obstacles along the way. After we reach our respective destinations (death), we'll learn what the hike was all about. That's how I see it. Not terribly novel or profound, but it's useful to me.

It's helpful (and healthy), I feel, to see the world from this (African) angle. Not because it's a "better" angle, but because it's *different* from the rich, spoiled, sexist, ageist, racist, know-it-all, first-and-fast world's point of view. ...

My burn wound is healing, ever so slowly. It reaches from my knee bone to my hip bone on the entire left side of my left thigh. From mid-thigh down, it's a lot better now, almost skin color. But above the mid-thigh line, it's still bright red and very painful. No, there's no "Silk Skin" here, I'm sure. I rub the area with a French cream called Biafine, which seems to help a bit. But it's still ugly and uncomfortable. *C'est la vie.*

It's so incredibly hot. Sweat is pouring down my face, back, legs, as I type this. There's no water again, either. No water for washing dishes, so the ants will invade with a vengeance. No water for a nice cool shower. Or for brushing my teeth. This is supposed to be the rainy season, but it hasn't rained for days and days. Just HOT, still air and blazing sun. Too hot to go out, so I stay in my house and read and write and sew, or whatever. But maybe I should try to rest now. I didn't sleep at all well last night.

> ... I love and miss you very much,
> Your big sister,
> BB xx

Mamma Food

I wish to emphasise a further fact that even the morally best and the idealists find it difficult out here to be what they wish to be. We all get exhausted ...
— Dr. Albert Schweitzer, *The Primeval Forest*

*In front of our home in New Jersey, 1950,
a few months before Heather was born*

On the wall of the long hallway in Bev's sprawling house in Lastoursville was a large, black-framed photo of her family. White-haired elderly parents, six middle-aged siblings with their spouses and children, and even some of those children's newest arrivals held in their young parents' arms. Four generations of pleasant-looking, clean-cut, conservatively dressed people standing close together on a grassy slope, somewhere. The men looked to me as if they could be accountants; the women, traditional homemakers. The photo was a paper-thin, frozen slice of time, and that time could well have been in the 1950s.

"And where are *you* in this gathering?" I asked Bev as she noticed me studying the group photo one evening when I'd gone to her house for supper.

"I'm the one who took the picture," she said. "It was at a family reunion back in Virginia a few years ago, the last time I was on furlough."

"Beautiful family," I said, to be polite. "And *big!* Everyone seems to have at least five kids."

"Except me," Bev said. "I never married."

Bev, I guessed, was fifty-six or fifty-seven, roughly five years older than I. She reminded me of my high school biology teacher, Miss Baker, with her pillowy, pale complexion; her short-cropped, straight, graying brownish hair; her always-serious demeanor; and the men's-style, leather shoes she wore. In the States, no one would confuse the two of us; but here in Lastoursville, Gabon, where she and I were the only white, female, permanent residents, local people sometimes mistook me for her. They would stop me on the road to buy a Bible. I would then explain that I was not the missionary who sold Bibles, I was the health volunteer who sold condoms — and did they care to buy one? Once in a while, I'd even make a sale.

"We're all missionaries in my family," Bev pointed out, as I stood there, still studying the photo, transfixed. Family photos, like families themselves, always mesmerized me. They made me feel as if I belonged to another species altogether — or didn't belong to any group at all. My family had never had a reunion. We had scattered like jagged shards of broken pottery, beyond hope of repair or reassembly. In fact, how could a family that had never been united in the first place ever be *re*-united?

I looked at Bev's family photo more closely, searching for flaws. It seemed to me to be too good to be true.

"No rebels?" I asked. "No renegades or black sheep? No one who ever stood up and said, 'Hell, no! Missionary work isn't for me!'?"

"Nope, not one," she said. "We're all missionaries in Africa for the same Christian Alliance Church."

"Well, I'll be damned," I quipped.

Bev didn't reply.

Bev's parents, now long retired, had served for more than forty years in the Ivory Coast, where Bev and her siblings were born and raised. She, like Youssef, spoke French with an Ivorian accent; and when he and I visited her together, the two of them often talked nostalgically of their younger years "*en Côte D'Ivoire.*" From what I could piece together of their conversation in French, it was a beautiful place to be then, especially when the country enjoyed stability and prosperity under its first president, Felix Houphouet-Boigny, following its 1960 independence from France.

After finishing college in the U.S., Bev had chosen to serve in Gabon, where she'd worked now for close to thirty years. She taught at the Bible school in Koula Moutou, the provincial capital, and she managed village churches throughout the surrounding area. Lastoursville was a new post for her, the last before her retirement. She'd lived alone in this large house not far from *centreville* for almost two years. But she was often on the road, speeding along the jungly, mountainous pathways like a fearless cowboy in her new, blue Nissan pickup.

One day, when I rode with her to Koula Moutou, I was amazed at the way Bev blithely raced past Africans on the side of the road who were frantically trying to flag her down for a lift. The back of her pickup was empty. She had the room. Traveling by bush taxi was costly for villagers — and notoriously unsafe. Just recently, a bush taxi, overcrowded and speeding as usual, had tumbled down a steep, 240-foot-deep ravine, killing two young Gabonese mothers, one of whom was pregnant, and all nine of their children. The driver, who was no doubt drunk, had managed to jump out before the car went down. All of Lastoursville, it seemed, was mourning these tragic deaths.

When I asked Bev why she didn't stop for the waving people, she hunched over her steering wheel, staring straight ahead, not letting up on the gas. "There are too many of them," she said, flatly. I got the sense she was burnt out by her missionary work in Gabon, the way I'd been burnt out by catering to rich people in New York.

On the rare occasions when she was in town, Bev and I tried to get together.

Sometimes she would drive up to my house on the hill for tea and cake in the late afternoon, or I would go to her house in the evening for supper. After dinner she would drive me home, so I wouldn't have to walk the mile uphill alone in the coal-black, moonless, starless, overcast night.

Bev had more amenities than I had: an old, black, rotary telephone; a fairly modern TV and VCR; an enormous (it seemed to me, because I didn't even have a small one) refrigerator; a huge, chest-type freezer stocked with top-quality cuts of meat she bought on her frequent forays to Libreville; a microwave oven; a four-burner stove and standard-size conventional oven; and a washing machine — albeit an ancient, round, wringer-style prototype. She even had a computer, she told me, which she hid somewhere in a back room and seldom if ever used.

"The Africans *expect* us *blancs* to live better than they do," she once explained to me, "just as they expect their own chiefs to. If we choose to live on their low level" (*Was she implying, 'the way Peace Corps volunteers do'?* I wondered), "they lose respect for us."

"Ah," I said, and nodded, not wanting to argue, though her position sounded a lot like rationalization to me.

Bev's home was at least twice the size of mine, with four large bedrooms to accommodate missionary guests and other travelers who might be passing through. One of those bedrooms was filled with trunks and boxes, as though she hadn't quite finished moving in to this house in Lastoursville. Her own bedroom was spare: one old-fashioned oak dresser with a mirror above it; a faded, oval rag rug on the floor; and, by the room's one window, a single bed with no mosquito netting over it. When I asked why she didn't take this simple precaution against the ever-present threat of malaria, she told me earnestly, "My Lord God is all the protection I need. No harm will come to me."

Except for the daily devotional book on a small table beside the toilet in the bathroom, and the King James Bible by her bed, there were no discernable religious items in Bev's home. There were no framed depictions of a handsome, long-haired Jesus and no crucifixes hanging anywhere, to be sure (too Roman Catholic). Bev's religiosity, it seemed to me, did not take the form of symbol or icon, but rather of word and deed. She appeared to live a careful, measured, super-circumspect life, like a grown "daddy's girl" always striving mightily to please her Father.

If, as in Islamic art, God were likened to a grand mosaic — too vast for any one person or group of people to see in its multicolor-tiled entirety — then I'd have to say Bev and I, both believers, saw different tiles. Bev seemed focused on God the Father, for whom she was forever the good, obedient daughter. I, on the other hand, had come to recognize only God the Spirit, who, I liked to think, could fill me and use me for good the way I used my hand puppets for children's health lessons. Bev's God was strict. My God was spirited. Bev's God, it seemed to me, was a monochromatic, rainstorm-gray. My God was a rainbow immeasurably wider than the Milky Way.

Nevertheless, despite our differences, Bev and I seemed to need each other's companionship from time to time, if for no other reason than we needed to speak to someone else in English for a change. So we sought common ground and steered clear of religious discussions. I tried at times to break through her taciturn veneer and solicit her opinions on other subjects. Once, for example, I asked her for her three rules for living successfully in Gabon. She thought for a moment, smiled slightly, and ticked them off on three fingers of her right hand: "One, always carry toilet paper in your pocket; two, never expect anything — that way you'll never be disappointed; and, three, never criticize the government. If you don't follow rule three, you're likely to find yourself dead. And you?" She turned to face me. "What are your three so far?"

"Hmm..." I stalled for time. "I guess I'd say: One, don't expect anything to get done, but if it does, call it a miracle; two, acknowledge that the only thing likely to change here is yourself; and, three, accept the fact that Africa will always be a mystery to us outsiders."

Walking into Bev's house for me was like falling back in time. Not only her family photo, but also her whole life and lifestyle felt as if it were frozen in the 1950s. From her simple, cotton dresses to her wood-framed living room furniture, everything seemed to be vintage '50s. Even — or especially — the meals she made for our occasional suppers together, reminded me of my mother's cooking from the '50s, before my mother returned to full-time work, before she turned the supper-making responsibility over to me.

Like my mother, Bev was a surprisingly marvelous cook whose specialty was middle-class American food — what New York foodies would refer to in the '80s as "Mamma Food," or comfort food. This was the kind of food that only the lucky among us might recall from our childhoods. For Bev, though, there in the rainforest of Gabon, it was standard fare. She made for us: meatloaf with real mashed potatoes and gravy one time; pork chops with homemade applesauce, baked potatoes, and broccoli another time; and porcupine meatballs another...

Porcupine meatballs! This was the first recipe my mother taught me, in 1956, when I was eleven, my youngest sister, Heather, started first grade, and I began making dinner for our family when my mother went back to work. I made my porcupine meatballs in the pressure cooker, the way my mother taught me, keeping my fingers crossed the whole time that the cooker wouldn't explode onto the kitchen ceiling, as it had one time.

The taste of Bev's food, so much like the taste memories I had of the '50s, flooded my mind and transported me back in time, every time.

• • •

Porcupine Meatballs

1½ pounds ground sirloin beef

½ cup fresh bread crumbs

1 large egg

½ teaspoon salt, or to taste

¼ teaspoon black pepper

½ cup uncooked long-grain white rice

½ cup finely chopped onion

1 large clove garlic, minced

¼ cup finely chopped fresh parsley (optional)

1 quart tomato juice (or V8)

Combine all ingredients (except juice). Roll into 2-inch diameter meatballs. Place in heavy pot or pressure cooker. Cover with tomato juice or V8. Cover pot and simmer 45 minutes (or cook 10 minutes in pressure cooker). Correct seasoning and serve. Makes about 4 servings.

Blueberry Muffins

As early as the seventeenth century, doctors looked at these hungry women and saw disease rather than choice. … It was a diagnostic shift, from the miraculous world of Catherine of Siena, anorexia mirabilis, to the self-destruction of Karen Carpenter, anorexia nervosa. … As society changed, as the lives of women changed, voluntary starvation became a different phenomenon. What exactly that phenomenon is still eludes us. … The fasting maid is no longer a miracle. But she is still a mystery.
— Sharman Apt Russell, *Hunger: An Unnatural History*

By the Penobscot Bay, Maine, summer 1961 — "at last I was able to fly away"

I wanted to disappear. I wanted to get out of there, but I had nowhere to go. It was 1960, and I was nearing fifteen, shy, quiet, bookish, utterly naïve. I didn't have the boldness or the wherewithal to run away, and besides, where would I go? How would I get there? Who would take me in? I was stuck, a prisoner. Also, my mother needed me at home.

I was her protector, especially when my father came home drunk, towering over her with his height and bulk, swinging wildly at her face, calling her horrible names. I stood between them, already several inches taller and over twenty-five pounds heavier than she was. He would stop swinging then, most of the time, when I stood up to him, because he was only aiming at her, accusing her of cheating. (I didn't know at what.) I just wished she would quit calling him names in return, taunting him, as if egging him on, while I was acting as her shield.

I was also my mother's helper, her deputy, her "good bunny." When she had to return to work, as a secretary in a typing pool, to support the family ("That drunken bum," she'd say between clenched teeth, "can't even put food on the table!"), it fell to me to clean the house and make supper when I got home from school. My father was unemployed at the time, and his drinking was getting worse.

I had grown up too soon, too fast for the rest of me. I stopped growing, at the height I was to remain, 5 feet 7inches, at eleven. Already at that age, I badly needed a bra, and I quietly begged my mother to buy one for me, but she kept forgetting. "Too busy," she'd tell me when she got home from work exhausted and empty-handed, after I'd been waiting anxiously all day for the bra's arrival.

Older boys, and men too, were noticing my body. They whistled at me from their cars as I walked to school, and they made other noises, like *click-click* and "*Heybabe!*" Some called me "Jane" and "Marilyn." It made me want to hide myself somewhere. But where could I go? I had to get to school.

My big brother, my hero, my idol, also noticed my developing body. He teased me about my enlarging bottom, calling me "Crisco, fat-in-the-can" so often I became too embarrassed and ashamed to walk in front of anyone. There was nowhere for me to hide, not even at home.

Then, at eleven, I suddenly began to bleed for no reason. My mother only said, "You're a woman now," without explaining what she meant. Would I never be a teen? Was it my destiny to make one long leap from eleven to twenty with nothing in between? *Why was I bleeding?*

My girlfriends at school felt sorry for me when I got my period, treating me like an invalid, taking me by each arm and walking with me slowly around the playground at recess. One friend's mother, after experiencing plumbing problems at their home, forbade her daughter from inviting me over, blaming me for the blockage, saying I must have flushed a used Kotex down their toilet to discard it — which I had not done.

People in our small, all-white, '50s-conservative, judgmental, New Jersey town didn't expect much of me, the eldest daughter of the town's most notorious drunk. This I felt especially, beginning at eleven, when their children my age were still *children*, and I emerged as a tall, shapely (36-24-36) young woman with long blond hair that fell into her eyes because she was always looking down. They misread me as sultry. They raised their brows and nodded slightly to each other, as if to say, "She'll be nothing but a tramp."

Over time, I became determined not to give them that satisfaction. In my teens I rebelled in the opposite direction. If they expected me to amount to a hopeless, fallen person like my drunken father, I would prove them all wrong. I would go to extremes to do this. *I'll show them!* I would become an outstanding student, a faithful churchgoer, a veritable saint. I would rise above their base expectations; I would float above them like a spirit with wings. I would not run away — *How could I?* — I would stay right there and become invisible to everyone. No one would look at me and say *click-click* or *tsk-tsk* or *heybabe!* again because they wouldn't see me.

This is how I became invisible to them:

One night in early January 1960, while I was out babysitting and the children in my charge were fast asleep, I stepped on the family's bathroom scale (we didn't have a scale at home), and saw, to my horror, that the number read 140. I decided, right there, as I stared at my bare feet on that cold, white scale, to go on a serious diet.

I had always had a good appetite and enjoyed my mother's cooking. In earlier years, when she still loved my father and fluttered around him adoringly, she had tried heroically to please him with good food. But things had changed. My mother had no time for or interest in cooking anymore. The elaborate, exotic, aromatic meals she had made to make him happy (every evening we tasted a different country's cuisine — Mexican one night, French the next, Italian the next, then German, then Chinese...; we toured the whole world at our dining room table) seemed like memories of delicious dreams. By January 1960, happy, family meals had become a thing of the past. Food was no longer celebratory; it had become perfunctory. My mother's new motto, which she often repeated to my two younger sisters and me became, "Girls, eat when you're hungry, sleep when you're tired. Iron your own clothes. I'm not a housewife anymore."

Clearly, she was fed up. She and my father were headed for divorce. Although they still lived under the same roof, they stopped speaking to each other, and she instructed us girls not to speak to him either. I secretly wished he would quietly pack up and leave.

At 140 pounds, I felt I was becoming heavy, like my father. I did not want to be like him or look like him or the big, buxom, Scottish women on his side of the family. I wanted to be slim and lithe, like my mother. Since I was now free to eat whatever I wanted, I devised a weight-loss diet I would follow religiously: High protein, low fat, low carbohydrate, no junk food whatsoever (my mother never let us eat junk food anyway, saying it wasn't food at all, it was "just junk"), lots of fresh fruit, lots of vegetables. My diet would be good and healthy. I would not self-destruct.

My new, New Year, new-decade, health regimen would include lots of exercise, too. I would run track and jump hurdles in gym class, I would walk everywhere instead of taking the bus, I would do calisthenics at home in the basement, I would pedal my legs to the count of one hundred every night in bed.

I ate a big bowl of Special K cereal with skim milk every day for breakfast. For lunch, perhaps I'd have an apple or banana, and for supper, a piece of broiled fish or skinless chicken with steamed vegetables, without butter. I abstained from spaghetti, potatoes, and bread. I pretended that cakes and pastries were made of plastic, inedible. I felt hungry at times, but it didn't deter me. I was determined. My unwanted, attention-getting curves began to melt away. In time, I became a stick figure. In bed, when I slept on my side, I had to put a pillow between my legs to cushion my boney knees.

No one could call me "Crisco" anymore because my buttocks had become flat. Men and teenage boys stopped whistling at me because my breasts had shrunken to almost nothing. I felt free of their harassment and proud of my resolve. My monthly bleeding, mysteriously, and happily, stopped completely. By that summer, I'd lost a total of 35 pounds. I was 5 feet 7 inches tall and weighed 105 pounds.

My parents, so engrossed in the ugliness of their own war, didn't seem to notice the change in my weight. I became virtually invisible to them, too. My mother, afraid to be in the same bedroom with him at night, began to share my twin bed, in the bedroom I'd inherited from my brother after he left home to join the Marines. Fortunately, because I was thinner than she by this time, the two of us were able to fit.

In mid-May of 1960, I turned fifteen and quickly got an after-school job as a checkout girl at the Acme supermarket over a mile away from home. Every day, then, I would walk to school and back, then walk to work, in the opposite direction, and back — a total of close to six miles. I found the work to be tiring and tedious and most of the customers impatient and rude. "Can't you go *faster?!*" they would snap at me, as I searched for the price of each item with my left hand and rang up the sale with my right.

Once, due to understaffing, a long, snakelike line of customers developed at my register, and I couldn't move quickly enough to satisfy them. They grumbled among themselves and scowled at me, as if I were a malfunctioning machine they wanted to kick. I said nothing. Instead, I closed my cash register tightly and walked away from them all, letting them see that the "machine" had legs. I climbed the steep stairs to the employees' lounge, sat alone at the cold, Formica table, and sobbed.

To make the job tolerable, I turned it into a high school science project: I studied what the customers bought when they did their weekly grocery shopping and compared that to their physical condition. The results of this project provided me with a vivid, indelible lesson: You are indeed what you eat. The overweight, out-of-shape customers filled their carts — and ultimately themselves and their families — with packaged cookies and cakes, cartons of cheap ice cream, bags of expensive junk food, ready-made, pop-in-the-oven, frozen TV Dinners, and boxes of Jell-O instant pudding (heavily advertised at the time for the woman with a "busy day"). The slim, athletic customers, on the other hand, bought mostly colorful, fresh produce and almost nothing edible that came in a box or a plastic bag.

"What is this?" I asked one memorably handsome woman as I reached for the pale green, knobby vegetable on the conveyor belt in front of her.

"Kohlrabi," she told me. "It's delicious."

I'd never heard of kohlrabi. I asked her how she prepared it, and she was kind and patient enough to tell me.

Eventually, I picked up speed. I memorized the prices of just about everything. A can of Campbell's tomato soup then, for example, cost ten cents. I did our family's grocery shopping there for my mother, taking advantage of all of the sales. Walking home with the heavy, brown-paper bags in my arms, I was often passed by people in the community whom I knew. Sometimes they waved wanly from their car windows. Most often, they didn't even see me.

"I'm Nobody! Who are you? Are you — Nobody — too?"

Mr. Ostrowski, our sophomore English teacher, introduced us to Emily Dickinson. "She was *rather strange*," he said, tapping his temple with his right forefinger and making a face that read *gah-gah*. "She lived alone in a big, draughty house in Amherst, Massachusetts, and she wrote little poems on small scraps of paper then crinkled them up and stuffed them in the crevices of her house to keep the cold out…"

What's strange about that? I thought. *She was cold and alone. She did what she had to do.*

"Then there's a pair of us! Don't tell! they'd banish us — you know!"

Emily understood how one could, like a magician, stay in one small place and travel far, far away at the same time. Books, she said, were like sailing ships ("frigates," she called them) that take us "lands away." Yes. Books became my escape. I held them the way rich men hold money. I ate them the way gourmands eat food. I rode away in them, without ever leaving town.

"How frugal is the chariot that bears the human soul."

I traveled to nineteenth century England, lived among Dickens' characters, and empathized with them. I fell into a rabbit-hole-like time tunnel with Kenneth Roberts' historical novels. I fell in love with Hemingway, Pearl Buck, and Steinbeck. I read biographies of famous women who had overcome adversity to make something worthwhile of their lives.

> *Hope is the thing with feathers —*
> *That perches in the soul —*
> *And sings the tune without the words —*
> *And never stops — at all —*

In the cluttered, damp, unfinished basement of our house, I set up a desk for myself, where I studied beneath a dangling light bulb. It was quiet and private there at night — away from the TV and my squabbling younger sisters upstairs — so I could do my homework undisturbed. I was determined to do well academically. (*I'll show them!*) I dreamed of going to college somewhere, some day. I made National Honor Society.

> *The Brain — is deeper than the sea —*
> *For — hold them — Blue to Blue —*
> *The one the other will absorb —*
> *As Sponges — Buckets — do —*

• • •

Every Sunday I walked alone to a Gospel church in the next town. There, I took Jesus as my personal role model. I envisioned him to be a thin man, with large, tough, carpenter's hands. He knew what it was to be hungry because, I read, he fasted in the desert. He wasn't happy-go-lucky, like the people in my town from "Ozzie and Harriet" families; he was dead-serious about the job he had to do. He was (and I marked this in my small, red, leather-bound Bible) "a man of sorrows and acquainted with grief."

The Jesus I looked up to was a strong, brave, no-nonsense renegade — overturning the tables in the temple, standing up to the pompous, self-righteous men in authority of his day. He was not afraid to go against the grain. "Take no thought for your life," he said, "what ye shall eat, or what ye shall drink; nor yet for your body, what ye shall put on. Is not the life more than meat, and the body than raiment?" (Matthew 6:25).

The minister at my church said that Jesus was due to return soon. *When he returns*, I thought, *he probably won't like what he sees here.* He'd have a lot to say about the bloated, consumerist way most Americans lived, I was sure. Joe McCarthy would likely try to have Jesus jailed as a Communist. Maybe, like Gandhi, Jesus would even stage a hunger strike to dramatize his points: "Judge not!" "Love one another!" Give generously to the poor and needy and hungry!" Maybe people still wouldn't listen.

I became the president of my church's youth group. I learned the words to all of the hymns. I memorized Bible verses and fell in love with the sing-song cadences of the King James version. I woke early every morning at home to read the Bible and beg God for spiritual strength to get through the day, because, I knew by then, we do not live on bread alone.

Missionaries on furlough from their service in the Congo showed movies at church of their work. I was riveted. I had dreamed about Africa, read about Africa, saw photos of Africa in *National Geographic*; but I'd never seen Africans quite this way before: so real, so alive, so near death. I studied the skinny bodies of the children staring back at me, and I spoke to them in my heart: *Yes, I know how it feels. It's like your stomach is scraping against the inside of your spine. It's a hollow, sharp-dull, chronic ache.* No one, I knew then, who has never felt true hunger could ever truly feel for the hungry of the world; no satiated person who has never missed a meal could begin to understand the hidden ironies of hunger, its physical pain and spiritual power.

"I want to be a missionary in Africa," I told the pastor's wife earnestly, after seeing the missionaries' home movies.

Occasionally, when I returned home from church, my father would be sitting alone at the dining room table, drinking. "Tell me about God, Sister Bonnie!" he'd drunkenly command me, and I'd disobey my mother by talking with him. I'd show him verses in my Bible and tell him, as calmly as I could, about God's love and forgiveness. He would feign interest for a while, then shout at me, "Yeah, well, that's all a crock of horse shit!" and I'd get up and walk away. "—And when you're a goddam missionary in Africa," he called after me, "they're gonna put you in a big, black, fuckin' cauldron and cook you for dinner! HAH! Then they'll dance around the fire and sing, 'Oooogah-moogah! Ooooogah-moooogah!' Hah-hah!"

These hurdles might look formidable to someone else. Obstacles. Impediments. Blockades on the road. But I see them as challenges. Magnets. Pulling me forward, toward them. They call to me. They say, "Hey, you, high school girl, let me see you jump me!" and I say, "Okay, I'll do that. Just watch." It's easy, once you learn how. One of the gym teachers showed me. You go like this: Take a few preliminary steps as you approach, then lift your right leg straight out in front of you while you bend your left leg out to the side and back. It's all about timing and positioning. Oh, and velocity and determination. One…two… three…SWOOSH—and you're over the hurdle and hurtling on to the

next one. It's so exciting! It's like __flying__! It's as if God gave you wings!
You say to yourself, I can do this! Nothing can stop me now. Nothing
can stand in my way — not even a long row of wooden barriers like
these. I feel so light and free! Watch me run. And jump. And fly! Just
you watch me.

I started to look sick. My high school biology teacher, Miss Baker,
who wore men's loafers and seemed to only call on the girls, stopped
me outside of her classroom one day to ask, "Are you all right?"

I was surprised that I was not invisible to her. "Yes," I said.
"I'm fine."

She pinched some skin on my forearm, which didn't spring
back, and she pulled down the lower lid of my eye to peer inside,
as though I were a science experiment.

"You're very dehydrated," she said, "and severely anemic. You
need to see a doctor."

My mother took me to our family doctor, whom she loved and
admired for his "gentle bedside manner." She told him my periods
had stopped and —

"Been foolin' around with the boys, eh?" he interrupted her,
with a sly wink. I stared at him blankly, thinking hateful thoughts.
I hated his triple chins, his huge belly with his pants pulled up to
cover the blimp-like bulge, his belt nearly at his chest. (*Doctors
should know better than to be obese,* I thought.) I hated his greasy-
shiny, slicked-back black hair and the filthy, full ashtray on his
desk. I hated the way he leered at my pretty mother and the way
she fluttered coquettishly in response.

"Oh, no," my mother said, "she's a good girl. She goes to
church. She's the only goody-goody in the family!"

He gave my mother a prescription for iron pills for me and
said I should drink milkshakes to gain weight. He didn't attach a
medical label to my condition. As far as I knew then, I was the only
person who ever chose this method of disappearing. "She'll be all

right," he told my mother as though I wasn't there. He lit a new cigarette, took a deep drag, and blew smoke high in the air.

The iron pills made me feel nauseous. The milkshakes made me throw up. My stomach, underemployed at the job of managing food, had taken on a new task: It became the repository for all of my unchristian thoughts and fierce emotions, tied together in rough, tight knots and rolled up in a small ball. It had become shrunken, hard, and surly, rejecting any foods that gave it more work to do, tossing up foods that were at all heavy or rich. I concluded I had no choice but to maintain my Spartan diet.

My mother started to worry when my eyes began to look sunken and their sockets ominously dark. "Where is my beautiful bunny?" she would say. "You mustn't throw away your beauty! I only *wish* I were as beautiful as you."

We never knew when my father would return, but we knew that when he did he would be drunk. Often, in the middle of the night, my mother and I would hear his old Hudson, which needed a new muffler, approach from a distance, then groaningly climb our steep driveway and smack into the back wall of the garage. I'd get out of bed to close and lock my bedroom door. He'd stumble into the house, cursing and wildly banging into things in his path. He'd come up the stairs heavily, as though he weighed a thousand pounds, shouting at my mother who was in bed with me.

Without bothering my sisters asleep in the next room, he'd pound drunkenly on my door, calling my mother names, accusing her of sleeping with her boss *(How could she be sleeping with her boss if she was sleeping with me?)*, threatening to kill her. She and I kept quiet, waiting for him to give up and stagger to what was once their shared bed. But one night he pounded so hard the door came off its hinges and fell onto my bed, onto my mother and me. Enraged, she picked herself up and went toward him, shouting. I kept her behind me with my right hand and held him at arm's length with my left.

Is the bird who flies from her cage brave?

It was 1961; I had just turned sixteen, and my mother arranged for me to spend the summer with my grandmother in Maine. At last, I was able to fly away.

"— Well, I wouldn't have guessed sixteen," the chatty middle-aged woman in the seat beside me on the flight from Newark to Boston said to me. "No, I would have said something like twenty — you look so poised and mature in your pretty, high heels and elegant navy sheath. Like a runway model! Or even like Jackie Kennedy! … Oh, you made your dress yourself? My, and you have talent too! Look out this window — so gorgeous! — all those puffy cotton-ball clouds floating by!

"Don't you just love to fly? … *Really?* — This is your first time? Well, my stars, I wouldn't have known. You don't seem the least bit nervous. You're so BRAVE! Me, I love to fly. Ever since my husband died — he was a doctor, general practitioner, died of a heart attack last year, just like that, may he rest in peace — I've been on the go. Flying here and flying there. When I'm up in the sky like this, looking down, it helps to put things in perspective, you know? And I feel like I'm halfway to heaven, almost back in my husband's arms.

"I go to visit my kids here and there, stay a little while with each of them, then I'm off again! I'm free as a bird now. I don't have to work anymore — I was my husband's receptionist for twenty-five years. You should have seen the crowd at his memorial service — standing room only — everybody in town came, everybody loved him. Especially me. I visit old friends now, too — people I haven't seen since college days. That's fun.

"And I even went to Europe by myself in the spring — you know, 'April in Paris'? — I always wanted to go there with my husband, but — Well, they're doing great reconstruction over there. You'd never know there was a war.

"This is such a smooth flight, don't you think? — like floating on a cloud. Yes, I do indeed love to fly. Travel is the answer, you know. Just up and go. Changes everything…"

"How did you survive?" I ask Emmy, as I sit beside her in the kitchen of the Maine house. Emmy was the cook and my maternal grandmother was one of the maids for a wealthy elderly couple who summered on the Penobscot Bay.

Emmy, a tall, strong, German woman with dyed-red hair, was a great cook, and when I wasn't helping Grandma with her work or walking into town through the pine-scented woods and open pastures, I'd sit with Emmy in the kitchen, the way I'd sat beside my mother in our kitchen when I was a little girl. My mother would say, "Be a good bunny, now, and don't talk to me. I need to be alone." So I'd pretend I was invisible, just a spirit with eyes, and watch her as she cooked and baked: I'd study her slender hands delicately handling the pie dough, her manicured fingers fluting the edges to seal the crust.

Emmy's hands were more like mine, large and square. She liked to be quiet too, but sometimes she would talk with me as I watched her work. One day, as she was sewing a boned, stuffed, veal roast with a long steel needle and kitchen twine, I asked her what it was like being a young woman in Germany during the war. Focusing on the meat, painstakingly stitching it together like a surgeon after a long, successful operation, she told me about the bombings, the terror, the death and deprivation. Her stomach, she said, was always knotted in fear and near-starvation. "We had no real food," she said, knotting the twine and tenderly patting the veal roast as if it were a baby on a changing table, "only bad bread."

Grandma had told me — *hush-hush* — that one of Emmy's sisters had killed herself, hung herself, in the hall closet of their home during the war. "But don't let on I told you," Grandma said.

"But how did you *survive?*" I asked Emmy, as she lifted the roast carefully, about to place it in a roasting pan.

She looked at me and smiled conspiratorially, revealing a gap in her front teeth I hadn't noticed before. "We either break or bounce," she said, allowing the meat to fall with a little bounce into the pan. "Now, *liebshein*, let's bake some nice blueberry muffins and then eat them warm, with butter."

Blueberry Muffins

- 1½ cups all-purpose flour
- ½ cup granulated sugar
- 1 tablespoon baking powder
- ½ teaspoon salt
- 1 large egg
- ½ cup milk
- ¼ cup butter, melted and cooled
- 1 cup blueberries, fresh or frozen, rinsed and drained
- 1 tablespoon sugar mixed with ½ teaspoon ground cinnamon, for topping

Preheat oven to 400 degrees. Generously grease 12 muffin cups.

Sift the first four ingredients into a large mixing bowl. In a separate bowl, whisk the egg, milk, and butter. Add the wet ingredients to the dry ingredients and stir just until blended. Gently fold in the blueberries.

Spoon the batter into the muffins cups, filling each about two-thirds full. Sprinkle each with cinnamon-sugar topping. Bake at 400 for 20 to 25 minutes. Makes 12 muffins.

The Wedding Cake

In Africa we learn not to be too exacting.
— Albert Schweitzer, *The Primeval Forest*

A first for Lastoursville

Time is money!" Antoinette enjoyed reminding me, teasingly, in English, at every opportunity. Her new job as Lastoursville's deputy mayor was taking up all of her time, and I assumed, paying her good money. I hadn't seen or heard from her in a long time.

Then one Wednesday afternoon in February, she arrived at my front door for a surprise visit. She was dressed for the office, in a Western-style plain blue cotton blouse and blue-and-white check skirt. She was so breathless and agitated I began to worry something was wrong. I led her to my living room sofa and made us some tea. "*Maman*," she said excitedly, using the favored Gabonese honorific for a woman, "I have a story for you! I have a good story!" I handed her a tissue so she could wipe the perspiration from her face.

"Tell me," I said, sitting down beside her, as she dropped five large sugar cubes and two heaping spoonfuls of NIDO powdered milk into her tea-filled plastic mug.

"You know I do counseling at my church?" she asked, stirring her tea vigorously, not waiting for my answer. "Well, a young man came to see me not so long ago. He is new to my church, a refugee from the terrible fighting in the Congo. He said to me, '*Maman*,

I need to talk with you,' and I said, '*Bien sûr. Je suis là pour ça*' (Of course. I am here for that).

"He said, '*Maman*, I have a problem.' 'Yes?' I said. 'I am in love,' he said. 'Oh?' I said, 'Is that a problem?' 'But I don't know the best way to tell her,' he said. 'Oh, I see,' I said. 'She is beautiful, intelligent, strong, and wise,' he said, 'and I am afraid she will laugh at me when I profess my love to her. What should I do?'

"I told him, 'You must be brave and tell her what is in your heart.' He said, 'Yes, you are right. I am trying to do that.' 'How have you tried?' I asked. 'I am trying now,' he said.

"I didn't understand, so I asked him to explain. 'You see,' he said, 'the woman I love, the woman I cannot live without, the woman I must marry is *you*.'"

With what appeared to be her punch line, Antoinette leaned over and with both hands rested her plastic mug securely on my makeshift coffee table, then allowed herself to fall, giddily, onto the sofa's cushion, laughing like a little girl.

"And that's not all," she said, righting herself and looking more mischievous than ever. "There is more to my story!

"He is young. Only thirty-three. Close to the age of my first-born. People may talk behind my back, but I don't care. I really don't care what people say. I've struggled on my own long enough. His love makes me happy."

"*Oui, cherie,*" I answered sincerely, "*Je sais*" (I know). I knew how Youssef's love made me feel. Perhaps this is why she knew she could confide in me.

"*Et plus,*" she added, "the story is still not finished! We have set a date for our wedding — April 18th! It will be the first-of-its-kind wedding in Lastoursville. And *you* will make the cake!"

My friend Antoinette, the town's first female deputy mayor, had somehow gotten it into her head to have the first Western-style wedding — complete with Western-style wedding cake — in the town's history, and there was no arguing with her.

Multi-tiered wedding cakes, even in the best of circumstances, pose heart-stopping culinary and architectural challenges. In New York City, where it seems everything in the world is available for purchase — including of course cake pans of every dimension and any ingredient any recipe could call for — I had made a few beautiful wedding cakes in my catering days. I knew the challenges, stresses, and rewards. A towering wedding cake, more than anything else a food professional creates, holds the potential of being a masterpiece. It is often displayed on its own table like a sculpture, admired with awe, and photographed for posterity. It becomes part of the couple's first sharing ritual; it is the sweet centerpiece of the wedding feast. I wanted to make such a memorable cake for my friend Antoinette, and she in fact was expecting it. But how could I achieve this feat without the proper equipment, a big enough oven, or, God knows, the right ingredients in the equatorial rainforest of Gabon?

While in Libreville for my Peace Corps in-service training, I hunted for large-diameter cake pans and, fortunately, found two that would be suitable, at Mbolo, Gabon's one and only superstore, catering to French expatriates. I had brought with me from the States — along with a nonstick omelet pan, stainless whisk, cutting board, good-quality chef's knife, and a few other necessities of culinary life — an eight-inch springform pan, which could serve to make tier three (as is) as well as tier two (trimmed along its circumference). For the top tier I knew I could use tuna fish tins, which I'd saved for baking small breads. I realized I'd have to bake the lower, larger layers at my friend Bev's house, because she had a standard-size oven.

I knew that real buttercream icing would be out of the question in a climate where unrefrigerated butter morphs into sauce within minutes, so I had to be inventive. A big tub of Rosa margarine, canary yellow and firm as cold cream, mixed with a large jar of lemon curd — a recent gift in a care package from a New

York foodie friend — for sweetness and flavor, became a spreadable solution. This wedding cake, unlike the grandmother-bride herself, would *not* be dressed in virginal white.

With Antoinette's approval, I decided on banana-nut for the cake itself. I'd made this cake before in Lastoursville, where sweet bananas are plentiful and the remaining ingredients usually available in the overpriced Lebanese shops, so I had confidence in its outcome. For decorative flowers, I shirred yellow and burgundy satin ribbons and secured them tightly to wooden toothpicks, making clusters of these "flowers" on the top and outer rims of the cake, set off by real lemon leaves from a neighbor's tree.

Each cake layer sat on a corrugated cardboard disk, cut to its exact perimeter and covered securely with aluminum foil. Then I placed six lollipop sticks, cut precisely the same length, equidistant within the center area of each cake layer, to support the next tier's weight. Once constructed, I encircled the base of each tier with wide, yellow satin ribbon (to hide flaws and add a sunny sheen), ending with a big bow at the base, with long ribbon-tails streaming down.

I was proud. This was a cake for the history books of Lastoursville — if anyone in town kept such records. This was a cake to be photographed and remembered. As soon as it was completed, I sat down and drew a large picture of it with my colored felt-tip pens.

Getting Antoinette's wedding cake to its final resting place — in the center of the white cloth on the head table in the front of the room of Lastoursville's *Maison des Spectacles*, the hall where her reception was to be held — posed the last seemingly insurmountable hurdle in this labor-of-love. I splurged and hired a taxi to take me there. I sat in the back, holding the base of this fragile structure slightly aloft, hoping my arms would serve as shock absorbers as the driver bounced over potholes and ruts in the road. When he screeched to a halt in front of the hall, I asked him to wait — and watch the cake — while I inquired within.

A burly young man stood guard at the front double doors like a nightclub bouncer.

"I'm here to deliver the wedding cake," I told him in my most forceful French.

"You cannot go in," he said flatly.

"But I must take it in and put it on the front table," I insisted.

"Give it to me," he said. "I'll do it."

This young man, I felt certain, had never seen the likes of a five-tier wedding cake in his life. He would never have guessed that it was held up by lollipop sticks and that one careless move, one uneven step, would send it and all the work that went into it crashing to the tile floor in a cakey, gooey mess.

"No, you won't," I said. "I am carrying it inside the hall myself."

He blocked the doorway and stood his ground. "I have orders," he said.

"*Vraiment?* (Really?) From whom?"

"From the boss. *Maman* Antoinette."

"Where is she now?" I demanded, my patience melting in the afternoon heat like real buttercream on a New York wedding cake.

"At the hotel Ngoombie, getting dressed."

"*D'accord,*" I said. "I'll be back soon — with new orders!"

I didn't want to upset her in any way on her wedding day, so I did deep-breathing exercises all the way to the hotel. Once again, I asked the taxi driver, waving a big tip in my hand, to wait for me and watch the cake in the back seat while I went in to see Antoinette.

In the hotel room she'd rented for the occasion, she was sitting in front of a large vanity mirror, putting the final touches on her makeup, more makeup than I'd ever seen her wear. Her lips were painted glossy cherry-red, her dark eyes made even darker with heavy mascara and coal-black eyebrow pencil. She wore large, rhinestone-studded triangular earrings and three strands of large fake pearls. The big, puffy shoulders of her billowy white wedding dress made her look like an angel with fluttering wings.

"You look lovely," I said. She really was radiant, happier than I'd ever seen her.

She smiled her little-girl smile and surprised me with more words that she knew in English: "I am BEAU-TEE-FULLL!" she said proudly. And indeed she was.

The wedding reception couldn't officially begin until the guest of honor, Antoinette's boss, Mayor Mouvagha, and his retinue arrived after 10 pm. Then the feasting began: Antoinette's women-friends from her church served food they'd made and brought in enormous cauldrons set along a long buffet line. There were, of course, cooked plantains, sweet potatoes, manioc, rice, *feuilles de manioc,* a ragoût of some kind of meat, and fish stew. There was wine that Mouvagha had provided, and singing and dancing while the people in the crowded reception hall ate their long-awaited dinner. Youssef, in his role as professional photographer, took photos for the happy newlyweds and their wedding guests.

By the time Youssef had taken photos of Antoinette and Jean cutting their wedding cake, it was nearly 2 am, and I needed to get home. Youssef, too, was tired, so we left quietly and walked home arm in arm, under an unusually star-flecked black sky.

• • •

Banana-Nut Gateau
(Antoinette's Wedding Cake)

½ cup oil

1 cup sugar

1 egg

1 tablespoon water

1 cup thinly sliced ripe sweet bananas

1 tablespoon fresh lemon juice (or vanilla or rum)

¼ cup finely chopped nuts (almonds or walnuts)

1½ cups flour

½ teaspoon salt

2 tablespoons NIDO (or other powdered milk)

1 tablespoon baking powder

Beat oil, sugar, egg, and water in a large bowl until thick. Add bananas and lemon juice to mixture. Mash well. Fold in nuts. Sift together flour, salt, NIDO, and baking powder. Fold dry ingredients into wet ingredients just until combined; don't over-beat. Pour batter into greased baking pan(s) and bake in preheated 350-degree oven about 30 minutes or so, depending on the size of the pan(s). Makes 6 small cakes if baked in tuna tins.

Mefloquine Dreams

I had by now become used to the idea of witchcraft, it seemed
a reasonable thing, so many things are about, at night, in Africa.
— ISAK DINESEN, *Out of Africa*

From the bridge in Lastoursville — the Ogooué at sunset

What was that?" I said, reaching over to touch Youssef in our bed. "Did you hear it?

"*Quoi?*" he said sleepily. He slept more soundly than I.

"That sound outside. *Écoute*" (listen).

We listened — he on his side of the bed, and I on mine. Every night, after telling me again *"je t'aime"* and wishing me a *"bon nuit,"* Youssef liked to move to the edge of the bed to sleep undisturbed, untouched. He slept deeply, quietly, without snoring or thrashing, like a long, thin, dead man, through the night.

The crunching sound on the gravel outside our louvered bedroom windows had stopped temporarily.

"C'est rien. N'inquiete pas" (It's nothing. Don't be worried). He patted my arm. *"Bon nuit, cherie,"* he said, and turned back to sleep, while I continued to listen.

Before Youssef came to live with me in my house on the hill, I was often woken in the night by either mysterious sounds outside or bad dreams, or both, in close succession.

One of the known side effects of the costly and powerful anti-malarial drug Mefloquine that I and all other Peace Corps volunteers in Gabon were required to take every week was terrible nightmares. (Among Mefloquine's other possible side effects were: depression, anxiety, paranoia, panic attacks, insomnia, hallucinations, convulsions, seizures, and central nervous system problems.) At any gathering, young volunteers would merrily share intimate narratives, usually involving health issues — especially intestinal health. *Giardia lamblia*, "a motile protozoan which rests in the small intestine," our handy medical handbook explained, "causing diarrhea, abdominal discomfort, foul-smelling stools and flatulence," was a predictably humorous topic. Other popular tales among volunteers included vivid details of their psychotic-seeming "Mefloquine dreams." I, however, kept my nightmare stories to myself, preferring to reveal them only to my journal.

Frequently, as my journal records, I woke in the night, crying out "No!" to the menacing antagonist in my nightmare, who was often my ex-husband, my daughter's father, come back from the dead. In one dream of him that I noted, I was screaming and shouting at him for taking our child from me for no other reason than his own selfishness and remorseless cruelty. In the dream, he just sneered at me. I lunged for his face, then woke, sobbing.

In another dream, I was walking across a rough, handcrafted African bridge made of logs and mud, careful not to stumble and fall through the gaps in the logs into the turbulent, rushing river below. As I was crossing, I heard African men's voices singing and laughing as they bathed in the muddy water by the riverbank. I kept walking, but the bridge became more difficult to cross because the center was broken; I had to inch my way along one side. At the end I discovered the only way down was a narrow, steep ladder, which I saw was not secured at the bottom. I looked down and saw a number of unhappy-looking white people dressed in business clothes in an office-corridor setting — rushing here and there, and waiting impatiently for the elevator. I called down from the top of the tall, narrow ladder: "Could someone please help me? Could someone hold the bottom of the ladder, please, so I can get down?" I called repeatedly for help, but no one even looked up. They were so focused on their work, they could not see anything else. I kept calling in vain for help until I woke up.

Once awake, heart-pounding, I would lie alone in bed in the darkness of my room, beneath my mosquito netting, like a fly pinned in a spider's webbing, and listen to the night sounds. Palm trees bowing to the belligerent winds, tropical rains pounding the sun-baked ground outside and pelting the house's metal roof like bullets, roosters crowing knowingly in the dead of night.

But often I heard more than this. I heard prowlers, I was sure. I heard sounds that only human feet can make.

What was that? I wonder, as I lie there paralyzed, too fearful to turn on the light, because I would then be seen for what I am — a woman alone. I am afraid to shout out, too, because I would then be *heard* for what I am, an *étrangere* (female foreigner) who knows too few angry words in French to be able to say something New York-street-tough, like, "Scram!" or "Beat it!" or "I'm calling the cops!" The fact is, I don't have a phone to call for help, nor a weapon — other than the machete I keep in the kitchen cupboard — to use for self-defense. My house is secure enough, with locks and bolts and chains on both the front and back doors and iron burglar bars on all the windows. *No one can break in*, I tell myself. *I'm safe. I think.* My heart is pounding. My mind is racing.

But what could it be? Why would anyone be skulking around my house in the dead of night? To frighten me? To scare me away? To hurt me somehow? *I refuse to let them frighten me away. And how badly could they hurt me? I'm not afraid to die.*

It sounds like a person, a grown man, is tiptoeing on the long grass and gravel behind my house, just outside my bedroom window. He could easily have approached my house through the thick forest beyond my back garden. His footsteps make crunching sounds, snapping twigs, crushing dried leaves. He's holding (I imagine, lying flat on my bed, staring straight up) a flashlight which he's shining through the wooden louvers, causing the light to bounce and dance nervously on my bedroom ceiling.

When my younger sisters and I were small and sharing a bedroom, we sometimes played with a flashlight at night. We called the dancing light on the ceiling "Sandy," and the ones who weren't holding the flashlight tried to anticipate what Sandy would do next.

What will this man with the flashlight do next? I take deep breaths and exhale slowly.

Perhaps I'm imagining things. Perhaps the light is not a flashlight at all; maybe it's just lightning. Perhaps the rustling on the ground is only a snake sliding by or something larger and four-legged, pawing, sniffing. I know it can't be a crocodile; I live too far from the river and too high up the hill for that slithery threat.

But what was *that*? *A cough?* Animals don't cough like that. Or do they? Only humans cough. Isn't that right? *It's a man's cough, I'm sure of it.* What is he doing? What does he want?

I wait and listen without moving in the dark alone in my bed.

The click-click ticking of my Swatch wristwatch seems too loud to me. Can the man outside my window hear it too? How long will it take for him to make another move, another cough? How many more ticks will it take?

I tried to recall the made-up lullaby my mother used to sing to us after a nightmare-disturbed night when we were kids. "Go to sleeee-eeeep, my bay-ay-beeeeeeeee…" she'd sing in her thin, thready voice to no particular tune. Lying alone and listening to the prowler outside, I would sing it silently to myself. Since I couldn't run from him; and he, I felt sure, couldn't break in, the only option left was to go back to sleep.

But when I managed to do so, the nightmares resumed, like a horror movie on TV that had only been on pause:

This time I saw the silhouette of a large man standing at the foot of my bed. *He broke into the house after all!* It was impossible to tell in the darkness of the dream whether the man was black or white, but he was as tall and as broad as both my father and my ex-husband, both white men, had been. This outline of a man didn't speak to me; he just hovered, threatening to rip my mosquito netting open. I awoke again, to escape from him.

After some months of this, I shared my nighttime horror stories with my friend Bev. One evening when we were at her house to watch the Tom Hanks comedy "The Man with One Red Shoe" on her DVD, I mentioned to Bev about the frequent mysterious sounds outside my bedroom window and my just-as-frequent nightmares.

Bev told me it might be people practicing the occult. She said they could be putting curses on me.

"But *why*?" I asked.

"Jealousy, maybe. Or just plain evil intent. Hard to say."

"What's the antidote? What can I do to stop it?"

"Only the name of Jesus can chase evil spirits away," Bev said. "You must go up to the window and shout out, 'In the name of Jesus Christ, the Son of God, the Lord of Lords, BE GONE!' I've had to do this before here in Gabon, and it's always worked for me."

"Did you shout at them in English or French?" I teased her.

"English, I think," she said seriously.

Bev lived alone, too, but closer to town and to other people than I did. She had lived in Gabon for thirty years; she spoke excellent French as well as many of the local languages. She had a watchdog, a golden mongrel named Ginger, who did a half-hearted job of keeping strangers at bay. She also had a telephone that usually worked and a sturdy new Nissan pickup truck always in good, getaway order. I had none of these backups.

"You should pray," Bev said.
"I pray every day," I told her.

When Youssef came to live with me in January 1998, I naturally felt safer with him in my bed, but the night terrors continued. Most of the time I blamed my nightmares on Mefloquine and the mysterious night sounds on the violent tropical weather.

But when Youssef — who was not taking Mefloquine — began having nightmares that he woke from with choked, inaudible cries, he too became alarmed. Both awake in the dead of night now, we listened to the footsteps and watched the flashlight beams. We talked softly in the dark and theorized together. He reminded me that some people in town believed this house was *"maudit"* (cursed), which is why it had been uninhabited for so long. He suggested that both the nightmares and noises could be caused by *"les mauvais esprits"* (evil spirits) who were restless, angry, looking for someone, perhaps not even us. Maybe when my landlord, Mayor Mouvagha, had lived in this house with his own family many years before (before building the white villa on a higher hill where he now lived), Youssef guessed, something terrible had happened — *a murder, perhaps?* — and the wronged person's spirit was returning for revenge.

"Do I need to tell this evil spirit how to find Mouvagha's new house?" I asked Youssef. "Shouldn't spirits know these things intuitively?" I joked.

But for Youssef, his nightmares were no laughing matter. Now that he was losing sleep too, he decided we should take action: buy a big, standing fan and keep it on in the bedroom all night ("Evil spirits don't like motors," Youssef said); keep the bathroom light on all night ("They don't like light either," he added); pour salt on the ground outside the window ("They don't like salt at all"); close the wooden louvered shutters on the bedroom windows tight (so the light beams couldn't come through); seek advice from the locals; wait and see.

Together, we decided to consult Bev again. We stopped at her house early one evening while we were out on a walk. This time Youssef and Bev spoke together in rapid French, he explaining in detail to her what he had experienced and what he suspected. She confirmed that his suspicions could well be correct.

"Believe me," she said to me in English, "there's a lot of spooky, devil-worshipping stuff that goes on around here."

Gabon, I would come to learn, although primarily Christian (predominantly Roman Catholic), is the spiritual center of an old and growing animist religion popular among forest peoples, called Bwiti, in which the hallucinogenic Iboga plant is used as a sacrament. Participants in their semi-secret rites, held in designated outdoor "temples," paint their faces in red and white, dance all night to pounding drums, and commune with their ancestors in visions. No mention is ever made of flashlights.

Youssef and I sat side by side on Bev's fifties-style, wood-framed sofa and she in a matching side chair. She reached for a black, leather-bound Bible on a nearby bookcase and turned to Ephesians chapter six. As she read aloud, Youssef listened raptly, as though he could understand English, even the King James kind:

Finally, my brethren, be strong in the Lord, and in the power of his might. Put on the whole armour of God, that ye may be able to stand against the wiles of the devil. For we wrestle not against flesh and blood, but against principalities, against powers, against the rulers of the darkness of this world, against spiritual wickedness in high places. Wherefore take unto you the whole armour of God, that ye may be able to withstand in the evil day, and having done all, to stand. ... Above all taking the shield of faith, wherewith ye shall be able to quench all the fiery darts of the wicked. And take the helmet of salvation, and the sword of the Spirit, which is the word of God: Praying always with all prayer and supplication in the Spirit ...

After her Bible reading, Bev suggested we pray together. She prayed in French, reiterating for Youssef the Apostle Paul's words, and asking that God free us from the evil spirits that haunted our nights. She prayed that God would give us the protective armor we needed to "stand against the wiles of the devil." On our walk home Youssef said he felt more "*tranquile*."

Ah, Afrique, I thought. *So full of mysteries, so close to, and far from, God.*

Friday Night Brights

Still, such as it was, my school
was to me a favorite place on the farm...
— ISAK DINESEN, *Out of Africa*

High school students at my Friday-night English class

Youssef Tounkara

eef or chicken, sir?" I ask each boy in turn, pretending I'm a flight attendant, going down an aircraft's aisle, taking dinner orders on a pad. It's Friday night, and my six o'clock English class, held in my living room and free to any high school student who cares to attend has just begun.

I try to make these classes fun for them. Instead of teaching English grammar from a dry text — something they surely get enough of in their English classroom at Lastoursville's regional *lycée* (high school) — I try to instigate lively discussions and enact real-life situations, all in English only.

A core group of about five earnest teenage boys — always clean and well dressed, in long-sleeved white shirts and pressed black trousers — attend these Friday night classes fairly faithfully. Other boys drop in from time to time, perhaps out of curiosity. Occasionally, a few teenage girls come, too; but they are mostly quiet, sitting close together on my sofa, giggling among themselves nervously. The girls' attention is focused solely on the boys; they show no interest in learning to speak English or are too shy in the presence of the boys to try.

The boys who attend regularly, however, are bright, bold, and ambitious. They have goals and dreams — especially of getting out of Gabon one day and making something of themselves in the world. They realize that the ability to speak English well, as well as their second language, French, would benefit their careers; so they take advantage of this free opportunity and apply themselves. They are also particularly good-natured about going along with whatever unconventional ideas I've dreamed up for making the class fun.

On this night we're pretending they are all scholarship recipients to universities in the United States, and we're on a flight from Libreville to New York, where they'll be making connections to their respective beneficent universities. This pretense pleases them. From their broad smiles and widening eyes, I can see that it's fueling their fantasies. Scholarship? University? United States? These powerful English words speak to them; they need no translation.

"Good evening, sir," I say to another of the boys (there are no girls this night), "what would you like for dinner? Beef? Or chicken?"

"I would like the chicken," Jacques says, articulating each English word with confidence.

"Very good!" I smile and nod in my real role as teacher, then pretend to write the order down in my play role as flight attendant.

"And you, sir?" I say, turning to Martial, sitting in the chair beside Jacques. "Would you like beef or chicken for dinner?"

Martial looks up at me, perplexed. As one of the brightest boys in the group, he surely understands my English, yet his face appears puzzled, even pained. I try not to prompt him. I wait for his order.

"Baton de manioc," he announces firmly. "I would like manioc with sauce for dinner."

"Oh, sir," I say, now thoroughly in my flight-attendant role. "I'm sorry, but I don't know what that is."

Martial looks stunned. Stammering, he tries to explain to me in English what it is. Then, as gently as possible, I let him know that *baton de manioc* is virtually unheard of in the United States. *What?* his facial expression says. *This cannot be! How can I live in a place where I can't eat manioc?* I could almost read his mind: He's planning to take the next plane back to Gabon as soon as our imaginary flight lands.

Now it's my turn to be stunned. Was it possible that manioc could mean more to Martial than the hope of a scholarship to college? Could the pull of this food be that strong? I had tasted *baton de manioc* — and I'd watched it being made from cassava tubers that had been soaked for several days (to remove the lethal cyanide in them), peeled, pounded to a paste, rolled in banana leaves, then boiled for four-to-eight hours — and it tasted a lot like sour rubber to me. But this was the staple food of Gabon, as meaningful to the Gabonese as pasta is to most Italians and rice is to most Chinese. Despite manioc's low nutritive value and unappealing (to me) taste, the people of Gabon, particularly those in the interior of the country, eat it every day of their lives. To them, it's as sacred as mothers' milk.

"Perhaps you might like to try the chicken dinner on this flight instead, sir?" I suggest.

On another evening, I made an even bigger mistake; this time by raising the verboten topic of politics, hoping it might lead to a lively conversation. We were sitting in a circle in my living room, four of the core boys and myself, when I too straightforwardly shared my unvarnished view that the Gabonese people seemed to me to be too apathetic about their situation. Why did they allow their government to do whatever it wished? Why didn't they stand up for themselves and demand their rights? "Apathy is complicity," I said, tossing out these weighty English words in the hope that the boys would catch their significance and a heated discussion would ensue.

My words fell heavily, and the boys stiffened. Their eyes darted across the length of the louvered windows in my living room.

Thierry shook his head slowly from side to side. Regis fixed his gaze on me and drew his right index finger gingerly across his throat. Martial froze. The boys' body language told me instantly: You mustn't say these things. People could be watching, listening. We cannot speak ill of President Bongo if we want to live.

Jacques, an active member of Bev's Christian Alliance church, spoke up. "Papa Bongo takes good care of us," he said in French. "We live in peace. He is a good president. God put him in office. It is not for us to question God's plan." The other boys nodded.

"Ah, yes, of course, you're right," I said carefully and slowly in English, then repeated again in French for whoever might have been lurking outside. I didn't want to put these boys in danger. Free speech was not an option for them, in any language.

A safer and more relevant subject of conversation for these high school students was AIDS. *Le SIDA* was one of the subjects I lectured on when I visited their high school. The boys knew me from these lectures, which I gave during their English class on the invitation of their teacher.

On one such occasion I'd brought with me a huge poster I'd made of a narrowing dirt road, littered with sharp shards of glass (made of cut-up plastic water bottles glued to the poster), which I taped to the classroom's front blackboard. I likened this treacherous pathway to the dangers of unprotected sex. "Yes!" I said playfully in English, plopping myself on the teacher's front desk and kicking off my sandals dramatically, "it's fun to walk barefoot!" I wiggled my bare, white toes gleefully, and the whole class of more than thirty students laughed with me. "But if I want to walk down *that* road," I said, pointing to my poster, "I MUST wear protection, I must wear shoes! If not, I am likely to bleed to death or die of an awful infection."

The students seemed to grasp the analogy. I gave them the statistics: nearly 80 percent of sexually active people in Gabon (between the ages of roughly 15 and 50) had a sexually transmitted disease, which offered a *"porte ouverte"* (open door) for the virus that causes AIDS. The one known sure method of AIDS prevention, I explained, was the protection that a condom afforded. I told them that I sold condoms — discreetly, in town, person-to-person, from a supply I always carried with me in my shoulder bag — on behalf of their country's *Programme Nationale de Lutte Contre le SIDA*. These condoms had a price — so that people would value them — but they were affordable (the equivalent of about five cents each). "Being smart," I told the attentive high school class, tapping my head, "and wearing protection," I said putting my sandals back on, "is the *cool* thing to do!"

I had learned enough about the sexual mores in Gabon to know that espousing sexual abstinence would have been a tragic, short-sighted mistake. It would have been like telling people to abstain from eating manioc: It wouldn't happen. People in Gabon became sexually active at a young age, often in their early teens, and there seemed to be no stigma attached to teen pregnancies and unwed motherhood. In fact, I was told, a large percentage of Lastoursville's high school girls were already mothers; their own mothers back home in their villages were raising their babies.

AIDS was on the rise in Gabon alarmingly, as it was in all of sub-Saharan Africa, and prevention offered the only hope. HIV testing, given at only two hospitals in Gabon, was far too expensive and too far to travel for most people. Anti-retroviral medications were unheard-of. Statistics were sketchy. When people with HIV who lived in cities or towns fell ill, they simply went back to their villages to be cared for by the women in their families and perhaps seek help from traditional healers. Death soon followed, and the cause given was invariably *"le palu"* (malaria). *Le SIDA* was a label the villagers either didn't know or chose not to acknowledge, whereas *le palu* was a more familiar and therefore more socially accepted death knell.

So the need for education was urgent, but with my Friday night English class I felt I was preaching to the choir. These bright boys understood the risks and took precautions. I knew, because they bought a few condoms from me whenever they came to my house. Nevertheless, one evening I turned to an article in a current issue of *Newsweek* on the subject of AIDS in Africa. We passed the one copy around our circle, which included that evening Morgan and Youssef, and each read a paragraph in English, stopping to discuss each unknown word, each unclear concept. This class wasn't fun, but it was, nevertheless, worthwhile.

"Last evening," I wrote to Marty on January 30, 1998, "for my Friday English class we made cookies in my kitchen. I conducted the class in slow, clear English, made each student copy the recipe in English, and gave everybody a turn at mixing the batter—stressing all the verbs involved. While the cookies were baking, we discussed cookies in general—I showed them the traditional Christmas cookies displayed on the cover of my December *Gourmet*—and then, of course, they ate some, warm from the oven. You should have seen their eyes. I think they've never seen a teacher teach like me."

One rainy Friday evening in April, when Youssef was away taking photos at a *chantier* and Morgan had no doubt stayed in Mana-Mana due to the heavy rains, only two of the boys—Martial and Regis—showed up, so I decided to make our class another hands-on cooking lesson. "Tonight I'll show you how to make French crêpes, so you can impress your girlfriends," I said. The two boys immersed themselves enthusiastically in this lesson, following every step, repeating every word, in both English and French, and laughing a lot.

I showed them the tricks of crêpe making and explained, "According to the French, the first one is always so ugly and misshapen, you must give it to the dog."

"Ah, no! Not here! We will eat it," Regis said, tearing the malformed first try into halves and sharing the other half with his friend.

I stressed that it takes a while to get all the variables aligned — the flame height, the heat of the pan, the consistency of the batter, the turn of the wrist. They caught on quickly and enjoyed producing fine, round, fabric-thin, golden crêpes.

"Voila le système!" Regis exulted, showing off to Martial how he had mastered the wrist-turning technique to distribute the batter evenly over the inside surface of the crêpe pan.

The three of us then ate the crêpes — slathered with my homemade tropical jam — together at my dining room table. "Very good! Yes! Delicious!" the boys said proudly to each other in English, as they slapped high-fives with their right hands.

• • •

Sweet Crêpes

1 egg
a pinch of salt
1 tablespoon sugar
1 tablespoon butter or light oil
½ cup water
2 heaping tablespoon NIDO (or other powdered milk)
1 teaspoon vanilla
½ cup all-purpose flour

Blend all ingredients in a blender and allow to sit about 10-plus minutes.

Heat a 5- or 7-inch skillet or crêpe pan until moderately hot. Brush pan lightly with butter or oil. Using a ladle or small cup, pour in a small amount of batter, turning the pan to spread it evenly in the thinnest possible layer.

Cook for a few minutes, until the bottom is lightly browned and the edges lift easily from the pan. Turn the crêpe with a spatula or by catching the edge with your fingers. Cook the second side for a minute or so. (It will brown in spots.)

Serve immediately, with sugar, jam, applesauce, fresh sliced fruits or berries, or melted chocolate. Makes about 8 crêpes.

Photographe

Opening Marty's gifts

Bonnie Lee Black

Quelle magie il fait
Avec un toucher il arête le temps
Il saisit le moment pour toujours
Les jeunes ne vieillissent pas
Les vieux ne meurrent pas
Et tout le monde sourie
pour l'éternité
Quel pouvoir!
Quel métier magiques.

— blb, 1/98

[What magic he makes
With one touch he stops time
He seizes the moment forever
The young don't age
The old don't die
And everyone smiles
for eternity
What power!
What a magical craft.]

Before I met him, Youssef had worked at a *chantier* outside of Lastoursville. In his travels in West Africa, he had heard that the French logging companies in Gabon paid well and that many fellow Malians, known to be dependable, strong, hard-working men, and non-drinking Muslims (unlike the often inebriated, nominally Christian local men), worked there. Youssef's lifelong dream had been to one day become a professional photographer, another Seydou Keita, the world-renowned Malian portrait photographer, he hoped. But Youssef knew the fulfillment of that dream was a long way off. His first step was to buy a decent, second-hand, single lens reflex camera, for which he needed to save a considerable amount of money. To that end, he went to work for the logging company, *Société de Bois de Lastoursville,* known as SBL, where he became part of a small expatriate Malian community.

Sometimes in the evening, in my study, when we sat and talked together quietly before going to bed, Youssef would share with me in tragic, lyrical terms how the earth and trees suffered at the hands of these foreign-owned logging companies.

As Youssef explained it, even carefully selected trees — which he described as several stories tall, oil-drum thick, and centuries old — take down many, many more trees with them. To get the big Okoume, first a path, then a clearing is cut, killing scores of trees; then, when the sought-after tree is chain-sawed and falls, screaming like a human, Youssef said, to the ground, it wounds and ultimately kills all the trees it touches. The prize tree is then sliced into truck-length portions, hauled out of the forest in chains, loaded onto the waiting *grumiers*, and whisked off to the greedy, thoughtless world.

The problems, Youssef added, are many and complicated. One is that all these slaughtered trees and plundered forests are not being replaced. Forests that took hundreds and hundreds of years to come into being can be, and are in the process of being, destroyed in the space of decades. Another problem is that the damaged and dying trees are left, like garbage, to rot in place. This, plus the roads and clearings made by and for all the heavy machinery, cause, Youssef said, "*inundations*" (floods) during the heavy rains, which cause more trees to die.

"But there seems to be an overabundance of trees around here," I said, gesturing out the window, in the direction of the forested mountains.

"If we were to return to Lastoursville in ten years, just to pay a visit," Youssef predicted earnestly, "we wouldn't recognize the *paysage* (countryside). You would say to me, 'Where did the forest go?' and I would answer, 'It was carted off by all those speeding *grumiers*.' Gabon, like so many of the countries to the north of here which were once forested, will be mostly bare, barren stretches of spent earth."

"But Francine's husband Louis tells me that the foresters care …"

"They only care about *l'argent*" (money), Youssef corrected me. "Okoume makes the best plywood in the world, and there is a great demand for plywood, especially in Asia. These French businessmen don't see the African workers who lose fingers and arms to the sawing machinery. They don't hear the trees weep."

When the Transgabonais Railway, the only railway in Gabon, was completed in 1987, I later learned, it opened the door for transnational lumber companies to exploit Gabon's rainforest, one of the few remaining undisturbed tropical rainforests on earth. This 416-mile rail link between Franceville in the southeast and Libreville's port of Owendo in the northwest — an effort that took seventeen years to complete and is said to be one of the costliest civil-engineering projects in the world — made timber transport faster, easier and more economical than ever before. In 1957, fewer than 10 percent of Gabon's forests were claimed by logging concessions. By 1997, when I met Youssef, nearly three-quarters of Gabon's forests were being logged, or were slated to be, and more than 90 percent of those logs were being shipped overseas.

The tree most sought after in Gabon's forests is the Okoume, which can tower as tall as 200 feet, and grow to 8 feet in diameter. When my friend Marty, a professional photographer, came from New York to visit me in Lastoursville, she took photos of me standing near dozens of Okoume logs lying in an open field near the Lastoursville train station awaiting shipment to the port of Owendo. These monstrous, pinkish-brown logs appear to stretch the length of a city block. In one photo, I am standing at the cut end of one log, the diameter of which is greater than my 5 feet 7 inches height.

This profitable, coveted tropical softwood, found only in Gabon, is used worldwide in light construction projects, such as paneling, joinery, particleboard, as well as plywood. Unfortunately, little of that construction takes place in Gabon. Most of the citizenry's dwellings in the country's interior are made of sticks and mud.

Youssef worked at the *chantier* just long enough to save 500,000 CFA, then worth about $1,000, to buy his first professional-quality camera. He entrusted the money to his Malian friend, Kofi, who lived with his wife and children in Lastoursville and who was traveling on business to Togo, where he was more likely to find a good, second-hand camera for Youssef at a far better price than in costly Gabon. When Youssef told me this story the day we met, he was still waiting for his friend's return, and I had my doubts. But I was proven wrong: Kofi eventually returned to Lastoursville, some months later, with the camera of Youssef's dreams.

When Youssef brought his new camera, a used Canon A-E1, home to show me, he was overjoyed. He cradled it in his arms the way he must have seen his mother hold his newborn siblings. He turned it slowly in his large hands, inspecting it as if to see whether it had all its fingers and toes. He didn't know yet how to use it — aperture? depth of field? what did all those numbers signify? — but an instruction booklet came with it, written in French,

English, German, and Japanese. He would learn soon enough, we both knew.

Youssef's first photo assignment was to take portraits of Kofi's family in Lastoursville for them to send back to relatives in Mali. He would do this as a thank-you gesture, to show his appreciation, right away. I made a camera carrying case for him from a sturdy, canvas shoulder bag I had, which I stuffed with mattress foam hollowed to fit his camera and lens. I also gave him a khaki vest Marty had given me when I left for the Peace Corps, with all sorts of zippered pockets in the front for holding film and other small items. I tucked into one of the zippered pockets a small notebook and pen so Youssef could record his clients' names, and the dates and settings for all the photos he took.

Youssef was set. He removed the lens with a slow turn, capped it, and nestled it into the shoulder bag. He capped the camera's body and tucked it too into the bag's foam bedding. He put the vest, which matched his clean, creased khaki pants, over his white T-shirt and slipped the shoulder bag's wide strap over his head. He patted the bag protectively as it hung at his side. Already tall and dignified, he stood even taller and more regally now. In his new role, he looked the part. "*Oh, vraiment, je suis professionnel maintenant. Je suis photographe!*" (I'm a professional now. I'm a photographer), he announced to me, smiling broadly.

Not long after we returned to Lastoursville from Libreville after my burn accident and hospitalization, and soon after Youssef's new camera arrived, Marty sent, through a fish volunteer named Chris who'd been back in the States visiting his family in New York, a surprise package for Youssef. At my request, and from my bank account, which Marty was handling for me, to thank Youssef for the care he'd given me in the clinic, she bought him a wide-angle lens and a flash attachment for his camera, as well as a dozen good-quality batteries for it and several rolls of film. On her own, she included in the hand-delivered package a large, coffee-table-size book of Seydou Keita's photography.

Youssef was overjoyed with his new camera equipment, repeating, "*Ah, merci, vraiment,*" with every item he opened, and so awed by the book he lifted it up to his face and kissed it. This was the first such book he had ever owned, he told me, and it became, along with his new photo equipment, one of his most treasured possessions.

Together, we studied Keita's photographs — the way he posed his subjects in his studio space, and the way these subjects chose to include their favorite belongings in their portraits to prove their modern identity, social status, or profession. There was one portrait of a middle-aged man in a light suit and tie sitting on his shiny, new motor scooter; another of a younger man in a dark blazer leaning possessively over a console radio with an alarm clock on top of it; two young mothers wearing identical, wildly printed traditional dresses, lavish jewelry and dramatic head wraps, each with a chubby baby on her lap; and a pensive-looking Peul woman with darkened lips and tufted hair sitting behind her hand-cranked Singer sewing machine. In these and thousands of other portraits, Keita captured the self-identity of his countrymen-and-women during a period of enormous social change in Mali.

Like my friend Marty, whose photographic career can be traced to the Kodak Brownie camera her father, who owned a camera shop in Baltimore, gave her when she was in nursery school, Seydou Keita's career began in Bamako, Mali, in the 1930's when as a boy he received a Brownie camera as a gift from his uncle. By 1948 Keita had set up a commercial studio in downtown Bamako, Mali's capital city, not far from the train station, and proceeded to teach himself the craft. At first, he used his own lacy bedspread as a backdrop, and he photographed outdoors using available light. In time, his photographic portraiture received worldwide acclaim. Keita's success stemmed from his sensitivity to his subjects' needs, his eye for composition and detail, and his unflagging determination to learn and improve.

Youssef, too, seemed to possess these same qualities. Although he had no one to teach him the technicalities, living as we did in Lastoursville, Youssef chose to follow Seydou Keita from afar, as if navigating his own small sailboat at night by the North Star.

In fact, the profession of itinerant photographer perfectly suited Youssef's nature. Like me, he was independent and self-motivated, and he preferred to be his own boss. He enjoyed the freedom to choose his own hours, follow his own pace, find his own clientele, make and keep his own appointments, hold himself to his own high standards, and methodically build a reputation for reliability — in a place where reliability was rare.

By his nature, too, Youssef was sensitive to his surroundings, vigilant, and observant.

"Did you see *that*?" he would ask me on one of our early evening walks together by the river.

"What?" I'd missed whatever it was he was pointing to.

"That bird, over there, up in the trees. It's so big! And it's plumage so beautiful, so colorful. Oh, it's flown off now."

I'd always considered myself to be an observant person. "A writer," I read somewhere once, "is one on whom nothing is lost." But Youssef consistently eclipsed me in this regard. He seemed to notice everything.

And he was unusually attentive to others' needs. Whenever we had unexpected guests who might spend the night, he would excuse himself quietly and straighten the guest room (Morgan's room), change the sheets if need be, fluff the pillows, make space in the closet for their clothes, put clean, folded towels on the bed. He would then return to the guests, whom I'd still be greeting, and ask whether anyone was thirsty; could he bring them a glass of water? Youssef's strict father, whom he invariably referred to as "the Ayatollah," had trained his eleven children to be thoughtful of others and hospitable toward guests. Youssef had learned these lessons well.

We both knew that his new photographic career would mean a change for us. He needed to travel more, using the house we shared in Lastoursville as home base. He needed to spend time at the outlying *chantiers* seeking photography clients among the West African expatriates working there. Having worked at the *chantier* SBL, Youssef knew many of the people, and he understood how much photographic portraits of their families would mean to them. They could send the photos to their relatives far away, as a way of saying, "Look! We are well. We are prospering. See how the children are growing? We are thinking of you…" Such photographs, Youssef knew, for people who might not be literate and who wanted to put their far-off loved ones' minds at rest, were worth more than thousands of words.

Once he had shot several rolls of film — on the weekends, when the *chantier* workers were freer, or on religious holidays, such as Tabaski or the end of Ramadan, when Muslims wore their best finery for the occasion — Youssef had to travel to a distant photo lab to have the film developed. The closest lab was in the town of Moanda, four hours away; the next choice was Franceville, six hours away; and the last option was Libreville, ten hours away. Then, after the film was developed, he had to return to the *chantiers* to deliver the finished photos to his clients and get paid. For me, having adapted to our happy, harmonious life together in Lastoursville, these long absences felt at times like abandonment. I missed his companionship, his affection, his voice, his smile.

Most of all, while he was away, I worried. I remembered the story Morgan had told me about the Malian driver who was hacked to pieces near her village the previous year. That man's family back in Mali probably never learned his fate and could still be waiting for his safe return.

I knew that some Gabonese bore resentments toward "foreign" Africans, especially West Africans; they expressed jealousy toward these outsiders' strong work ethic and their economic success. I

worried for Youssef's safety, especially at night, when these fester-
ing resentments could likely be fueled by drunkenness. I'd seen
enough in my childhood of the destructiveness of drunkenness.

Once, when he didn't return for days, as my journal records, I
not only worried, I panicked:

Youssef was supposed to come home tonight, and I am worried sick and shaking. What if he doesn't come back? What if
he's been harmed? My imagination is running wild. What if I
never see him again? I've been working on my quilt with tears
streaming down my face.

[The next morning:] Youssef still has not come home. I'm terribly, terribly worried. The only way I was able to sleep, on and
off, last night was by telling myself he spent a safe and peaceful
night in the home of his hosts at SBL. But now that I'm up, my
mind is racing, my heart is pounding; and, from time to time
I'm sobbing. What if something awful has happened to him?
What if he was beaten and left bleeding by the side of the road
somewhere — or murdered and his body discarded in the forest
— all for his camera equipment? How could I go on? I'm drinking coffee and smoking. I can't eat. I've been crying all morning.
I can't go to work. I'll send word I have a migraine.

When my neighbor Augustine, a thirty-eight-year-old Gabonese mother of ten who came to my house every Monday morning
to sweep and wash the floors and whom I paid generously with
money sent from my friend Paul in New York, arrived for work at
8 o'clock, she was very comforting. But despite her best efforts to
console me, I couldn't stop sobbing.

"Il est ma famille ici" (He is my family here), I kept saying to
her between sobs.

"Il va venire," she repeated. He'll come back. He's just working
hard. Maybe he couldn't get a ride last night, she said. He'll be back

tonight. Or tomorrow. "*Reste tranquille,*" she insisted.

Augustine, whose husband was a gendarme, helped me by going to the gendarmerie with a photo of Youssef, which I labeled with his name.

"Please tell them *il est photographe,*" I said.

She assured me the gendarmes know everything that happens. "If something happened to him, they'd know, and they'd know to tell you," she said. "Try to keep busy and think of other things."

I watered the garden and did some hand laundry, then took a shower. I made a list of all those I could or should contact if Youssef didn't return soon. On that list was Liz, the U.S. Ambassador, who sat next to Youssef at her Christmas dinner. She'd remember him, his dignity and nobility. She would be able to do something. She would care, I felt sure.

"The fact is," I told my journal, "Youssef is carrying obvious and temptingly expensive camera equipment in a town and its outskirts where people are poor and some are desperate. He is a foreigner in a xenophobic place. He always returns when he said he would. He hasn't returned. He could have been harmed and left for dead or in fact killed."

Two days later, by which time I had stopped smoking cigarettes and sobbing and had just gone numb with worry, Youssef appeared at my front door as I was preparing lunch. I was making kidney stew with rice, one of our favorites, in the hope that its aroma would work some white magic. It did.

Over lunch, he told me he was sorry to have upset me, and he agreed that it was dangerous and risky for him to go around with all his most valuable possessions on display. He told me he is always careful ("*Je suis toujours prudent,*" he said), but he would try to be even more careful in the future. He said from now on he would not commit to any specific day or time for returning because "Things are too uncertain here." Transportation was too unreliable, communication essentially nonexistent; anything could happen, at any time. If I'd had a phone, Youssef could have called me to tell me about the logging truck that had broken down, blocking the only road, forcing him to turn back and wait. But I didn't have a phone.

We talked it all out. He said he understood the depths of my concerns; but he asked me to have patience, faith, and endurance. "*Il faut supporter,*" he told me, which I interpreted to mean: Please be supportive (emotionally, not financially; he never took money from me) of my photographic career.

He gave me the names and addresses of all his *logers* in France-ville, Moanda, and the *chantiers*. "So now," I told my journal, my confidante, my therapist, "all I can do in the future is entrust him to God's care. We had a nice lunch and took a nice nap. All is well again. He is alive, thank God."

Most of the time, when Youssef arrived home from his two- or three-day trips to the photo lab, he was proud to show me his pictures. Like his unsuspecting mentor, Seydou Keita, Youssef had a gift for posing his subjects in front of the most flattering back-drops, tilting their heads just so, saying the right word to the fussy baby to capture that curious expression, pressing the shutter at the perfect instant to preserve the ephemeral, forever. His eye for color and composition was unerring. His pride in his work was palpable.

But his work was not without its frustrations. Sometimes a whole roll came out overexposed; his subjects looked like ghosts standing in front of a bleached-out background. Youssef knew his clients would not accept these inferior photos, and not only would they not pay the balance due, they would demand their deposit back. In these instances, he knew that all of the time, effort, and travel expense he had incurred was for nothing. At times he became disheartened and withdrawn. He couldn't understand what caused the problem. Was it his fault? Was it the camera? Was it the lab?

I tried my best to cheer him by making up stories that may have been half true. I told him Marty sometimes forgets to put film in her camera when she goes on a shoot; once she misplaced a whole roll of exposed film after an event she'd covered, and she never did find it. "Marty can be forgetful like that," I told him. "These things happen. I'm sure Seydou Keita had lots of horror stories too." I would turn to the Introduction to the Seydou Keita book Marty had sent him and translate again for him the sections where Keita speaks about the tough time he had at the beginning of his career. "*C'est normal*," I assured him.

He was grateful. "You see," he told me," a younger woman wouldn't know what you know, couldn't give me the *conseil* (counsel) you give me. Young women only care about themselves. They are too young to know anything else."

Meanwhile, I mailed one of Youssef's bleached-out photos to Marty to ask her what she thought might be wrong. She wrote back that she suspected the lab Youssef was using might not be changing their chemicals frequently enough, in an effort to save money. She suggested he find another lab.

To take his mind off these setbacks when he was home, I played his favorites among the cassettes I'd brought with me to Gabon — Willy Nelson, Paul Simon, and Tracy Chapman. He especially liked listening to Tracy Chapman, even though he didn't know the words she sang in English. He said he could tell just from the depths of the sound of her voice that her ancestors came from Mali.

We worked in our back garden together. We walked to the *marché* and visited *maman* Leora together. And, as always, we enjoyed playing in the kitchen together:

Last night [I told my journal], Youssef showed me the traditional method of making peanut butter. We roasted a ½ kilo (about a pound) of fresh peanuts in the oven for about 10-15 minutes, until reddish-brown, then removed their papery skins by rubbing them between our hands when they were cool enough to handle, then tossing them up in air outside so the skins flew away. Then we pounded the roasted peanuts in my *mortier* until pasty, which took about a half hour. This made almost a whole big jar full.

One Friday afternoon, when Youssef was feeling too disheartened about his recent photo failures to visit the *chantiers* to take more pictures, Morgan arrived on her motorcycle with a live rooster hanging by his feet from her handlebars.

"Surprise!" she said merrily, by way of greeting. "Look what we're having for dinner!"

I tried not to look too closely at the scrawny, black-feathered thing for fear I might get as emotionally attached to this one as I had to *Dîner* and *Déjeuner*, both of whom had obviously become a neighbor's dinner while I was hospitalized in Libreville after my burn accident. I girded myself for the experience of eating a creature I'd known even for a little while, while he was alive.

"But who's going to kill it and clean it?" I said.

"*Moi même,*" Youssef said. "*Pas de problème.*"

He asked that I put a large pot of water on to boil, and then he set to work.

First, he laid the rooster on the ground, facing east (Mecca), near an indentation in the earth he'd dug to catch the animal's blood. Crouching, he placed one foot on the rooster's legs and the other on its flattened, doubled wings. Then he said a prayer in Arabic, asking for God's benediction, and, taking my sharpest cleaver in one hand and twisting the rooster's neck with the other, he made a slit in the animal's neck and let the blood flow into the indentation in the dirt. He then folded the wings around the bird's neck and let it lie there until good and gone.

Morgan had obviously seen many similar beheadings in her village, but this was a first for me. I watched Youssef's skill with a mixture of awe and surprise. *How could a man who could hear trees weep slit an animal's throat so unblinkingly?*

Youssef poured the boiling water into a pail, took the pail outside, and plunged the entire freshly killed bird into the water, holding it by the feet. The black feathers came off easily. Then he opened it up, removed its entrails, and rinsed it inside and out.

"Voilà!" he said happily, as if he'd altogether forgotten the ghostly photos and his recent discouragement. Photography might remain a new challenge for him, but he was a master at butchering. *"C'est prêt!"*

While I made dinner for the three of us in the kitchen, in the living room Morgan showed Youssef a new craft she'd just learned from a woman's magazine sent from home. It was how to make small, decorative frames for photos, using cardboard, fabric, foam, and glue. "It's easy!" she said. "Here's all you do!" By the time dinner was ready, they had made two colorful frames. Youssef could see the benefit of this new product for his photography business. His hopes were once again raised.

For dinner that evening I made a West African-style chicken stew with gumbo (okra) in a peanut sauce, served, of course, on a bed of rice. And (of course), Youssef told me it was delicious.

Chicken Stew with Okra
(adapted from *Gourmet*)

1 (14- to 15-ounce) can whole tomatoes in juice
¼ cup water
2 tablespoons tomato paste
1 (3 to 3½ pound) chicken, cut into serving pieces
¼ cup peanut oil
1 medium onion, chopped
1 teaspoon cayenne (or more, to taste)

4 garlic cloves, minced and mashed to a paste
   with 1 teaspoon salt
½ cup peanut butter, at room temp.
1¾ cup reduced-sodium chicken broth (14 fluid ounces)
1 pound sweet potato
1 (10-ounce) box frozen small okra, thawed
Accompaniment: cooked white rice

Place tomatoes with their juice, water and tomato paste in a food processor and pulse until tomatoes are finely chopped.

Heat oil in a 10- to 12-inch heavy skillet over moderately high heat and brown the chicken, without crowding, in three or four batches, until golden on both sides. Transfer with tongs to a 6- to 7-quart covered pot.

Pour off all but 2 tablespoons of fat from the skillet, then add chopped onion and cook over moderate heat, stirring occasionally, until golden, abut 2 to 3 minutes.

Add sautéed onion, chopped tomato mixture, garlic paste, and cayenne to chicken pieces. Whisk together peanut butter and 1 cup broth in a bowl until smooth, then add to chicken with remaining broth, stirring to combine well.

Bring to a boil, uncovered, then reduce heat and simmer, covered, stirring occasionally (to prevent sticking), until chicken is very tender, about 30 minutes.

Peel sweet potato and cut into 1-inch chunks. Stir into stew along with okra, then simmer, covered, until potato is tender but not falling apart, about 12 to 15 minutes.

Makes 6 servings.

Compost Queen

To turn the forest into good arable land is a work of generations.
— ALBERT SCHWEITZER, *The Primeval Forest*

Sharing some of the hospital garden's harvest

Martha Cooper

brought Henri with me today to teach us *la prévention du SIDA*" (AIDS), I said as I pulled from my large, handled shopping bag the dark-brown, Peace Corps-issued, 8-inch-long, carved-wood penis I'd affectionately named. By now, the women who sat through my *exposés* at the hospital's mother-infant clinic had come to expect the unexpected, and they knew that ridiculousness could well be a part of the mix.

By now, too, I no longer had to beg the women to come in to the room and take a seat on one of the long wooden benches to listen to my lectures. Over the past year, word must have spread throughout the town and surrounding villages that the *Americaine* who gave health lessons in wobbly French at the PMI, Lastours-ville's medical center clinic, was indeed *folle* (crazy), and her out-landish free show was not to be missed. In fact, most mornings now in the classroom space I had come to commandeer, all of the benches were filled. For latecomers, it was standing-room-only.

One look at the big, brown phallus that I held like a magic wand for all to see, and the young mothers holding babies on their laps doubled over those babies in laughter. These were not shy, hands-over-the-mouth, stifled laughs, but rather throaty, knowing, unrestricted laughs of recognition, as if to say, "Ah, yes, I'm well acquainted with Henri! I see him almost every night!"

Knowing I had their attention, I then explained to the women the importance of protecting themselves against AIDS and STDs. "Eighty percent of sexually active adults in Gabon have a sexually transmitted disease," I told them, as I'd often lectured at the high school, "and STDs are a *porte ouverte* (open door) for the deadly disease AIDS." I told them too that the one known proven protection against these diseases was the condom (*la capote*, they called it), which I sold on behalf of Gabon's *Programme National de Lutte Contre le SIDA*, for a nominal price. "I carry them in my shoulder bag at all times," I told the women, showing them my supply. "And you can stop me anytime, anywhere to discretely purchase as many as you think you might need."

We then used Henri to demonstrate exactly how to achieve this promised protection. Using out-of-date condoms provided for this purpose, I first showed the women how to open the small, square packet without tearing its contents, then how to place the condom on the tip and unroll it carefully down to the base. "If you insist on protecting yourself, and you know how to do it, your man will respect you," I said, hoping fervently that my words would be true for them.

I asked for volunteers from the audience to come to the front of the classroom and show us what they'd learned, and several women playfully complied, translating the message and the steps involved into Inzebi so that all would understand without question. Thus armed with knowledge, most of the women bought at least a few condoms to take home to their own, live "Henris."

Since all of the pregnant women and mothers of infants from Last-oursville and the surrounding villages came to the clinic one morning each month for checkups, vaccinations, or baby-weighing, I taught the same subject every weekday morning for the duration of an entire month. To supplement my still-insecure French and total inability to speak the local languages, I continued to rely on colorful posters, lively songs, dramatic skits, sock doll dummies, outright bribes (seed packets as gifts for listening), and anything else I could think of to convey the importance of illness-prevention measures. Henri was just one of the many props I pulled out of my large shopping bags.

When I taught *Sevrage* (weaning) for a month, I brought with me a large doll I'd made from black socks Marty had sent. I named this sock doll "Lulu," after the beloved black cloth doll my mother had made for me before I was born. I told the women this new Lulu was "my little girl," nearing two, and she was ready to switch to solid foods. I sat her on my lap and pretended to feed her the weaning food I'd prepared from the ingredients on the table in front of me: a plastic bottle filled with clean water, a tin of Quaker oatmeal or a bowl of ground rice, sweet bananas or ripe avocado, and whatever other available, affordable, easily digestible, nutritious ingredients I could find for the purpose.

Caroline, the clinic's head nurse, abandoning her inner office, sat in the front row, listening, taking notes, and occasionally making comments and translations for the mothers.

"Breast milk is pure and best for babies, as you all know," I said. "But when a new baby comes along and the slightly older one needs to be weaned, there is a strong danger of illness that could lead to death if the porridge is made with dirty water." When Caroline loudly agreed, the mothers in the audience paid even closer attention. She knew, and she let the mothers know, that diarrheal disease due to dirty water was one of the main reasons Gabon's mortality rate in children under five was so high. "Therefore, the most important ingredient in your babies' weaning food is *clean water!*" I emphasized. "We must boil our water well before we prepare our babies' first food," I said, lovingly patting my Lulu's woolly head.

The women in attendance found this, too, to be hilarious — that I should so sincerely refer to this black doll as "my baby" and proceed to feed her as if she were actually alive. From then on, whenever these women saw me in town, they would call to me and wave from a distance, *"Bonjour, la maman de Lulu!"* and laugh good-naturedly. Their laughter made me happy. I loved being a fool for love.

In fact, my genuine love for this new Lulu resonated deeply for me. She was the reincarnation, in a way, of my very first doll, who had had dark-chocolate-color cotton fabric for skin and short, braided black wool tufts for hair. That Lulu was larger than infant size and soft to the touch; her embroidered facial features were permanently wide-eyed and smiling. She kept me company in my crib and for years afterwards wherever I went, my mother, her creator, later told me.

I've often imagined that this doll must have been a comfort to me when my father came home drunk and began punching my mother in a rage. Lulu must have been the one I reached for whenever the shouting and screaming began. Sometimes, when I've tried to trace my lifelong magnetic pull toward Africa and African people, I go back in my mind to that black doll. She was my friend and constant companion — always smiling, always soft, always there for me. To me, she didn't represent "the other." She represented love.

I became a soldier, carrying an imaginary rifle on my shoulder, marching in the war against deadly bugs. I became a slovenly housewife, slouching lazily in a chair, clothes and hair askew, allowing sickening germs to invade my imaginary house and make all my children ill. I became a dancer and singer — uncaring that I'd never had any real performing-arts training — to get my points across in my morning classes.

Once, in high school, I performed in a short scene from the play we were studying in English class, Arthur Miller's "Death of a Salesman." I was a thin, shy, quiet, bookish teenage girl then, but when I played Linda Loman, something magical happened to me. I only had to play my mother, and Linda Loman came alive. "Attention, attention must be paid to this man!" I pleaded passionately, and I could see my classmates' mouths drop. I tried to tap in to that latent magic in my classroom at the Lastoursville clinic.

For another month, I taught the women a song in French — to the tune of the alphabet song little children learn in English — that provided a potentially life-saving recipe for a rehydration solution to use when their children had diarrhea. The formula — one liter of clean water, eight cubes of sugar, one level teaspoon of salt, plus a squeeze of one lemon — set to music, I knew, would remain with these mothers and would be readily recalled when they needed it most. Music and laughter, despite all of the daily hardships and struggles these women endured, seemed to be part of their being, their prime defenses against defeat.

I demonstrated how quick and easy the rehydration recipe was to make with ingredients close at hand, and I impressed on them the importance of spoon-feeding this solution in steady, small amounts. "When someone, especially a little one, has diarrhea," I said, "he or she loses too much water too quickly and can die of dehydration within days. So it's *très important* to replenish that water with this solution — and hurry to the hospital."

Together, we all sang the rehydration song repeatedly, swaying and clapping to the beat at intervals, the way the women at Bev's church did when they sang hymns. To God's ears, I felt sure, this childlike song to staunch diarrheal disease and death must have sounded exactly like a hymn.

Marty had given me an inflatable beach-ball globe, which I pulled one morning from my shopping bag and began to inflate in front of the quiet classroom filled with women. Their eyes asked, *Now what is this?* and *What will this crazy white lady do next?*

"This," I said, when the big plastic ball was fully inflated, "is the world. We are here" — I pointed to Gabon — "and I come from here" — I walked my fingers across the Atlantic to New York.

"I've traveled to many countries in the world" — I pointed to Mexico, Canada, England, France, Germany, Holland, Italy, Greece, New Zealand, Morocco, and Zimbabwe — "and I've stayed in many towns in those countries, and I think Lastoursville, Gabon, is one of the most beautiful towns in the whole world!" The women's faces brightened, and they nodded in pride.

"But the *ordures* (garbage) strewn everywhere here makes it ugly, unsafe, and unhygienic." They nodded again, but this time sadly. "Garbage breeds germs, germs bring disease, and we don't want diseases in our lives, do we? No! *Absolument, non!* So what can we all do about this problem called garbage?"

I put the world down and reached into my bag for more posters, which I taped along the classroom wall, explaining as I went. "From now on, before we toss something out, we must analyze it and decide:

(1) If it's a pit, such as an avocado or mango pit, PLANT it;

(2) If it's kitchen scraps, such as peanut shells or banana skins, COMPOST it;

(3) If it can have a new life in another form, RECYCLE it; and

(4) If it's truly dead and has no other use, BURY it."

For this month-long *Ordures* lesson, I brought several shopping bags filled with visual aids — avocado pits I'd planted, which were now healthy seedlings; and things I'd made from recycled materials, such as a door mat woven from large plastic bags on a simple, nail-studded wooden loom; and tin cans turned into wall sconces for candles. The women *ooh'd* and *aah'd*, as though I were a magician pulling white rabbits from upturned top hats; light bulbs seemed to pop over their pretty heads. Their receptivity to my homespun ideas thrilled me. They seemed hungry for practical, doable, down-to-earth suggestions for making their lives better, and I was hungry for the deep satisfaction that sharing such suggestions gave me. Catering to wealthy people in New York had never been this gratifying.

When it came time to explain my newest passion, composting, I took the entire class outside, to the model garden I'd planted with Dr. Djimet's blessing on the hospital grounds, not far from the PMI. To my great amazement and joy, this fenced-in garden was flourishing, and I was able to give its produce — eggplants, zucchini squashes, carrots, cherry tomatoes, lettuces, arugula, basil and mint — to women who were cooking and caring for their loved ones in the hospital.

The secret to this garden's success, I told my classes, was not that I was an experienced gardener — because gardening was completely new to this New Yorker — but rather it was the *compost*, which I pointed to admiringly. "The compost feeds the earth, so that she will be more fertile and will bear produce such as this!" I said, scanning the healthy little garden.

I took a shovel and dug into the compost pit to demonstrate the richness of the decomposed matter in it.

"When you feed the earth organic material, such as egg shells, plantain skins, dried grass, and *caca de chèvre* (goat droppings), mixed with this infertile soil, in one pile, the earth with the help of the sun and the rain will chew it up and turn it into good food for your garden. If, when you dig your own garden rows, you dig deeply and add some of your compost to it, your plants will eat well and in turn feed your family healthy vegetables."

After these demonstrations, the women called me *"La Reine du Compost"* (Compost Queen), and I wore that title happily.

In a letter to my Peace Corps supervisor, Paulette, in Libreville I shared some good news:

The Minister of Health for Gabon was in Lastoursville last week — for the first time, I understand, because this is a new job for him. There was a big to-do made at the hospital, *bien sûr*, and he was given a tour of all the buildings. I was told the next day that when M. le Ministre got to the PMI in the afternoon and saw the big display I'd put on the classroom wall to illustrate my *exposés* for the month of August *(Ordures →* Compost → *Jardinage* — big posters for each, big arrows leading from one to the other, lots of color, drawings, etc.), he actually took out a pad and a pen and copied my display down. What a coup, don't you think? I was thrilled to hear this.

Some mornings at the clinic were neither thrilling nor lighthearted. There was nothing light about malaria, which threatened the lives of all of the people, especially the youngest and oldest, at all times. I could only resort to simple mathematics for that lesson: A protective, preventive bed net, at the equivalent then of $6, was half the price of filling the prescription at the pharmacy for the after-the-fact, uncertain malaria medication.

And when death came, as it inevitably did at the hospital, especially when it visited Pediatrics, the building closest to my classroom, and the mother of a child who'd just died wailed and keened and pounded the dry earth in the courtyard near my classroom's open door, rocking back and forth on her knees, tossing handfuls of dirt, pulling at her hair, the Compost Queen, with her imaginary magic wand and shopping bags full of tricks and gimmicks, stood paralyzed, powerless, speechless in front of the roomful of young mothers waiting for their babies to be weighed. She was no match for Africa; she was brought down to size.

OCTRA

I have been considerably chaffed both by whites and blacks about my partiality for this tribe [the Fang], but as ... these Africans have more of the qualities I like than any other tribe I have met, it is but natural that I should prefer them.
— MARY KINGSLEY, *Travels in West Africa*

Teaching cooking in Lucienne's kitchen in Cité OCTRA

*A*cross the tracks from the cement-block train station in Las-toursville, along a clearing that bordered the encroaching forest, some enterprising women set up tables with food they'd prepared for sale to hungry travelers. There were *batons de manioc*, of course, and egg sandwiches on chunks of French baguettes slathered with margarine, golden deep-fried beignets, some sort of sliced grilled meat dabbed with hot sauce and sold in rough paper cones, roasted-until-blackened whole corn-on-the-cob, as well as tiny plastic bags filled with frozen sweet drinks (along the lines of Kool-Aid, but made with dubious water) and stored in large coolers.

As I waited for the train that would take me to my Peace Corps in-service training session in Libreville, sweating in the midday sun in my jeans and T-shirt with a suitcase-size pack on my back, I chatted with these women to pass the time. The train was running predictably late, and I found the women, like food professionals everywhere in the world, happy to chat about food.

These young entrepreneurs were different from the women I'd come to know in Lastoursville in the time I'd been there so far. They wore Western-style skirts and blouses, instead of the traditional *pagne* wrap skirts in African-print fabric; and their hair, instead of being close-cropped and hidden under head wraps, was done in intricate braided and looped designs that framed their bright and friendly faces like haloes. They told me they lived in nearby *Cité* OCTRA; their husbands worked for the train line; they came from the north of Gabon, near the border with Cameroon; they were Fang.

My Gabonese friend Antoinette in town had told me early on that the people of the north of Gabon, the Fang, were more ambitious than "us in the south." She said it might have been better for me if I had been posted there, because they would be more receptive to my crafts classes. "We here are *paresseux* (lazy)," Antoinette admitted to me. She fanned her face with one hand and smiled her mischievous smile. "It's just too hot in the south."

Mary Kingsley, a young, highly adventurous Briton who was the first lone woman to explore Gabon, wrote in her classic travelogue, *Travels in West Africa* (1897), that she was especially partial to the Fang tribe. "They are brave," she said, "and so you can respect them, which is an essential element in a friendly feeling. ... Their countenances are very bright and expressive, and if once you have been among them, you can never mistake [them]."

As I was talking with one of these Fang women — a tall, attractive, outgoing woman who introduced herself as Dede, another woman, in a fitted, dark business suit and low, dark pumps, approached us, then took me aside. She said her name was Lucienne, she was the manager of the OCTRA station, she'd seen me from her office window, and she wanted to speak with me. She knew who I was, she said; she'd heard about my cooking and crafts classes for church women's groups and my puppet shows for little children. She wondered whether I might do the same for the women and children of the OCTRA community.

She looked at me intently with piercing eyes and a confident smile. Would I be willing to come to her house one afternoon a week and teach them, she asked?

The *Office du Chemin de Fer Transgabonais*, known as OCTRA, was the then-state-run railway system in Gabon. *Cité* OCTRA, about five miles outside of Lastoursville, situated on a barren stretch of land between the Ogooué River and the road to the train station, was a community of some twenty long, white, house trailers provided by the government for railway workers and their families. Lucienne, a single mother of two young children, was a community leader there, and, I would come to learn, a woman of impressive energy and will. I could tell from her businesslike manner she meant business. I told her I'd be happy to give lessons at her house. We agreed to talk again in a week or two, after I returned from my in-service training in Libreville.

Every six months I made this trip on Gabon's one and only railway to and from Libreville for Peace Corps trainings. It was a journey that should have taken just under ten hours each way but generally took many more and was invariably daunting. Three days a week a few of the railway cars carried passengers — in addition to its more highly valued cargo of timber, manganese, and uranium. These passenger cars were generally stiflingly hot and overcrowded, the seats torn and worn, and the bathroom plumbing nonfunctioning. Along the way, the train would stop and sit on the tracks for hours, with no official bothering to explain why. The passengers, all African except me, would sit quietly and patiently, unquestioningly, staring straight ahead or dozing, as if inured to such setbacks in their plans. I, on the other hand, would envision something like this occurring on a New York commuter train out of Penn Station and the melee that would ensue.

Traveling like an African in Africa, I gradually learned, is an exercise in tolerance and patience. For me, the antidote to seething impatience and loud teeth-grinding included plenty of interesting reading matter and writing paper, my favorite Uni-ball pens, a hearty homemade sandwich, a liter bottle of clean drinking water, and a good supply of Wash 'n Dry's (sent in care packages from friends in the States).

When I wasn't reading, studying scenery, or resting my eyes, I was recording my observations in my ever-indulgent journal.

On one trip I told my journal about the young couple with two small children sitting across from me: "The baby girl was fussing (it's hot in here), so I asked to hold her to give the mom a break while the dad visited the restroom. When he came back, he looked around and said, worriedly, 'Where's the baby?' I pointed to my lap, where the baby was sleeping, and he exhaled. 'She is my heart,' he said." His loving words brought tears to my eyes. *What a fortunate little girl to have such a father,* I thought.

On another trip I sat next to a large, barefooted middle-age woman in traditional African dress and head wrap who was using a cellular phone — the first I'd seen in Gabon — to phone her travel agent in Libreville about a flight to Rome. She then explained to me that she was heading to Rome to see an exorcist affiliated with the Vatican in order to heal one of her eight children, who had been possessed by evil spirits since she was eight years old. The girl was now twenty-two.

"The mother took the cap off her Orange Fanta bottle with her teeth," my journal faithfully recounts, "took a big swig, and settled her large frame back into the tattered seat. '*C'est triste*' (It's sad), we both agreed, that her daughter was ill. ... The mother told me she is forty-six; she said she thinks I look good for fifty-one."

On clear, sunny days, the view from the train window was at times beautiful. Where the tracks hugged the Ogooué, I saw wide expanses of sparkling river, with raw, rolling, forested mountain ranges in the distance. Near Lope, the view opened up to high savanna — scrubby trees with broad, grassy vistas and balding hills. But for the most part, the daytime scene was solid trees on both sides of the tracks, the sort of scenery a bug might see when scooting through a garden row of broccoli. At night there was nothing to see out the windows but blackness, so I would try, unsuccessfully, to sleep sitting up as the train rumbled loudly and bumpily toward Libreville.

After Youssef came to live with me in January 1998, I could count on his meeting my train from Libreville at the Lastoursville station. He would be right there at the passenger car door, waiting to greet me when it opened and I was the first to disembark. Often the train arrived many hours late in the middle of the night, and he had been waiting there for at least five hours. He never complained. Instead, he only told me how happy he was to see me, and I in turn told him how happy I was to be home again with him.

One such reunion was especially dramatic. After having gotten on the train on Sunday evening in Libreville's Owendo station at about 6 pm, I settled in for a ride that should have brought me into the Lastoursville station at 4 o'clock Monday morning. Instead, my train limped in at 8 am. Youssef was there on the platform to greet and embrace me. He had been waiting patiently at the station since 3 am.

Since we knew that my neighbor, Augustine, who helped me keep snakes and scorpions at bay by washing all the floors of my house every Monday morning, would be waiting at my locked front door, Youssef and I decided I would go ahead to the house to let Augustine in. There was some unexplained delay in getting the baggage off the train, so Youssef stayed behind at the station to collect my big bag from the baggage car.

But when Youssef didn't return that morning, I began to worry. I walked back into town, where I saw the taxi driver who had brought me in. He confirmed my fears: Youssef was in trouble. He had been apprehended by the gendarmes at the OCTRA police station for not carrying travel documents, Gabon's *carte de séjour*. I asked the driver to take me to him right away.

Outside of the tumbledown station, I found Youssef, visibly shaken, but upright and dignified. He was barefoot and sweaty, with pieces of grass caught in his hair and grass stains on his good khaki pants. The gendarmes had made him take off his shoes and cut the grass surrounding the station house with a machete, since he wasn't carrying sufficient money to pay the arbitrary fine (ie, bribe).

While Youssef continued his forced labor outside, I sat in a rickety wooden chair in front of a boxy wooden desk, where a diminutive gendarme in a crisp uniform spoke to me firmly. He demanded 24,000 CFA (about $50) to let Youssef go.

"I'm sorry, sir," I said, "but I only have 10,000 CFA with me. *Je suis volontaire. Je ne suis pas riche.*"

At first he refused, saying Youssef would have to stay there — or perhaps be sent to Koula Moutou to prison.

"*Ah, non,*" I countered, without flinching. "*Nous sommes ensemble* (He and I are together). In fact, I will go outside and cut the grass with him, if you don't take this 10,000 note and let him go." I tried my best to be calm, reasonable, and polite, but at the same time communicate the fact that he'd best take my offer. It would be embarrassing for them, I knew, if people driving by saw me outside the gendarmerie cutting grass with a machete. By this time, everyone in town knew who I was and what I was doing in Lastoursville.

Finally, his superior officer, a burly man who'd obviously overheard this conversation from his inner office, marched in and commanded his underling, "Let them go." I offered them the 10,000 CFA note, which they accepted, and I thanked them both sincerely. Youssef put his socks and shoes back on, and we flagged the next passing pickup truck to give us a lift back home. We made lunch, took a nap, and all became well again.

Lucienne and I established that my lessons at her house would take place every Wednesday at 4 pm, following my first in-service training in Libreville. I would begin each session by giving a cooking lesson in Lucienne's kitchen to a group of young OCTRA community mothers, most of whom I'd first met selling their fare at the train station, and then I'd give a puppet show to the many OCTRA children.

Lucienne's trailer home was large, clean, and modern. On the round dining table to the left of the front door was a big bouquet of pink and white plastic peonies. The living room walls were white, as was the clean linoleum-tiled floor. Pretty curtains framed the windows behind her plush living room sofa. In the kitchen, which was large enough to accommodate up to eight mothers sitting on chairs and benches for their cooking lesson and dozens of little children sitting patiently on the floor waiting for the puppets to perform, Lucienne had pots and pans hanging from the faux-pine-paneled walls. She had a sink, a refrigerator, a stovetop and an oven.

<u>Thursday, April 17, 1997</u>: At my OCTRA class yesterday I taught the Banana Gateau recipe for the first time, and it went over very well, especially at the end when the mothers tasted the cake. Lucienne's eyes lit up and her smile was a mile wide. This is very gratifying to me. The women seem to love it, just the way most women everywhere love cooking and learning new ways to prepare tasty things.

The kids were adorable too. There must have been about forty of them this time — ten more than the week before — all sitting on Lucienne's kitchen floor. They sang Chantal Chanson's hygiene song by heart ("To have good health, wash your hands with soap and water…"), and they were attentive to my Nutrition lecture, actually delivered by puppet Renee Repas. Lucienne said the puppet shows are getting so big we'll have to hold them in the local grammar school from now on.

<u>Thursday, May 15, 1997</u>: Yesterday at my OCTRA class I taught pancakes (with oatmeal and bananas) and a new nutrition song for the children. There were so many children they can no longer sit on the kitchen floor. Lucienne had to move them out into the living room/dining room area. There must

have been at least fifty. Lucienne led them through the new song, "*Mangez bien — les trios groupes d'aliments!*" (Eat well — the three food groups) based on the "*Lavez les Mains*" (Wash Your Hands) tune, while the mothers made pancakes in the kitchen. Everyone was happy — especially me.

<u>Friday, July 25, 1997:</u> A setback: Lucienne now has a TV in her living room. All of the OCTRA kids, who normally wait patiently on the kitchen floor for my puppet shows to begin, were glued to the TV in the living room. When the time came, Lucienne had to turn the TV off to lure them reluctantly in to the kitchen for the puppets. Competition. Modernization.

"To give you an idea of the ups and downs, joys and disappointments of life here," I wrote my journal in mid-November 1997, "let me tell you briefly about my day yesterday:

10 am — While Youssef worked outside in the garden, transplanting haricots seedlings to a better-soiled location, I walked to and from town to get things I needed for my cooking class at OCTRA; namely, eggs and green papaya. At first I was told there were no eggs anywhere in town; then someone led me to a shop that still had some (1,100 CFA for ½ dozen eggs — that's about $2.20 for six eggs). Youssef had told me that the West African family that runs the *quincaillerie* (hardware store) had lots of green papayas behind the store where they live, so I got two from them. The young mother used a long stick to poke them loose and let them fall to the ground. I tried to pay her for them, but she refused to take my money. She insisted they were a gift.

11 am — When I got home — sweaty and out of breath — I took my second shower of the day, then worked in the kitchen with Youssef: He prepared lunch — his specialty, saka-saka; and I prepared (peeled, chopped, cooked, and pureed) the papaya for my OCTRA cooking lesson: Green Papaya Tart.

3:30 pm — After eating lunch, taking a nap, and taking shower #3, I walked down to the *carrefour* and waited in the shade of a tree near the prefecture for a ride to *Cité* OCTRA. A pickup truck finally came along, and I hopped in the front.

4 pm — When I got to Lucienne's house, she was resting on the sofa in front of the fan (what HEAT!), wearing her at-home clothes, jeans and a short-sleeved shirt, watching TV. She sent some kids to call the other mothers; little by little the mothers trickled in. I began.

The kitchen itself was like an oven. The floor — from the sunlight pouring in from the window — was burning my bare feet. Sweat poured out of me as I tried to teach. The pastry wouldn't (couldn't) behave, due to the heat and humidity, so I put it in the freezer for a while to chill out.

The kids sat as usual on the kitchen floor (under foot for me), talking, arguing among themselves, and fooling around. The mothers, intermittently, shouted at their kids for misbehaving. The heat was making us all grumpy. Lucienne's oven lacked a shelf, and its temperature couldn't seem to get high enough to bake the tart properly. Amid all these handicaps, I tried to teach *Tarte a la Papaye Vert* in particular, and *patisserie* in general. The only thing I succeeded in doing, for sure, was not losing my cool or my temper. I'm trying to adopt Morgan's attitude toward working in Gabon: "*Whatever.*"

5:30 pm — While the tart was in the oven trying to bake, the kids and moms went into the cooler living room and I gave a puppet show from the kitchen doorway. Renee Repas taught the three food groups, and Chantal Chanson followed, leading the kids in song. They were a good audience.

6 pm — Ready or not, we took the tart out of the oven because I had to leave and I needed the pan. The mothers loved the tart. On my way out Lucienne handed me some money: a collection taken from the mothers for my "taxi" fare — about 1,700 CFA. I tried to give 1,000 back to her; but they refused. On the walk to the main road, holding my hand, a pretty little girl of about six or seven asked me to teach her greetings and numbers in English.

6:15 am — Lucienne flagged down a huge *grumiere* (logging truck) to give me a lift to town. I walked up the hill again — for the second time in the day — this time carrying a case full of cooking equipment and puppets.

6:45 pm — When I reached the house — drenched in sweat and panting profusely — Mr. Mekani, my Chadian French tutor, was sitting on my front porch in the darkness. Once again, our lesson consisted mostly of my explaining how discouraged I am at my inability to speak and understand spoken French. His reply is always the same: *Practice.*

8:30 pm — After Mr. Mekani left, I cleaned up the kitchen, unpacked my things, put everything away, did a load of white laundry (by hand), took a hot bucket bath and washed my hair.

11 pm — Went to bed, turned off the light, and thought about the future before falling asleep. As next September gets closer, it's becoming clearer to me: I cannot go back to the past.

My Wednesday afternoon OCTRA classes soon became the highlight of my week, and my fondness for these bright, ambitious women and the OCTRA community's children widened and deepened. The children were quick to learn all of the words to the puppets' educational songs, and each succeeding week the mothers reported to me that they'd made the recipe of the previous week and even tried selling that item to travelers at the train station.

Most weeks the mothers were cheerful and enthusiastic, but one Wednesday they were grieving. One of them, one of the women I had first met, the tall, ebullient young woman named Dede, had been killed in a train accident a few days before. She had tried once again, as she'd done successfully many times before, to hop onto a moving train as it left Lastoursville's station to take her to the next station where she planned to sell her cakes. But this time she lost her footing, and she fell onto the tracks, under the train's wheels, where her body was shredded beyond recognition. This news struck me like a stomach punch. It sent me reeling; I felt unable to breathe.

In the sunny place that Dede had occupied in Lucienne's kitchen, there was now emptiness and sorrow. We were all sisters, mourning her untimely death.

But, for the children's sake, we put on a happy puppet show and led the children in boisterous singing. Chantal Chanson tossed her purple yarn hair, warbled her hit tunes, and clapped her big, green felt hands. *"Après les besoins"* (after you do your business), she sang with immense sincerity and gusto, "wash your hands with soap and water!" But we women knew what these little children would only come to understand in time: Soap and water can't wash pain and grief away.

Lucienne and her son with balloons Marty brought

Maison des Femmes

Ce local fait déjà la fierté des femmes de Lastoursville.
— from L'Union *newspaper report of the inauguration ceremony,*
calling the newly opened Maison des Femmes the
pride of the women of Lastoursville.

Youssef Tounkara

Mothers and daughters
in women's center crafts class

She was due to arrive at 10 am. That's when the ceremony was to begin. Crowds had gathered on the dusty playing field behind the *Maison des Spectacles*. About a dozen dignitaries sat in rows of folding chairs beneath a makeshift awning put up for the occasion, to shelter them from the sun. The rest of us stood and watched as group after group of women dancers in traditional dress filled the waiting time by performing celebratory gyrations — wriggling, bending, stomping, clapping — to the energetic beat of drums. The actual inauguration and ribbon cutting ceremony couldn't start until the guest of honor, Madame Edith Lucie Bongo, the beautiful, young, physician wife of President Omar Bongo, arrived. But it was now nearing noon on the equator, and Madame Bongo still hadn't appeared.

Youssef moved among the crowd smoothly, proudly, like a leopard, taking pictures of the dancers from different angles with his new camera. I stood in the baking sun feeling faint and increasingly irritable. My burn wound was still painful, still a long way from being fully healed; and it was difficult for me to stand for this length of time, especially in hundred-degree heat. It was Saturday,

January 10, 1998, and Youssef and I had only been back from my hospital stay in Libreville a little over a week.

Nevertheless, I couldn't miss this occasion: the inauguration of the almost-completed *Maison des Femmes* in Lastoursville. This new building, across the roadway from the *Maison des Spectacles*, the community reception hall, and just down the hill from my home, held the promise of a dream fulfilled for me. At this women's center, a first for Lastoursville, I would be one of the primary teachers. Gabon's Minister of Education, Madame Paulette Monsango, had learned of my work in Lastoursville, considered me "experienced and capable," and sent word through her local representative that she wanted me to teach there. As a Peace Corps volunteer, I wouldn't be paid, of course; but I knew it would be incalculably rewarding for me. I would have my cooking school in Lastoursville after all.

At last Madame Bongo's delegation, in a caravan of new black Mercedes sedans with Gabon's green-yellow-and-blue flag fluttering from their antennae, pulled into the field, and Madame Bongo, one of the president's several current wives, stepped out. Indeed young — perhaps in her early-to-mid- thirties — and beautiful in the softly rounded, vernal way young Gabonese women can be, she walked elegantly from her chauffeured car, wearing a fitted, two-piece, African-print ensemble with starched, puffed sleeves and a matching, regal-looking head wrap. She greeted the honored guests individually, bowing to and shaking the right hand of each one, turned and stood in front of the microphone, and spoke to the attentive crowd of the importance of this historic occasion for Lastoursville and the urgency of educating Africa's women. Her voice was soft and sincere. Her words made me glad to be there.

I wanted to approach her at the end of the ceremony and introduce myself. I wanted to tell her how proud I was to be chosen as one of the new center's instructors, how deeply I believed in empowering women. I wanted to add that I'd just recently spent several weeks in her private clinic in Libreville and thank her for the superior care I received there. But I said none of these things. I couldn't work up the boldness to walk up to her. I feared my French would fail me. And I wasn't feeling well. Between the merciless midday heat and my still-painful burn wound, I thought I might faint. I remained the lone white face in the large Gabonese crowd.

That the small town of Lastoursville should devote its resources to and express such fanfare for this big, brand new, white-stucco building overlooking the Ogooué, called *Maison des Femmes*, rather than *Maison des Hommes*, was only fitting. Women — at least in an unofficial sense, in my observation — ruled.

Loosely defined and mostly relating to traditional life in the interior, Gabon might be considered one of the world's surviving matriarchal societies. Whether by default or by design, the mother is most often the head of a household, the men who father her children come and go, and the children take the mother's name. For this reason, I found, women — especially women who are mothers, as most are — are highly regarded. The word "*maman*" used in addressing a woman denotes honor, as "sir" in English does for a man. Most Gabonese boys, even those who grow up to become swaggering gendarmes in crisp khaki uniforms with wide black leather belts and shiny black leather boots, are reared by strong women and are therefore forever respectful of women's capabilities.

Therese, the stout, middle-aged *maman* who'd been appointed by the presiding politicians the *directrice* of the women's center, gave me a tour of the facility a week after the inauguration. As I followed her from classroom to classroom, I noticed she was unsteady on her feet, and her French words were coming out slurred. My friend Antionette had intimated to me one day that Therese, who was *not*, Antoinette stressed, a member of any church women's group, had a drinking problem. I could see now that could well be true.

The classrooms were still under construction, the electricity not yet hooked up, and the supplies not yet fully unpacked. But what I saw inside the new women's center gave me hope: a pile of gardening equipment, including machetes, shovels, and even a weed-whacker; six classic, black, Singer sewing machines; a table covered with fabric, spools of thread in every color, trimmings, scissors, and pins; new cooking appliances still in their big boxes — refrigerator, freezer, stovetop/oven; and plenty of pots and pans. My heart sang.

I suggested to Therese that as soon as the construction was completed, I would be happy to give classes every Thursday afternoon from 4 to 6 pm. I offered to teach cooking, crafts, gardening, recycling, sewing, and even *"le rangement de la maison"* (interior decorating). She nodded vaguely, then shook her forefinger as if something had just occurred to her.

"Je suis enseignante de la couture!" (I am the sewing instructor), she slurred. *"Ah, bon,"* I said. *"Bien sûr. Pas de problème."*

In the following weeks I made colorful posters, decorated with gold star stickers, to put up all over town. ***"Une Annonce Importante,"*** the big, bold heading read in bright red, with the starting date and the hours in blue; *"Mme. Bonnie Black, Volontaire du Corps de la Paix, donnera des cours pratiques pour toutes les femmes de la communauté de Lastoursville."* I listed the course offerings with gold stars for bullet points, then added at the bottom, in green: *"TOUTES SONT INVITÉES!!!"* (all are invited).

The courses were free and open to all the women of Lastoursville and the surrounding community. Up to this time, I had been giving classes to select groups — the young mothers who brought their babies to the hospital's clinic, various women's church groups who'd invited me, and the women who worked for the railroad company, OCTRA. But at no point were my classes as all-inclusive as this.

The response was electric. It was as if Lastoursville had suddenly become a university town, and all of the women had received full scholarships. The women who attended my classes came from all of the various Gabonese ethnic groups as well as the West African immigrant community. Women who hadn't mingled before found themselves sitting side by side, on relatively comfortable wooden folding chairs in a clean, white classroom, sharing this new educational experience.

Every week an average of about twenty women arrived, punctually, for my four o'clock classes. And they came prepared with slim notebooks and Bic pens. Some brought their school-age daughters, instructing them to "sit very still and listen." Little boys gathered outside, looking in wonder and longing into the classroom at the open windows. Exercising our female power gleefully, we didn't let them in.

I recognized many faces — Germaine, Edwidge, and Denise, nurses from the hospital; as well as Mary Paul, Emilienne, and others from the Nazareth Church women's group. My friend Antoinette, however, was too occupied with her new job at the *mairie* to make it. Similarly, Denise Nimba told me she couldn't leave her restaurant for those hours. My elderly *maman* Leora, too, said she would love to come and see me teach, but the hill was too much for her, and she couldn't afford a taxi.

For those who did attend, I tried to create some incentives to maintain interest and sustain attendance. I instituted a "tontine," a system familiar to these women: Each one who chose to, could, before the class began, put a 100 CFA coin into one bowl and her name on a folded slip of paper in another bowl. At the end of the class, one of the attendees, chosen at random, pulled a name out of the bowl to decide who won the "pot." So, with an initial investment of roughly 25 cents, a lucky woman could, theoretically, go home with the equivalent of about $5, which would be for her a bonanza.

I also gave small packets of seeds to all attendees, one packet per woman. But, if a woman brought to class an item she had made at home after having learned how to make it in one of our previous craft classes, she earned an extra packet of seeds. These brought-from-home items provided a show-and-tell element to our classes. The woman who brought what she'd made stood up, showed the group her item, and explained her process; then everyone applauded her efforts. For some of the shier women, I could tell, this was their first experience at giving a public presentation and earning others' applause.

"What if," I proposed to them, planting a seed of a plan at the start of my crafts classes, "we have a *foires des métiers* (crafts fair) at the *marché* in a few months, so you can sell what you've made, to make extra money for your family? Lastoursville is *un carrefour* (a crossroads) — people pass through from all directions — they'll see the banner for the fair and stop and buy!" This, I knew, was an ambitious plan, but I could see from the women's response that many of them were willing to try.

Among the crafts I taught were: paper beads — made from rolled strips of the colorful advertisement pages I'd clipped and saved from *Gourmet*, varnished with clear nail polish — for making pretty necklaces; corn husk flowers for a table bouquet; and hand-quilted shoulder bags. The craft that resonated most deeply for all of us, though, was sock dolls.

"Anybody can *buy* things," my mother used to say to my younger sisters and me in a *tsk-tsk* tone of voice, when we were young and my alcoholic father couldn't keep a job. "But only creative people can *make* them!"

My mother had a way of turning our circumstances downside-up. *Buy a commercially manufactured doll off the shelf of a toy store?* Well, anybody could do that! (She didn't add that we didn't have the money to do that.) What *we* could do, because *we* were blessed with creativity, was *make* our dolls. Our dolls would be unique in their adorableness. One-of-a-kind! *Eventual collectors' items!* The whole concept was thrilling to me. It made me feel proud.

We watched as our mother made dolls for us from my father's old socks — black, brown, beige, and white — stuffed with cotton. She showed us how she embroidered each doll's smiling face, sewed on buttons for eyes, made hair from yarn. Then, from scraps of fabric she had used to make dresses for us three, she sewed pretty skirts and blouses for these soft and lovable, multi-ethnic sock dolls.

To my then young and spirited mother, Lee, who had come of age during the Depression and had lived through World War II, creativity trumped poverty. It was this spirit, her spirit, that I tried to bring to my classes at Lastoursville's *Maison des Femmes*.

My sister Heather and my friend Marty sent bags of old socks — mostly black and brown — at my urgent request. I showed the women how to cut, sew, and stuff the socks, with foam available from the *marché*; how to embroider happy faces; how to make yarn-hair. The women dressed these dark sock dolls in traditional African outfits, with matching head wraps, and gave them to their young daughters, most of whom had never owned a doll before. One little girl who came to class with her mother carried her new sock doll lovingly wrapped on her back, the way her own mother carried her babies.

To teach interior decorating tips to women who lived for the most part in mud-wattle houses with dirt floors was, I knew, a stretch; but the women were receptive nevertheless. For this class I brought photos Youssef had taken in our home and passed them among the attendees. I explained how I'd made a coffee table from a flat, discarded door laid on top of two large paint tins; how I'd made shelves from imperfect planks of wood (available free from the *chantiers*) and sturdy NIDO cans. Everything I showed them was doable for very little money — just the price of enamel paint.

As a follow-up to my lecture, we took a "field trip," a walk up the hill to my house, where they were able to touch and inspect what they'd just seen in photos.

Not surprisingly, my cooking classes were the most heavily attended. My reputation as a cooking instructor had spread, and even those women who had attended my demonstrations before came again. I taught the same, simple recipes I'd taught at other women's groups, such as healthy soups, whole-grain yeast bread, and tasty sauces, including Italian tomato and West African peanut sauce. The women took notes from the recipe-posters I taped to the wall, and they enjoyed sampling the finished products at the end of each class.

One especially memorable lesson was for crêpes with *confiture*. For most of the women in the class, this was their first taste of crêpes, and they loved learning the technique involved in making them. I then demonstrated how to make papaya jam, bottle it, label it, and decorate the bottles with pinked circles of African fabric tied to the tops with ribbon. "Imagine," I said to the class, "selling these pretty jars of jam — first here in our own *marché*, then in Libreville! It's possible! You could do it!"

I gave each woman a packet of papaya seeds I'd saved and dried for this purpose. Because my time in Lastoursville was drawing to a close, I asked the women to plant these seeds "in memory of me," which they agreed to do.

The women who returned to class the following week and reported they'd made the *confiture* at home, admitted it didn't last long enough to sit in a pretty jar on a shelf. Their large families ate it all right away.

In April 1998, Alison, a fellow volunteer posted in Libreville, sent me a full-page clip from the *L'Union* newspaper there, with the heading, "*La Nouvelle Naissance de Lastoursville*." The article touched on the pros and cons of this crossroads town in the Ogooué-Lolo region, which was founded on "le 9 Juillet 1883," the article said, by a young Frenchman named de Lastours. Among the criticisms: Why was the electricity and water in the town so often cut? (A good question I had often asked myself.) But among the pros listed was "the pride of the women of Lastoursville, the new *Maison des Femmes,* where women could receive lessons in various subjects taught by Mme. Bonnie Black, *une volontaire du Corps de la Paix.*" At some expense, I made photocopies of the newspaper clipping in town, to share with Antionette and Therese and another to send to Marty in New York. I made one for me to keep, too, because I knew how fragile newsprint — and memories — can be.

"My good news," I wrote to Marty in April, "is that my crafts classes at the women's center are a big hit. I've turned on the taps of my creative energy full force. Everything I create now is with a view to passing the idea on to the women here so they might profit from it. ... Like you, I've always been a person who derives a great deal of satisfaction from making things that hadn't existed before — but now this part of me is operating at full tilt. I'm manufacturing new things as if I were a one-woman factory. I feel I've only got six months left, and I want to give these women everything I've got."

One Thursday before class, Therese approached me, unsteadily, with a fistful of money. I also noticed she had a black eye. *Accident? Drunkenness? Domestic violence?* My face must have registered my concern.

"I fell down some stairs," she said, brushing her bruised eye with her free hand, "and hit my face."

I remembered how my mother used to lie about the true cause of her black eyes, but I didn't press Therese. "*Je suis desolé,*" I said, and turned my attention to the money.

"This is for you," she said, "for teaching here — 15,000 CFA [about $30]. We want to thank you."

I explained to her that as a Peace Corps volunteer I was not permitted to accept payment for my work, but I suggested we use the money to have a *fête* for my students. Therese agreed.

With the money, I bought ingredients for the dessert recipes I'd taught them — the same banana-nut cake I'd made for Antoinette's wedding, and the crêpes they'd so enjoyed learning how to make. I divided the ingredients among four willing attendees, asking them to make one of the recipes and bring it the following week to our *fête*.

On the day of our party, we had two cakes and two batches of crêpes (with four different fillings I'd brought) proudly arrayed on the front table. I also brought fresh lemon syrup I'd made for lemonade (thanks to a fruit-laden, old lemon tree I'd discovered in an abandoned, overgrown orchard behind my house), plus two dozen plastic cups and seven quart bottles of filtered water — all of which Youssef helped me carry down the hill.

At first the women were subdued, sitting quietly in a circle of chairs around the room. But then, little by little, they began to get up and dance African dances and sing African songs. Watching their happiness, I thought I couldn't be happier. But I was wrong: One of the women, a young mother named Veronique, brought her chubby newborn baby girl up to me to show me. Then she told me her new baby's name: Bonnie.

Simple Tropical Jam

Combine any of the following fruit: papaya, mango, passion fruit, banana, and/or pineapple — peeled and cut in chunks — with an equal amount, by weight, of sugar, in a heavy pot and cook, uncovered, over a low flame, stirring frequently, until thickened. Spoon into sterilized jars, seal tightly, and upturn the jars until cooled.

Henriette

[T]he older women … usually have children willing and able to support them. If they have not, their state is, like that of all old childless women in Africa, a very desolate one.
— MARY KINGSLEY, *Travels in West Africa*

Martha Cooper

All this while I'd been calling her by her last name

*O*n a Sunday morning in late July 1998, while Youssef was visiting a *chantier* for the weekend to take photos, a young man, dressed for church in a dark suit and tie, walked determinedly toward my house. I hadn't planned to go to church that morning. I hadn't planned to go anywhere, in fact. It was one of those days when I needed to be quiet and alone, when I didn't have the social energy to say "*Bonjour! ça va?*" to anyone. As I watched the young man approach on the gravel driveway, with his head lowered and his hands clenched, I wondered who he could be and what he might want. *Had the church sent him to get me? No, that couldn't be. Was he bringing bad news of Youssef?*

"It's *maman* Henriette," he told me when I greeted him at the door. "She is gravely ill — in the hospital." He was out of breath and perspiring in his hot suit, which wasn't suited to this climate. He looked uncomfortable in his role as a messenger of ominous news.

My mind ran in circles looking for someone I knew by the name of Henriette, but I couldn't connect that name to anyone's face in my memory.

"Henriette?" I asked the young man. "*Qui est Henriette?*"

"La vieille au marché" (the old woman at the market), he said. "She asked me to get you right away."

"Leora?" I asked him. *"Maman* Leora?"

He nodded sadly. *"La même"* (the same).

I quickly gathered up some things for her — clean bed sheets, a pillow and pillow case, towels, bath soap, drinking water, and food — and walked with the young man to the hospital, as though I were family.

Almost every morning since my arrival in Lastoursville twenty months before, I had visited with *maman* Leora at the *marché*. It was one of the aspects of my daily regimen that I most cherished: I sat beside her on the rough wooden bench behind the rickety wood table where she sold her *saucisson* sandwiches, and I held her small, leathery, skeletal, arthritic hand in mine. We shared news and told each other stories from our lives. We told each other, *"Je t'aime."* She often said, "I think of you all the time," and "When you appear at the *marché*, my heart is filled with happiness," and "I want you to stay here forever."

She told me many times, as though she'd never told me before, about her early years in the coastal city of Port Gentil, when she was young and her husband, a policeman, was alive, and she worked as a cook for a certain rich French woman. She shared simple recipes with me, such as sautéed fish fillets with sorrel sauce that she used to prepare for that woman for dinner. I told her I used to cook for rich people, too, in New York; she and I had a lot in common.

I brought Leora samples of things I'd made at home, such as yeasted cornbread rolls and banana beignets, which she savored. From the Lebanese grocery store closest to the *marché* I bought her a cold bottle of her favorite drink, Coke, which she called "Coca," and brought it to her, with its beads of condensation dripping down the shapely green sides. She sipped the fizzy elixir delicately, as though it were Champagne.

I gave her a carved stone mask pendant, a souvenir from my trip to Zimbabwe, telling her it was for good luck and good health. She wore it every day from then on.

On Mother's Day, the "*Fêtes des Mamans*" holiday in Gabon, Sunday, May 26, 1997, nine months into my service in Lastoursville, I walked to Leora's house after church, bearing gifts of cold Coke and a loaf of my homemade bread. When I asked directions to get there, I was told her house was a mile out of town, in the opposite direction from mine, on the road to Koula Moutu. "It's a small house," I was told, "with a bar next door. You won't miss it."

If Leora hadn't been outside her front door tending to some scraggly plants when I walked by, I might well have missed it. I might have thought, *No, no one could live in such a tumbledown shack.* By this time, I had lived in Lastoursville long enough to have seen innumerable humble mud-wattle houses, but I'd never seen one so solitary and squalid as this. This small, wood-plank structure, barely standing, stood alone in a clearing just off the main road, with only a ramshackle bar nearby.

To be an old, poor, childless woman with no living family members or clan connections in this society, I could see, was to be an outcast. Here in the interior of the country, where poverty, by American monetary measures, was the norm, Leora lived so far below this norm I could hardly believe my eyes. *How can this be? How does she survive?* I wondered. Surely oil-rich, timber-rich, magnesium-rich Gabon, with a population of little more than one million — very few of whom live much beyond 60 — could afford to provide for its elderly citizens, I thought. Shouldn't she receive some sort of pension, from her husband's police work, at least? Leora was a devout Catholic; couldn't her Church help her? But I could never bring myself to ask her such personal questions.

She was surprised to see me that Mother's Day, but also pleased, I could see. I wished her a "*bonne fêtes des mamans,*" gave her my small gifts, and she invited me inside. The interior of her home was so dark it took a moment for my eyes to adjust. The air was so heavy I found it hard to breathe. Were the windows boarded up for her protection? Did she fear that someone from the bar next door might do her harm in the night?

She motioned to me to sit in her one chair, a straight-backed, wooden chair that was unsteady on its legs. She sat on a low wooden stool beside me, and as always, we held hands.

"No one ever comes to visit me," she said with a wry little laugh, "so I only need one chair."

She had no kitchen, just a two-burner hotplate fueled by bottled gas that sat on an old, roughly constructed, wooden kitchen table. She had no running water and no electricity.

I could see in the small adjoining room, she had one narrow wood-frame bed with no mosquito netting above it, and piles of dust-covered cardboard boxes lined the walls. In the main room, where we sat, there was an ancient breakfront, where she told me she kept her glassware and plates.

She got up and reached into the breakfront to pull out a gift for me — a small, glass pitcher with yellow and red birds painted on it. "*Pour ma fille*," she said. I hugged her small, sinewy body and thanked her. As ever, her skin smelled of wood smoke and loam.

Above the breakfront, tacked to the wall, were photos of Leora and her husband when they were young. She pointed them out to me proudly.

"*Il eté beau*" (he was handsome), she said, as if she were still young and in love. I could tell from his face that he must have been a kind, earnest man — a lot like Youssef.

On those rare occasions when Leora was not at the *marché* when I arrived, and I was told by the other *marchandes* there that she was ill at home, I would go again to her house to see her. The problem, she explained to me the first time, was her asthma; she had run out of her medication, Ventoline. Although it was against Peace Corps policy, I agreed to provide her inhalers from then on.

The young man led me to Leora's hospital room, where she was asleep, curled up, fully clothed in her faded *pagne* and blouse, on a stained, worn, unmade mattress on the rusted metal hospital bed.

"*Voici son carnet de santé*" (here is her health record), he said, taking the passport-size booklet from the metal table by her bed and handing it to me.

I read the name on it, the way the Gabonese write them, last name first: LIGHORA, HENRIETTE, and I felt ashamed. All this while I had been calling her by her last name, which sounded like Leora to me, thinking it was her first name. All this while I hadn't even known her real name.

"Are you family?" I asked him.

"*Non, madame,*" he said, and he shook his head and left.

"*Maman?*" I said, touching her boney shoulder to wake her. "*Je suis là*" (I am here).

For the moment, we were alone in the dingy hospital room. The unmade bed beside hers was empty, so I lifted her gently under her arms — she was as light as a small child — and sat her on the other bed, while I spread clean sheets on hers. Following in the tradition Albert Schweitzer had begun in Lambaréné, families, not nurses, took care of their hospitalized loved ones at the medical center in Lastoursville. But how much could I do? Could I install netting over her bed and nail screening to the open window, to help prevent her from getting malaria on top of the illness that brought her in? Could I bring a brush and bucket and scrub the stained and muddy brown walls with disinfectant to make the room more sanitary? Did Schweitzer envision the limitations families face in maintaining hospital standards?

I tucked Henriette between the clean sheets and offered her a sip of water and a bite of bread before she laid her head on the pillow.

"*Qu'est-ce-que se pas?*" I asked her.

"I almost died," she said.

The next day, after Youssef returned from the *chantier*, when we visited Henriette at the hospital together, bringing her fresh food and water, we found she was no longer alone in her room. A young Senegalese mother named Fatimata, whom Youssef and I knew from Lastoursville's Muslim community, was in the next bed, having just arrived, dizzy, weak and seriously ill from *le palu*. She was alone, and no one was attending her, so Youssef went to see what he could do.

"The nurses claim they have run out of cotton and alcohol," Youssef reported when he returned to the room a short while later. "So they can't hook Fatimata up to an IV."

Incensed, I marched over to a nurse I knew in another department and asked her for some cotton and alcohol, which she willingly gave me. I asked her whether she knew what was wrong with Henriette Lighora. She said, "Yes. She is very old."

Henriette ate some of the soup and bread that I had brought and told me it made her feel much better. Youssef filled a bucket with water from the hospital's outdoor spigot and brought it to *Maman* so she could bathe herself with the washcloth and soap I'd brought. What else could I do? Was she, in fact, able to bathe herself or should I do it for her? I hadn't brought her a change of clothes. I hadn't brought her a tooth brush. Was she strong enough to get out of bed and walk to the latrine outside? If not, how would she relieve herself? Should I be doing more? If so, what? How? I agonized over the cultural barriers I couldn't seem to scale.

Youssef and I stayed until Fatimata was hooked up to the IV that would deliver her antimalarial medication.

The next morning Youssef prepared a Senegalese fish stew with rice to bring to "our patients," both of whom had been given prescriptions for medicines they couldn't afford to buy, so I went to the pharmacy and bought them for them — $30 worth, out of my own pocket. Although doing so was *interdit*, and I as a volunteer living on a small monthly allowance couldn't afford it, how could I not? We all were, in a sense, family.

Sautéed Fillets of Fish with Sorrel Sauce

4 serving-size fillets of white fish, such as sole or flounder (about 6 ounces each)

    2 tablespoons all-purpose flour
    ½ teaspoon salt
    ¼ teaspoon freshly ground pepper
    ¼ cup unsalted butter (4 ounces)

For sauce:

    1 pound fresh sorrel, washed, stemmed, and chopped
    1 cup heavy cream
    Salt and pepper to taste

Rinse the fish fillets and pat dry. Season with salt and pepper, and dust with flour on both sides. Melt the butter in a large skillet and cook the fillets for about 4 minutes on each side. Carefully transfer them to a heated platter and keep warm.

Add the chopped sorrel to the skillet and cook, stirring constantly, until wilted. Add the cream and continue to cook, stirring, until the sauce has reduced to a thick, green puree. Serve sauce over the fish or on the side. Makes 4 servings.

· · ·

Senegalese Fish Stew with Rice
(adapted from *The New York Times*)

½ cup vegetable oil, such as peanut oil
1 large onion, chopped
3 to 4 cloves garlic, minced
2 to 3 hot peppers, such as habañeros (or to taste),
   seeded and minced
3 tablespoons tomato paste
1 can diced tomatoes, with juice
4 cups homemade chicken stock, or canned chicken broth
2 carrots, peeled and cut into chunks
1 small butternut squash, peeled and cut into chunks
1 head cauliflower or green cabbage, cored, and
   cut into six pieces
1 small eggplant cut into six pieces
3 cups uncooked, long-grain white rice
2 whole red snappers (about 2½ pounds total),
   cleaned, scaled, and cut into thirds

In a large, flameproof casserole or stockpot, sauté the onion, garlic and hot pepper in oil until soft. Add the tomato paste, canned tomatoes, and chicken stock, plus 3 cups water and bring to a boil.

Add carrots and squash chunks, lower heat to simmer, and cook 5 minutes. Add cabbage or cauliflower and eggplant; cover and cook another 5 minutes. Add fish pieces and cook 5 minutes more, or until fish is cooked through and vegetables are fork-tender.

Carefully transfer vegetables and fish from stew to a platter; cover with foil and place in a warm oven. Ladle 6 cups of stew liquid into a large pot, cover, and bring to a boil over high heat. Add rice, stir well, cover, turn flame to low and cook until tender and all broth has been absorbed (about 15-20 minutes).

Spoon a portion of rice onto each of six plates. Add one piece of fish to each, along with some vegetables. Ladle stew liquid over each plate and serve. Makes 6 servings.

The Still of the Night

In the still of the night
I held you, held you tight
'Cause I love you, love you so ...
— FIVE SATINS' LYRICS

I t's a hot night. I'm sitting at the makeshift desk in my study, working on my first-ever quilt, listening to the summery sounds outside my window. Nearby, soprano crickets and baritone toads sing repetitive duets. Youssef is away for the weekend, taking pictures at a logging camp upriver. I am alone in my house on this hot African night.

The teenage boy who lives across the road is playing his favorite, fifties doo-op music: It's "In the Still of the Night" right now. Memories try to waft through the window with the music, but I wave them away.

Down the road, at the *Maison des Spectacles*, there's a revival meeting going on. The preacher's fierce "Hal-le-lu-iah!"'s punctuate every sentence. No, every phrase. People are whooped-up, cheering, clapping; now they're breaking into song. I hear mostly female voices. Although I attended a gospel church for years when I was in my teens, I can't recognize the hymn.

Question: *Is this a dream?*

Where are we? What year is it? Suburban New Jersey, where I grew up, circa 1956? Has anyone walked on the moon? Has Princess

Di been born? Is the World Wide Web even a filament in anyone's imagination?

The Five Satins' smooth words pull me back, against my will, to the time when my big brother used to dance with me to this song. It was the mid-fifties, he was in his mid-teens — just a few years away from joining the Marines — and I was about ten. He'd put this 45 on the record player in our living room and hold out his arms to me tentatively. "Let's dance," he'd say, and all of a sudden, like magic, I'd feel like Cinderella at the ball. He was a handsome boy but shy with girls, and I knew even then that I was only for practice.

He took small steps. His body was stiff, and he hardly spoke, except to scold: "Follow my lead!" or "Keep your weight on the balls of your feet!" I kept my mouth shut, tried my best to follow, and wondered where, exactly, the balls were on my feet.

My brother was my hero then; and for me, slow dancing with him in the living room to "In the Still of the Night" was heaven itself. My face reached only to his chest, so my cheek would sometimes brush against his soft, plaid-flannel shirt. I was close enough, too, to smell the Old Spice aftershave he'd just begun to wear. I knew the name because I read the label on the cone-shaped bottle when I sat on the edge of the tub admiring him as he shaved in front of the bathroom mirror. He used a strop and straight razor he'd inherited from our Scottish grandfather, along with our grandpop's black, beetle-shaped car we all called the "Oldmobile."

My brother was dead serious about his new shaving ritual. He waved the four-inch straight razor in front of me once and said, "This thing could slit your throat."

But I felt safe in his arms when we danced, and the music was transporting. The voices were men's, deep and rich. I'd close my eyes and pretend we were somewhere else, a place where grown men were strong enough to be still. A place where love lived longer than the duration of a dance.

My big brother and two younger sisters and I were alone at home. Our father was out drinking, our mother was with him, and my brother had to babysit his baby sisters. His thoughts as he and I danced, I knew, were elsewhere too — maybe on the upcoming junior prom and who he might ask to go with him. Or maybe he was thinking of the other things he could be doing if he didn't have to stay home on a Saturday afternoon and babysit us. Baseball with his buddies, probably. My brother loved baseball.

Or maybe he was thinking the worst: What our father might say or do when he came home drunk. Tell us again that we kids were "stupid and good-for-nothing," that we "never should have been born," that we would "never amount to anything," that he hated his life in this little suburban New Jersey town, that marriage to our mother and having us kids were his "biggest mistakes."

Maybe in his drunken rage he would try to hit us again, and as he approached to swing at me, my brother would stand in the way and take the blow instead.

As my brother and I danced and he rocked me slowly, as if in a cradle, I tried to think only of how lovely and soothing the music was, how lucky I was to be dancing with my hero, who smelled so sweetly of Old Spice, and how much I wished that time would stop right there, right in the middle of "In the Still of the Night."

Music, like fragrance, transports us involuntarily.

No.

I snap myself back to reality. It's a Saturday night in late January in the steamy rainforest of equatorial Africa two years from the new millennium. I'm working on piecing my first patchwork quilt. It's one of the many projects that occupies my hands and mind here, keeps me from knowing the meaning of the words "bored" or "good for nothing."

It's the first time I've ever had the luxury of enough spare time to sit quietly and hand-sew a whole patchwork quilt. I don't own a TV. I don't have a phone. I don't have a car, or a washing machine, or air conditioning, either. Sometimes I listen to the Voice of America on a battery-operated shortwave radio. Mostly, when I'm alone, I just sit quietly and listen to the sounds of the night.

Each piece of fabric in this quilt I'm making will add to the story of my two years in Lastoursville. This triangle, for example, with the yellow umbrellas on it, represents all the RAIN we get here. The red strip with the babies on it stands for the maternal-infant clinic where I teach. This piece, with the blue fish swimming nose-to-tail, is for my "fish head" postmate, Morgan, better known among us Gabon PCVs as "the motorcycle mamma of Mana-Mana." This brick-red bit stands for the impossible soil I first encountered in my back garden, and this muddy-brown patch is what all the roads here look like right after the RAIN. You get the idea.

The revival meeting is still going strong. I imagine it to be heavily attended by the wives of those men who are spending this otherwise quiet Saturday night at one of the many local bars, drinking beers and paying bleary-eyed attention to pretty, young women who don't sing hymns. I know these pretty, single women. I sell them condoms so they might help protect themselves against *le SIDA*, as a part of my job as a health volunteer.

For those who prefer not to find their spirits in a bar, God is very big here. Faith is a powerful elixir when things look close to hopeless: When your husband spends his whole paycheck on alcohol and other women, when you can't feed your kids the way you know you should, when you can't afford the twelve-dollar bottle of medicine for your youngest's bout with malaria or the six-dollar bed-netting to keep the malaria-carrying mosquitoes from biting your sleeping children in the first place.

What can you do when you've been born in a tiny, little-known country that's close to *dernier* place in the world's mad race? (Question: *Race toward what?*) Well, you could choose to join your sisters on a hot Saturday night and sing and pray and shout Hal-le-lu-iah and trust that God, like some rare, good daddy, will make it all better.

As for the teenage Gabonese boy across the street: He's fascinated by all things American; especially, right now, American music. But not rap, disco, or jazz, or even rock and roll. At the moment his tastes are turning to fifties doo-op. He's a bright kid, a student in the English class I teach in my living room every Friday night. His English is good. His dream, like that of most of the students in my highly motivated but sparsely attended free class, is to get a scholarship to an American university and live in the USA. He believes life is perfect in the Land of the Free.

Who am I to disabuse him?

This boy's hope, his prayer, in the still of these hot nights in this small timeless town is to leave his country, his continent and to run in the big race wearing genuine Nikes and try to catch up.

Of course, when this, my first of maybe many quilts, is finished, it will be decorative only. Not exactly a thing of beauty, this homely hodge-podge mélange of scrap African fabrics will be a conversation piece at best. If anyone asks, I'll share its story. I won't use it on my bed at night here, that's for sure. The nights are far too hot here.

Mapping Africa

It was a curious thing that I myself did not, during this time, ever believe that I would … leave Africa. … I kept on believing that I should come to lay my bones in Africa. For this firm faith I had no other foundation, or no other reason, than my complex incompetency of imagining anything else.

ISAK DINESEN, *Out of Africa*

Merchant selling puppet in Segou, Mali —
"I think you'd love this town"

When Youssef was home, we would sit in my study in the evenings and talk quietly together. As my close of service approached, we talked mostly about the future. Where could we go after Gabon? *What should we do?*

One thing had become clear to me in the course of the year since we'd met: I could not leave this man and return to my previous life in Manhattan. I could not live alone again in a tiny one-room apartment, struggling to survive in the gray, cold, soulless city. I felt I could not start over elsewhere in the States, either, at the age of fifty-three, single, unemployed, and feeling sidelined. I could not envision living through days that didn't begin with the words, "*Je t'aime beaucoup, cherie.*"

Repeatedly I confessed to my journal: I can't go back to that. I can't go backwards. Backwards is not an option.

Youssef felt similarly. "*Il faut que nous restons toujours ensemble*" (we must stay together always), he told me earnestly.

So we studied the globe together. Neither the United States nor anywhere in Europe we could think of would work for us because we felt the industrialized, so-called "first world" was notoriously racist, sexist, and ageist; and we knew we were too thin-skinned to withstand the inevitable discrimination we would face as a couple that seemingly broke all their unwritten rules. We narrowed our choices to the continent of Africa, where Youssef would more likely be accepted anywhere and where I might feel adopted.

In numerous letters to Marty, who was managing the sublet of my apartment in New York, I tried to share my reasoning and solicit her always cool and rational thoughts. "I would like to live where my low-tech talents can be best put to good use," I wrote to her some months before my scheduled departure. "That just about narrows the globe to the Third World. And of all the places in the Third World, Africa interests me the most. Francophone Africa, to be more specific, because I still haven't mastered this second language, and I'm still determined to do so. ... Please trust that I'm doing my best to make the best of the hand that's been dealt me. You were given different cards than I. ... The world is big, and I don't want to be confined to one room in it anymore. ... Please let me know your thinking. ..."

For many months I'd been writing letters to nongovernmental organizations worldwide that focused their efforts on food and nutrition, inquiring about the prospects of my finding a job in Africa along the lines of the community health and nutrition work I'd been doing in Gabon. Most of these letters went unacknowledged. One of the few to respond to me was the World Health Organization in Geneva. They informed me that the minimum requirements for the type of position I was seeking were a master's degree, at least three-to-five years' experience in the field, computer savvy, and foreign-language fluency.

In addition, they made it clear that even for those who met these minimum requirements, the competition was stiff. "Very often," their letter stated, "there may be hundreds of applicants for a single vacancy notice." With no master's degree, only two years' experience as a community health volunteer, no computer skills, and still-far-from-fluent French, I knew I would have to find my own way. With only the puppet-making, bread-baking, and compost-preaching talents I possessed, I couldn't begin to compete for anything like a WHO job.

When I left New York for the Peace Corps, Marty had given me a large map of Africa, which I'd hung on one wall of my study in Lastoursville. Most evenings in the months before our departure, Youssef and I would sit in front of it, as if watching a movie screen, waiting for the sound track to reveal some clues. Sipping our night-cap glass of cheap Spanish red wine and studying the map, we discussed the possibilities.

South Africa? Perhaps. But Youssef couldn't speak English and wasn't especially keen to learn.

Zimbabwe? No. I'd been back the Christmas before I met Youssef and found the whites I encountered there to be as racist as ever. Privately, I'd heard some refer to Africans as "ants."

Nigeria? No. Youssef had told me most Nigerians despise whites; it wouldn't be at all safe for me there.

East Africa? Neither of us had been there, but it seemed too Anglophone.

Togo? Youssef had been there once, briefly, and said he liked what he saw; but he had heard rumors of political instability in the face of their upcoming elections.

Burkina Faso? A possibility. We'd have to look at it more closely.

Morocco? I'd been there on a food writers' junket a few years before and loved it — especially the food, art, textiles, music, and culture. As a Muslim, French-speaking country, Morocco might be a good choice for Youssef, we felt; but as a mixed couple, we probably would have trouble fitting in.

We needed to find a racially tolerant country, ideally Francophone and preferably hospitable to Muslims. Over time, after weighing the pros and cons, by a process of elimination, we found that country: Mali. Tolerance, Youssef told me, was an integral part of Mali's national creed. The nomadic desert people of the north, the Tuaregs and Moors, were fairer skinned than those of the southern ethnic groups, such as Youssef's, Malinke. "People of all colors and all religions live together in peace," he said. "And older people, especially older women, in Mali, are revered. Age means wisdom. Age is a plus." Before long, I referred to Mali in my journal as "my destiny."

As if on cue, a friend in the States sent me a copy of a newly released memoir called *Fishing in the Sky*, by a man from New England named Donald Lawder, who, at the age of sixty-six in 1983, after having raised a family and gotten divorced, joined the Peace Corps and was sent to serve as an English teacher in Bamako, Mali. There, Lawder fell in love with the culture, the people, and ultimately a beautiful young Malian woman. He writes with wonder at this opportunity for a second life, in this place where age and human interrelations are viewed so differently than they are in the U.S. Lawder was so in love with Mali he decided to remain there for the rest of his life.

At first, Youssef and I too considered making a new life in Mali's capital, Bamako. I'd read — and tried to translate the English aloud for Youssef — in the Introduction to his new *Seydou Keita* book:

> According to the writings of the Arab marabout Sidi Mahamane, Bamako was destined to become a large city inhabited by many races and tribes on both banks of the river. The early citizens set out to fulfill the prophesy that 'every new settler, whatever their origin, their religion or their trade, will feel at home.' ... The city later became a hub, an enormous crossroads where all races and tribes came together. Bamako was the capital of French Sudan, and it was a good place to live.

When I wrote to Marty of this plan, she quickly shared her

views. She'd traveled to Mali after her visit to me in Gabon, and she found Bamako to be too hot, too overcrowded and congested, and too chaotic. "I know you'd hate it," she told me. She enclosed with this letter a photo she'd taken in Segou, Mali, of a Malian shop-keeper wearing a blue-and-white skull cap and a purple, flowing boubou, and holding up a carved, wooden puppet that he had for sale. In Mali, Marty informed me, the people use puppets (*mari-onnettes*) in their storytelling traditions, unlike most other African countries where mostly masks are employed. On the back of this photo Marty wrote: "Marionette from Segou. I think you'd love this town."

Puppets? I'd been in love with puppets all my life, ever since I'd been entranced by the fifties kids show "Kukla, Fran, and Ollie" on TV. I especially loved the five hand puppets I'd made for giving health presentations, in skits and songs, for the elementary school children of Lastoursville — as did the children themselves.

When I asked Youssef about puppets' use in Mali, he remem-bered that every year in a village called Markala, not far from Segou on the Niger River, the Bambara people hold an enormous *Fêtes des Marionnettes*, which has become world-renown. The puppets they make for this celebration are larger-than-life-size, he said, repre-senting both mythic animals and symbolic people, who, through accompanying drums, dancing, and singing, tell stories of the peo-ple's origins and their relationship to the animals and the earth.

"Have you been?" I asked him.

"*Pas encore*," he said, adding, "but we must go when we get to Mali."

That clinched it. Malians love puppets, and I love puppets. *That's where I belong,* I said to myself.

Although he himself was born and raised in Abidjan, Côte d'Ivoire, Youssef's parents were originally from Mali. He spoke the predom-inant Malian language, Bambara, and he had many relatives there.

He told me he even had family in Segou: a kind cousin with a big house and a generous heart.

"Perhaps we could stay with him until we get settled," Youssef said. Segou, he added, is an ancient city, rich in history; small enough to be unintimidating, yet large enough to offer opportunities. It also has good soil and thriving agriculture, he said, in addition to a welcoming family.

"Well," I said, "it looks like it's Segou, Mali, for us."

Mud Oven

If you can make mud pies, you can make your own
wood-fired oven out of earth.

— KIKO DENZER, *Build Your Own Earth Oven*

Teaching bread-baking at chantier *CEB*

They called it "*la crise*" — the crisis. The impact of the Asian economic crisis of 1997 on Gabon's logging industry became evident even in Lastoursville by mid-1998. Okoume log exports to China, the largest single importer of Gabonese wood, dropped by about 50 percent between 1997 and 1998; as a result, the volume of unsold logs doubled in early 1998, which led to a production freeze. Many logging companies had to lay workers off. For the people at the *chantiers*, this was *la crise*.

For Youssef, whose photographic clientele were primarily West African workers at the nearby *chantiers*, the situation became distressing also. When he returned to the logging camps with the developed photographs his clients had commissioned, they couldn't pay him. When he sought new work, they couldn't oblige. As much as they depended on recent photos of themselves and their children, dressed in their newest finery, to tell the stories of their lives in Gabon to far-off family members in Mali, Senegal, or Chad, they couldn't afford to do so. Their work had come to a standstill. They weren't being paid.

Youssef and I discussed *la crise* in the evening in my study before going to bed. He explained to me the cause of it and its trickle-down effect on the local economy as well as on his own photographic career. I could see he was discouraged that his dream of becoming a successful professional freelance photographer was being stymied by this situation, but he was not despairing. In his years of traveling in Africa, he had learned many skills, not the least of which was to survive, with his dignity intact. He had experience working in restaurants, in forestry, and in construction. Together we explored his alternatives, and together we came up with a plan.

In early May, with Youssef's help, I wrote a proposal to the French director of one of the five largest logging companies in Gabon, *La Compagnie Équatoriale des Bois* (CEB), located at Bambidie, about a 40-minute drive south of Lastoursville. Bev had a church in Bambidie and was on cordial terms with the CEB director, Mr. Pasquier, whom she described as "a decent man." She had suggested we approach him with our plan.

I proposed to Mr. Pasquier that he hire Youssef as a consultant to teach some of CEB's laid-off workers how to build traditional, wood-burning, mud-brick bread ovens — one of the skills Youssef had acquired in his West African travels. In addition, I proposed that I, as Youssef's partner in this endeavor, could — as a free bonus, since I was a volunteer who could not accept payment — give bread-baking classes at CEB to whomever wished to attend.

In the proposal I stressed the benefits of this project: It would give CEB workers something creative and constructive to do with their time; it would provide them with a new and lasting skill; it would lift their spirits and take their minds off of *la crise*. The project, I went on, would cost CEB next to nothing, since the building material, primarily sandy-clayey subsoil — of which Gabon had no shortage — would come straight from nature, and CEB had no shortage of fire wood; it would give Pasquier himself a proud showpiece for foreign visitors and journalists; and, best of all, it would provide the opportunity for everyone in the logging camp to have access to healthy, home-baked bread.

Good bread, Youssef had often told me, was impossible to obtain at the *chantiers'* food stores, even at the best of times. It was not like bread at all, he said; more like long, white, rubbery wands of under-cooked dough. Our proposed bread project, I wrote to Pasquier, had the potential to turn at least one aspect of *la crise* into a plus.

Not trusting the postal system, I entrusted the proposal to Bev, who hand-delivered it to Pasquier the next time she drove to Bambidie. He responded immediately. He arrived at my front door unexpectedly one day soon after, while I was alone, making lunch. I saw that he was about my age, tall and tanned and very handsome, I thought, in a rugged, care-worn, weathered way. He said he was in a hurry *("très pressé!");* he couldn't stay for lunch as I'd suggested *("mais, merci pour l'invitation");* but he wanted to tell me — in his fast Parisian-French, which my mind had to race after to follow — that he liked my idea, and, yes, he would like to go ahead with the plan, just as soon as he returned from a holiday with his family in France. We made a date to meet at Bambidie on Sunday afternoon, May 31 to discuss the details.

The French have a handy expression, *"les mots d'escalier,"* meaning the things you remember you should have said — after it's too late. It was only after Mr. Pasquier had hurriedly driven off in his red pickup truck that I thought I should have told him two important things — mud ovens must be made in the dry season, which meant *soon*, and Youssef and I would be leaving Lastoursville in just four months.

Monday, June 1, 1998 — 7:37 am:

Yesterday at Bambidie went well, despite the fact that Mr. Pasquier hadn't returned from France yet. Embarrassed by this, Benoit, Pasquier's young and eager assistant, asked Youssef and me to stay for lunch, but the other [French] foresters at our lunch table didn't bother to speak to us or acknowledge our presence.

The good part was that we were able to give our presentation, including the drawings and the list of materials, to Benoit, and he listened politely and intelligently. He promised to pass all the information on to Mr. Pasquier when he gets back. Benoit seemed to think the project will be no problem to do.

One month later, on the first of July, Mr. Pasquier, clearly a man under great stress, stopped by my house again briefly to make another date to discuss arrangements. "Come to Bambidie this Sunday," he said, "at 11 am." I told him we would be there, and I would bring bread. And this time I remembered to tell him that Youssef and I would be leaving Lastoursville in September, just before the rainy season, and that mud bricks must dry in the sun, during the dry season. "*Oui, d'accord*," he said before speeding away, hunched over his steering wheel.

Monday, July 6, 1998 — 6:45 am:

We went to CEB yesterday, just-baked bread in hand, and we waited, mostly at the clubhouse, for Mr. Pasquier to show up; but he never did. Benoit tried to reach him on the car radio, but without success. Benoit thought maybe Pasquier had gone hunting, having forgotten our appointment to meet. But why hadn't he taken his hunting dog, "Champagne," along with him? It remained a mystery.

Nevertheless, Y. and I had lunch at the clubhouse with the other foresters — the handful of regulars, plus a new handful of young men, French university students studying forestry, out here for the summer. There were about a dozen white Frenchmen in all at the table with us, but not one of them engaged us in conversation. ("Please pass the butter," doesn't count.) Ignorance? Bad manners? Racism? Ageism? Anti-Americanism? All of the above?

Anyway, the meal, prepared by the Senegalese (Muslim, of the Malinke tribe, like Youssef) chef de cuisine there, Segou, was delicious:

First course: Fresh sardines on lettuce with lemon
Main course: Beef brochettes with onions; haricots verts
Dessert: Crêpes with four kinds of *confitures*.

Before the meal, while still waiting for Mr. Pasquier to drive up any minute, Y. and I took a tour of the vegetable garden, then visited with Segou and his assistant as they tended the wood on the grill. They talked with us, of course. Segou shared his thoughts about our travel plans. He's a warm, open, intelligent, thoughtful person — not like the above-mentioned Frenchmen. Benoit, though, was kind enough to drive Y. and me all the way home.

At last, in mid-September, only days before our departure from Gabon, Youssef and I visited CEB for the fourth and last time. As we had in the past, we hitchhiked from Lastoursville to Bambidie in the back of a beat-up pickup truck, were let off near the camp entrance and walked the mile-long, winding road that led to the Frenchmen's high-beamed clubhouse.

On our previous visit in August, Youssef had shown Benoit and some of his handpicked African workmen how to make and dry the mud bricks: how to identify the best clayey soil, how to mix it with sand and straw-like fiber, how to mold it into small uniform bricks and let them dry in the baking sun.

This time, with Mr. Pasquier and several of his foremen present, Youssef was able to demonstrate, with all of the materials Benoit had gathered together beforehand, the construction of a traditional outdoor bread oven — from the foundation made of stone and rubble; to the perfectly level, flat-brick oven floor; to the dome made of the dried mud-bricks, plastered over thickly with more clayey mud. This oven was to be the prototype for others to follow throughout the *chantier*.

"When this mud dries," Youssef said confidently, as if he'd been giving these demonstrations for years, instead of now for the first time, "you can fire up the oven — *petit à petit*, so it doesn't crack

— and in a few hours' time, you'll be able to bake your bread. Just push the hot coals over to the sides with a long stick, wipe the bricks clean, and place the bread dough on the oven floor. Then close the door... *et, voilà, après quelque minutes, le bon pain!*"

That afternoon, in the Africans' meetinghouse filled with straight-backed wooden chairs, I gave a demonstration at the front table on how to bake bread. Some of the French foresters attended, as well as African CEB workers and their wives and children — about two dozen adults in all. I posted my *"Pain Americain"* recipe on the wall behind me, and as I taught I could see many people taking notes.

"This bread," I said, as always, waving a French baguette I'd brought from the bakery in Lastoursville, "is good. But *this* bread" — I showed them my own, round, golden loaf I'd brought from home — "is much better because it's filled with more goodness. And soon you'll be able to make bread like mine in your own bread ovens here at CEB!"

By this time, in the two years I'd been in Gabon, I'd taught the same bread baking lesson nearly one hundred times. But I was far from tired of it. I knew I would never tire of it. For me, making bread was a labor of love, a near-religious experience, and teaching bread baking was something I did with passionate, indefatigable, missionary-like zeal.

Mr. Pasquier paid Youssef generously for his work and assured us he would follow through in seeing that bread ovens were built at his forestry camp in the very near future, before the heavy rains came, and while his workers still had time on their hands, thanks to *la crise*. He wished us well in our travels and told us he looked forward to the day when he could leave Gabon forever too. He shook our hands. Then his assistant Benoit drove Youssef and me home in the cab of his pickup.

Vanilla Sister

Of all the orchids, the vanilla family is the only one that produces an agriculturally valuable crop, as distinct from orchids which are cultivated and traded simply for their decorative value.

— TIM ECOTT, *Vanilla*

Yolande with her son Alix

Martha Cooper

efore I left for Gabon in mid-1996, I had what I briefly thought was a brilliant idea. It was both a thought — an inspired one, I felt — and a gut feeling, not something I had spent time researching. I thought I would introduce vanilla growing at my Peace Corps post and thereby single-handedly raise, exponentially, I felt sure, the standard of living of the people around me. To the extent that I had thought this through, my reasoning went like this: Vanilla is a tropical plant; Gabon is a tropical country. Vanilla beans are precious and costly; the poor people in the country's interior would profit from growing and selling them. *Why hadn't anyone else thought of this?* I wondered.

When I first shared these thoughts with my Gabonese "sister," Yolande Borobo, with whom I lived during my Peace Corps training in Libreville and with whom I gratefully stayed during every subsequent trip from Lastoursville to Libreville for my in-service training, she rolled her eyes and laughed.

"Vanilla? *Here?* Vanilla growing takes *work*," she said to me in English, one of the several languages she spoke fluently, "hard, dirty work. And we Gabonese don't like that kind of work. We don't like to get our hands dirty. We prefer to work in air-conditioned offices." She laughed again, flashing a gleaming smile and waving a manicured hand. "Oh, *cherie*, you'll have to choose a better project than that. Ditch the vanilla idea."

From then on, she called me her "Vanilla Sister," a term of endearment that both fit and stuck.

Yolande, who worked in a modern, air-conditioned office as the private secretary for an oil executive in Libreville and whose work wardrobe consisted of fitted suits and tailored dresses she'd bought on her frequent trips to New York and Paris, was right, of course. Vanilla, I subsequently learned, is the most labor-intensive agricultural product in the world; and this was not the type of work the Gabonese preferred.

Furthermore, the vanilla vine itself would not like Gabon. *Vanilla planifolia*, which originated in Mexico, prefers a highly specific habitat, within a band around the globe roughly 23 degrees north and south of the equator. These tropical plants, grown from cuttings, like moist heat, a specific temperature range, fertile well-drained soil, evenly distributed rainfall throughout the year, and just the right amount of sun and shade. Madagascar, which produces more than half of the world's supply of vanilla beans, offers the ideal growing conditions; Gabon's climate of extreme heat and merciless rain, coupled with washed-out, infertile soil, would not.

In addition, the orchid-like flowers of vanilla plants grown commercially outside of Mexico must be *hand-pollinated*, since the flowers can only be fertilized naturally by a particular tropical bee that lives only in Central America. The hot, slow, painstaking outdoor labor of hand-pollination would be the farthest thing from working in an air-conditioned office in Gabon's capital, so it would likely attract few Gabonese workers.

And that's not all. According to British writer Tim Ecott, author of the fascinating travel memoir and natural history of the subject, *Vanilla*, "growing the beans is relatively simple, but the drying and curing is more complex, and labour intensive. A few farmers experiment with curing their own beans but in general the process requires a skill which takes many years to perfect, and secure premises in which to store the crop as it increases in value."

My "inspired" vanilla idea, then, so utterly unsuited for Gabon, became a sisterly joke between Yo and me — an example of how far off base a well meaning, green, gung-ho, humanitarian wannabe can be. But her nickname for me, Vanilla Sister, suited me, I thought, because compared to her Gabonese "chocolate" beauty, which never failed to turn men's heads when we were together, I was indeed "plain vanilla."

Nevertheless, vanilla became a kind of benchmark for me during my two-year stay in Lastoursville. My lofty impulse to leave behind something of enduring value to the people never wavered. My curiosity about what would take root there—and what wouldn't—never abated. *If it couldn't be vanilla, what could it be?*

I knew it couldn't be me. As much as I longed to remain in Africa, I knew it couldn't be Gabon. In this respect, too, I was similar to vanilla; I could never feel rooted there.

It wasn't just the incessant heat and infuriating bugs, the ever-present mud during rainy seasons and ubiquitous dust in the dry, the constant humidity that made my joints feel like rusted metal, or the worrisome threat of malaria I'd face if I stopped taking Mefloquine (because it's harmful to the liver if taken over a long period of time). It wasn't even that as a white person I was clearly an outsider. Youssef was considered an outsider, too, and as such required a *carte de séjour* to stay in Gabon legally.

It was only when he was detained by the gendarmes at the OCTRA police station that I realized Youssef had never obtained this necessary and costly document. He had felt, he told me after that incident, that as a proud African, he was a citizen of Africa and he had every right to travel with impunity across national borders, the way Americans can travel freely across state lines. The fact was, however, that the continent of Africa had been deliberately divided and conquered by European colonial powers and formed into small, hamstrung, U.S.-state-size countries, each with its own sovereign rulers and arbitrary laws. Without a *carte de séjour*, Youssef was undocumented; he was defying Gabon's immigration laws. He was an illegal alien, and as such, we both knew, he could be picked up again and this time put in jail.

And there were other signs that told us it was indeed time to go, with no regrets and no looking back. The *mauvais esprits* Youssef frequently spoke of seemed to be escorting us to the exit. We no longer felt safe in our home.

One evening in mid-September, not long before our scheduled departure, when the sun was beginning her descent, waving good-bye with pink ribbons in the sky, while Youssef and I took a walk to the bridge spanning the Ogooué to enjoy the pleasant, early evening cooler weather and take some scenic pictures of the mountains and the river for the last time, our house was robbed.

And this was not the first time for me. The first occurred eighteen months earlier, before I knew Youssef, while I was attending a Peace Corps conference in Libreville. When I returned from that trip, I found that my house had been broken into and all small, valuable items in it had been stolen: binoculars, flashlight, tools, food, toiletries, towels, sheets, plates, bowls, cooking pots and pans, kitchen utensils, machete, kitchen knives, clothes, tennis shoes, teapot.

The strange thing then was that one of each item — one spoon, one fork, one knife, one plate, and so on — was left for me, as if to send the message: *You, single woman living alone, don't need more than one of these things.* This made me think of Jacques, the high school boy I'd hired to paint my kitchen: He'd told me frankly that this house would "normally" house a large family of Africans, not

just one person. *Was he implying I was greedy to want it all to myself?*
I wondered at the time. *Was he behind this break-in?*

When I reported that robbery at the local police station near
my home, the police chief I spoke with "promised" — as his lieuten-
ants snickered in the background — that they would find the thief
"*demain.*"

After trying desperately to find a working phone in town to get
through to the Peace Corps office in Libreville, I finally approached
a new neighbor, a young road engineer named Kamil, newly arrived
from Lebanon, who'd recently moved into a rental house about a
quarter mile down the hill from mine. Kamil told me I could use
his phone — but with conditions.

Still desperate to make the call, I used Kamil's phone to reach
Country Director Frank Conlon, explaining to Frank what had happened and telling him in English, which Kamil didn't speak, that I
was only able to use my neighbor Kamil's phone if I agreed to sleep
with him. Frank laughed at this, as if I were joking; I assured him
it was not a joke. Kamil, meanwhile, standing close behind me, was
attempting to stroke my bare arms and nibble at my neck. I pushed
him away, and, in pantomime, indicated I'd like a cup of tea.

"*D'accord,*" he said, nodding, and left for the kitchen.

Frank told me break-ins happen frequently. "Unfortunately,"
he said, "they're more the rule than the exception." He was patient
and helpful and assured me the Peace Corps would reimburse me
for lost items, up to $500 (although I calculated the value of what
I'd lost to be over $800). When Frank offered to buy me whatever
would make me happy, I was so touched by his kindness, I began
to cry. I told him about the teapot that was taken and how much it
meant to me, how I drank tea every morning at dawn at my desk,
watching the sun rise sleepily over the mountains. I told him where
in Libreville I'd bought the teapot. He promised to get another one
for me himself and to send someone out to me in a day or two with
a care package.

As I left Kamil's house, he lunged for me expectantly. I backed away, feigning a smile, and promising, "*Demain*." From the hopeful look on his face, I could tell he didn't know how to read American women, and he had yet to learn African French.

Soon after that first break-in, my friend Antoinette came to see me. In her no-nonsense way, she counseled me not to let this incident get me down — not, in other words, to let evil win — because it would spoil my life and work in Lastoursville. "Eight out of ten men are animals," she said, holding up her hands with two fingers bent. "Ask God for the means to replace what was taken, thank God for this lesson, and go on," was her sermon for me.

I followed her advice. The Peace Corps reinforced the locks on my doors. Frank sent the promised care package, filled with second-hand sheets, towels, and clothing — plus the new teapot he had bought. I put this unsettling experience behind me, remembering Kipling's admonition to "start again at your beginnings, and never breathe a word about your loss."

"The robb'd who smiles steals something from the thief," I wrote in my journal at the time of that robbery. This aphorism had become one of my many mantras during the years my daughter was missing and I had to go on living. If the thief takes your spirit too, then he has surely won. "I can't smile yet," I added in my journal, "but I'll try not to cry anymore, and not even frown."

This second break-in, however, was more serious and more ominous. This time the "impenetrable" locks the Peace Corps had installed on all the doors of my house after the first robbery were opened, as if by a pro. And this time, all of the money Youssef and I had been saving for our trip to Mali was stolen. Only someone who had been watching me, day and night, from outside my bedroom window would have known how to find where I'd hidden this *banque*. No one I knew, not even Youssef, knew the secret hiding place I visited like a safe deposit box. But clearly someone I didn't know, perhaps the same someone who lurked outside my bedroom window brandishing a flashlight in the middle of my sleepless nights, knew. And he even knew to bring his own keys.

When Youssef and I returned from our sunset walk by the river, we found the doors to the house open and our *banque* lying open and empty on our bedroom floor, open lock and keys neatly placed nearby. The envelopes that had held our "accounts" — the remainder of my monthly living allowance (about 50,000 CFA or $83), Youssef's savings, including his earnings from Mr. Pasquier, plus the money we'd recently earned from the sale of furniture and other items, all of which we'd earmarked for our trip — were empty. These envelopes had been tucked behind toiletries in a zippered pocket of the locked outer compartment of my big, sturdy backpack. And the backpack had been well hidden — on the bottom shelf of my clothes cupboard, way in the back, behind my shoes. *Who could have known this?*

Youssef was so distraught he wanted to chase after the thief, but I insisted he didn't. Too, too, too dangerous, I told him. "Money can be replaced," I said; "the life of a loved one can't."

Again, I reported the break-in at the gendarmerie, and again I was assured, tongue-in-cheek, they would find the perpetrator "*demain*." And once again I repeated to my journal, "The robb'd who smiles steals something from the thief," knowing soon we'd be gone. Like a green vanilla vine, I knew I wasn't meant to grow roots in Gabon.

But what would remain of what I'd tried to accomplish? Vanilla growing, admittedly, was a profoundly dumb idea; but would any of the good ideas I'd planted actually take root and flourish? Would mothers continue to make healthy bread at home for their families? Would little girls not yet born one day play happily with their homemade sock dolls? Would kitchen gardens become a common sight? Would community composts enrich the exhausted soil?

Would townsfolk automatically throw their trash in the newly installed *poubelles*? Maybe. And maybe not. I'd have no way of knowing, since I knew I probably would never return.

What I did know was that the things already rooted and growing in Lastoursville would likely continue to do so. Among these, two stood out for me as having the most beneficial potential: avocados and papayas.

In my last months in Lastoursville, I saved and dried bags of papaya seeds and then took a bag of them with me on all of my walks, tossing them along the roadside, in the spirit of Johnny Appleseed. That quirky American pioneer, whose real name was John Chapman, traveled the Ohio river in the early years of the nineteenth century, dispersing apple seeds into the receptive soil of the frontier. I fancied myself Bonnie Papayaseed, hoping the soil along the roadsides of Lastoursville would be similarly receptive.

I forced several dozen avocado pits to sprout into seedlings, then potted them in liter-size Spanish wine cartons, and gave them as gifts to those who visited me to say goodbye. "Plant this in remembrance of me!" I'd urge them religiously, not missing the irony of pressing a tree onto people who live in dense forests.

I brought samples of these avocado seedlings, at various stages of growth, to the hospital clinic and used them in my Recycling lectures. "If it's a pit, plant it!" I'd say, showing the women how to suspend the avocado pit halfway up its bottom (pointed side up) in a jar of water, using toothpicks embedded into the sides for support. In about a month, I explained, showing another "model," the roots and stem emerge from the seed, and it can then be planted in the earth. "By the time your babies start school," I told the women in the clinic classroom, who held their infants in their laps as I lectured, "you will have plenty of your own avocados to feed your family."

Like a zealot, I preached the health benefits of eating avocados and papayas — fruit that too frequently fell to the ground unappreciated there and was simply left to rot. "The avocado is a *wonder food*," I'd tell my women's classes. "It is filled with goodness, *beaucoup de vitamines!*" In fact, the avocado is packed with nutrition, containing significant amounts of thiamin (Vitamin B1), riboflavin (B2), niacin (B3) pantothenic acid (B5), Vitamin B6, folate (B9), Vitamin C, iron, magnesium, phosphorus, potassium, and zinc; and its fat is mostly monounsaturated, which is the healthiest. "Papayas, too," I expounded, "are very healthy and good for the digestion!" The women nodded politely at first. Then, when I showed them how to use these foods in salad and salsa, and they tasted the results, they became convinced.

Avocado and papaya trees, which grew as carelessly as weeds in Gabon, needing little-to-no human attention, didn't have the value or cachet of vanilla. But they offered practical, sustainable benefits, which is what matters most in Africa. My job, vanilla taught me, was not to change anyone's way of being or add to their already heavy burdens, but rather to suggest, perhaps, new ways of seeing and using what they already had.

Avocado Salad (Guacamole)

4 to 5 ripe avocados, peeled, seeded, and coarsely chopped
 into ½-inch chunks
4 to 5 medium-size tomatoes, seeded and diced
½ medium-size red onion, finely chopped
1 small jalapeño pepper, finely chopped
2 to 3 cloves garlic, peeled and finely minced
2 to 3 tablespoons freshly squeezed lime juice
½ cup fresh cilantro, finely chopped

• • •

Combine all in a large bowl and toss gently but thoroughly. Season with salt and pepper to taste. Serve with tortilla chips. Makes enough to feed a small crowd.

Avocado-Papaya Salsa

2 tablespoons freshly squeezed lime juice
1 large (or two small) ripe avocado, peeled, seeded and diced
¼ cup finely diced red onion
¼ cup minced fresh coriander (including leaves and
    tender stems)
1 large clove garlic, peeled and finely minced
    (about 1 teaspoon, or to taste)
¼ (approx.) medium-size, ripe papaya, peeled, seeded and
    cut into ¼-inch dice (about 1½ cups papaya meat)
1 tablespoon finely diced fresh jalapeño pepper (optional)
Salt and freshly ground black pepper to taste
Pinch of cayenne pepper (optional)

Combine all in a bowl and toss gently but thoroughly. Serve with grilled chicken or broiled fish. Makes about 6 servings.

Plus Belle

We inherited the earth from our ancestors
and are borrowing it from our children.

— Fambidzanai Permaculture Centre brochure

Dudley at Fambidzanai Permaculture Center,
Harare, Zimbabwe, 1997

In late-December 1996, nearly a quarter-century after leaving Salisbury, Rhodesia, I returned to the same place, since renamed Harare, Zimbabwe, for a two-week visit. I had to go back. This return journey, in fact, was one of the underlying reasons I'd decided to join the Peace Corps in the first place; serving in the Peace Corps in Africa would take me a giant step closer to this vital life goal.

I had to answer questions that had haunted me since I left Rhodesia in April 1972: Should I have stayed? Would I have been better off if I had never left the happiness I had known there? Should I have settled in and grown roots, married my English boyfriend Melvyn, perhaps; made a home and family, surrounded by a garden framed by flame-hued bougainvillea, under southern Africa's sunny skies? Did I do the right thing by leaving then and returning alone to the country I had no choice but to call mine, in the seemingly futile hope of finding my daughter once again?

An hour before dawn on Sunday, December 22, 1996, my Gabonese sister, Yolande, drove me to the airport in Libreville so I could catch a 6:10 am Air Gabon flight (Yo called Air Gabon "*Air Peut-Être*" — Air Maybe) to Johannesburg, South Africa, and later that day another flight to Harare. My friend Sue, with whom I'd lived for six months when I first arrived in Salisbury in March 1969 and with whom I'd stayed in touch over the years, and her current boyfriend Des, met my flight. As we drove in Des' white Mercedes sedan through heavy rains and darkening skies to Sue's garden apartment in the Harare suburb of Avondale, I couldn't recognize anything from the past. Everything seemed so foreign to me, more enlarged and expanded than it had remained in my memory, and worlds away from the Africa I'd just left in Gabon.

That week, while Sue worked as the manager of a real estate office in Harare during the day, I wandered on foot and bicycle alone, searching for something I thought I might have lost.

Tuesday, December 24, 1996 — 5:45 am — Harare:

Yesterday morning, after taking a luxurious bubble bath in Sue's enormous tub, I walked to the nearest shopping center — so American-looking and feeling, it could have been in any southern place in the USA — and did a lot of the shopping I've been wanting to do, for spices, tools, towels, and seeds. I also bought some salad greens, fresh broccoli *(broccoli!)*, tomatoes and a huge mango, all of which I ate, ecstatically — one can't easily find salad components in Lastoursville — for lunch. Then I rested and read *The Herald* in the sun for a short while in Sue's walled-in, beautifully landscaped front courtyard and chatted for a while with Sue's maid, Fortunate, about how I might locate my former maid, Margaret. Fortunate said she would try to make a call-in announcement to Margaret for me over the local African radio station.

After Sue got home from work at about 5:30, we went to her club, Old Hararians, for a drink. The men there — all middle-aged, puffy and veddy white — had been drinking at the club for most of the day, so they were all quite drunk. They spoke loud nonsense, made unfunny jokes, pawed Sue and me, and

I couldn't help wondering what in the world I was doing there.

Sue and I drove around and through the center of the city before coming home from the club. Harare is about twenty times grander than Salisbury was. It's a grown-up, sky-scrapered, modern, impressive city now. While I've been away, it's gone on with its life. And no one here remembers me or even cares that I've come back. That's all right. It helps me put things into perspective. I'm very glad I came. It's closure for me.

In the days that followed, Sue and I went for long walks together in her neighborhood each morning before she left for work. We passed new, white-stuccoed housing complexes, with tall, thick, barbed-wire-topped walls around them, where only whites lived, in what seemed to me to be both prosperity and fear. The only Africans I saw on these walks were the uniformed housemaids who worked at these complexes and the armed guardians at their gates.

Sue and I celebrated Christmas day with her extended family, at the grand, English Tudor–style home of one of her grown sons, whom I hadn't seen since he was four years old. Twelve of us sat outside under the canopied veranda within view of the swimming pool and gardens: Sue's ex-husband Alwyn, now head of the law firm that had generously handled my custody case pro bono in Salisbury's high court nearly thirty years before; two of Sue and Alwyn's four children, along with their spouses and young children; plus Alwyn's second wife, Bryonny, and their two teenagers. Our Christmas lunch buffet included cold roast turkey, cold baked ham, two bounteous fresh green salads, hot garlic bread and dinner rolls, and Sue's homemade meringue cake with vanilla ice cream and sliced fresh strawberries.

I sat beside Alwyn at lunch, as a springlike drizzle pattered on the canopy, and asked him about the new Zimbabwe. Tourism, he told me with quiet pride, was the country's third largest revenue source, after agriculture and mining. The population was now at eleven million, he said, eleven times greater than Gabon's. And his law firm, Winterton, Holmes, and Hill, now had a staff of seventy, about ten times larger than when they'd represented me. Despite the years of war and deprivation they'd all endured and the uncertainty surrounding President Robert Mugabe's handling of the new, black-ruled country, Alwyn appeared to me to be optimistic about Zimbabwe's future. Or perhaps he was too British and reticent to share with me his innermost fears and apprehensions.

The day after Christmas, the holiday Boxing Day, Sue and I got dressed up in sundresses, hats, and heels, and went to the races. Sue, I learned, was now part of a local syndicate that owned sixteen racehorses, so she went to the races as often as she could. For me, this was a first.

"You pick the winner," she said to me, as we looked down from the glass-enclosed clubhouse at the horses being led by black grooms to the track. "Let's see whether you've got beginner's luck."

Knowing nothing about horses, I could only guess. I studied the sleek, muscular animals as they paraded past, and I chose the one who seemed most anxious and out-of-place, the one who twitched and bridled most at being led, the one who seemed to wish he were elsewhere and just wanted to run away.

He won the first race.

"Do that again!" Sue encouraged me. "You're a natural at this!"

Again, my pick of the underdog-horse won. Sue and I had only made small bets of about ten Zimbabwe dollars (about $1 U.S.) so our winnings were modest, but fun.

We sat with her race club friends, "the hoipolloi," Sue called them, who were smoking Dunhills and drinking beers and gin-and-tonics at a round table in the middle of the room.

"Tell us about your life in Gabon," one of the elderly British women at the table said, leaning toward me with a look more of astonishment than curiosity that I should be living in what she considered a godforsaken place. "What, for example, do you do for a *social life?*"

"Social life?" I stammered, buying time. I had no intelligent response for her. It was as if she had asked me a complicated question in a language I didn't speak. I hardly knew what a social life in Lastoursville was. I had been living there by then for four months and during that time seldom went anywhere other than work and church and Bev's house once or twice for dinner and a video. "I don't really have a social life," I finally said to her. "I stay pretty much alone." The woman shook her head sadly as if she couldn't imagine not having a tight circle of close clubhouse chums to drink with regularly at the races.

"Ah, Gabon," a sandy-haired man in his fifties said, swirling his beer. I studied his tanned, craggy face, thinking he might have been handsome if his eyes weren't so bloodshot and mean. "Tha's my favorite African country 'cause it's got the fewest Africans in it. Wha's the population there — 1 million? Ach, we should all be so lucky!"

Others at the table referred to Africans as "ants" and "human flotsam and jetsam," even though the white-uniformed African waiter, standing at attention near the doorway, ready to take orders for another round, was within earshot.

Like my first winning racehorse, I wanted to run away.

I spent the remaining days of my Harare stay visiting old friends who were still living there, walking in the city's showcase botanical gardens, and doing research that would aid my work when I returned to Lastoursville.

I had to see Dudley again. My former boss at *The Rhodesian Farmer*, the weekly farming magazine where I'd worked as a copyeditor for two years in Salisbury, the man who gave me my editorial start and who had been like a father-figure for me, was now in his late-seventies, retired and frail. Sue and I drove in her yellow Mercedes to his fifteen-acre farm just outside of Harare on Sunday, the 29th, for lunch. After eating and taking a walking tour of his lovingly tended gardens, Dudley gave me some information about Permaculture to help me in my gardening efforts in Gabon and other literature that might help in my development work. Dudley, who was born and raised in South Africa and whose first language was Xhosa — learned as an infant from his African nanny who strapped him to her back while she worked, as if he were her own — had fought against apartheid there as a young man. He seemed both proud and pleased to support my Peace Corps purpose in Gabon.

The next day, while wandering in town, I discovered, as if nudged by Mother Nature herself, a small bookstore called Grassroots that specialized in eco-friendly books. It was perfect. The Gardening section had just the how-to books I'd been hoping for — books that would help me learn how to garden in the tropics and then teach others in Lastoursville what I'd learned. If I had had the money, I told my journal, I could have spent hundreds of U.S. dollars (thousands of Zimbabwean dollars) on potentially helpful books. Instead, I narrowed my choices to three, all that I could afford — *Community Gardens, Fruit and Vegetable Processing* and *Introduction to Permaculture.*

That night I went to bed with Bill Mollison's Permaculture book and read for hours. "Permaculture," I learned from Mollison, the Australian who developed the concept and coined the term in the late '70s, "is a design system for creating sustainable human environments. The word itself is a contraction not only of permanent agriculture but also of permanent culture, as cultures cannot survive for long without a sustainable agricultural base and land-use ethic." Hungrily, I read on:

> Permaculture is not energy- or capital-intensive, rather it is information-intensive. It is the quality of thought and the information we use that determines yield, not the size or quality of the site. ... If we take the time to read, observe, discuss, and contemplate, we begin to think in terms of multidisciplines, and to design systems which save energy and give us yields.

Perhaps because I am an Earth sign (Taurus) and I'd yearned all my life to sink my heart and hands into gardening, or perhaps because it had been a long time since I'd been to bed with a man — or perhaps for both reasons — I found myself falling in love with Mollison and his Permaculture philosophy. His revolutionary words and passionate voice seduced me:

> We ourselves can cure all the famine, all the injustice, and all the stupidity of the world. We can do it by understanding the way natural systems work, by careful forestry and gardening, by contemplation and by taking care of the earth.
>
> People who force nature force themselves. When we grow only wheat, we become dough. If we seek only money, we become brass; and if we stay in the childhood of team sports, we become a stuffed leather ball. Beware the monoculturalist, in religion, health, farm or factory. He is driven mad by boredom, and can create war and try to assert power, because he is in fact powerless.

When Dudley phoned the next morning and I told him about my new-found love interest, he suggested we visit the Permaculture Centre, "Fambidzanai" (a Shona word meaning "exchange" or "reciprocity") in Harare, the first of its kind in Africa. That afternoon he picked me up at Sue's and we drove twelve miles on the Lomagundi Road toward Chinhoyi to the center.

As soon as we arrived at the round, thatch-roofed visitors' station, we were welcomed by a young, neatly dressed Zimbabwean guide. While Dudley and I followed him down a gravel pathway, our guide proudly explained that Fambidzanai was established in 1988 to enrich the quality of life for Zimbabwe's people, especially those in rural communities. "We offer free training programs in Permaculture design and organic gardening, natural pest control, dryland cropping, brick making, textile printing and dyeing, beekeeping, and so on — and we provide living examples," he said, sweeping his arm across the forty-acre spread.

I asked questions as though I were a child.

"Why are so many weeds allowed to grow?"

"Permaculture teaches 'no bare earth,' so even weeds can be our friends," our guide said, smiling, "because they act as umbrellas to shade the soil from the strong African sun and keep the temperature cooler between the plants."

"Why are there so many glass bottles inverted at an angle into the beds?"

"Because they allow the plants' roots to drink water more directly. Oftentimes we suffer from drought here in Zimbabwe, so we fill the bottles with tap water and poke them into the soil to make sure the roots get enough to drink."

Permaculture in action in Africa, it appeared, was not *House & Gardens* beautiful, but it was down-to-earth practical and, most of all, sustainable. It required little in the way of equipment or material, just a willingness to learn from and work with the realities of the terrain.

"I can do this," I said to Dudley resolutely, when we got back to his car. "I can do this in Lastoursville."

"Of course you can," he said.

On the drive back to Harare along the Lomagundi Road, Dudley became quiet and pensive. I studied the landscape, admiring the wide savanna dotted with massassa trees, feeling comforted that this aspect of Africa hadn't changed since I first fell in love with her earthy beauty nearly three decades before. Outside of the man-made, modern capital city, Africa herself was essentially the same.

"I wish," Dudley said wistfully, "I were twenty years younger so I could show you how much I love you."

"You already do, Dud," I said.

Friday, January 3, 1997 — 5:30 am — Harare:

The wonderful, magical thing about being quiet and listening to your instincts is that things happen, or seem to happen, according to a preordained plan. All of the literature that Dudley gave me has opened other doors to names, addresses, and telephone numbers I can pursue here for further information to help in my work.

For example, yesterday I wrote to the F.A.O. in Rome for information regarding food preservation. Dudley had said the F.A.O. is very good — helpful, prompt, efficient, thorough — so I'm hopeful I'll get what I requested soon.

After Dudley and I visited the Permaculture Center, we came back here to Sue's, I made lunch, Sue came home for lunch, and we three ate together. Dudley left at about 2:00, and I cried. I'll probably never see him again in this life. This life. What does it mean? We never get a straight answer to this question. We just have to keep listening to our instincts for hints.

I walked alone in the city's centrally located Harare Gardens, remembering the walks my daughter and I used to take there when she was a little girl, the way we walked hand-in-hand, slowly, bending over and studying the flowers, and I would teach her the names of their colors. The gardens were still beautiful, but more grown up, fuller, and more lush. They were clean, too, with trash receptacles at almost every turn. A "Keep Harare Clean" sign was displayed on each one, and people obviously took heed. *If only Lastoursville could be so clean,* I thought. *What would it take?*

Lastoursville was a pretty town, if one didn't look down. In addition to the central garbage dump near the *marché*, where mounds of refuse rotted in the hot equatorial sun, spreading its stench — to say nothing of germs — in all directions, litter was strewn wantonly everywhere. *Why?* I often wondered. Was it that for millennia what one tossed into the steamy rainforest quickly biodegraded or was eaten by scavenging animals and soon disappeared? Were the culprits modern plastic bags and metal tins that didn't biodegrade? Was it that the people didn't know what a clean town could look like because it had always looked like this? Was it laziness? Apathy?

If so, on whose part? The fact was, there was no municipal garbage pickup in Lastoursville.

As my Harare stay drew to a close, I thought more about Lastoursville and what else I might bring back with me of lasting value. While doing more research toward this end, at the UNICEF Library in Harare, I learned of a UN-sponsored organization called Clean Up the World, headquartered in Australia. One of its main objectives, I read, was "to bring together citizens from every corner of the globe in a simple activity that will positively assist their local environments." Namely, voluntarily cleaning up the place where they lived.

Human beings need two things for happiness, D.H. Lawrence purportedly once said: love and a crusade. If on this trip, I, a grown woman from New York who had never in her life had occasion to use a shovel or a hoe, fell hopelessly in love with Permaculture, then Clean Up the World became my rabid crusade. I decided that upon my return to Lastoursville I would lead an effort to leave the town more beautiful — *plus belle* — than I had found it. I would rope the Lastoursville community into this international effort. I would whip up interest and mobilize the town government. Like Dr. Urbino in Gabriel Garcia Marquez's *Love in the Time of Cholera*, I felt obsessed by the dangerous lack of sanitation in Lastoursville, and I was determined to do what I could to upgrade it. I was on fire.

On the third Saturday in September, 1998, shortly before my Peace Corps service ended, Lastoursville participated in the international Clean Up the World Day, thereby adding Gabon to the nonprofit organization's 120-country world map. Along with a write-up on the success of Lastoursville's first clean-up effort in Clean Up the World's annual report, was a group photograph, taken by Youssef, of Lastoursville's participants, pointing to and admiring the novel object labeled "*POUBELLE*" (garbage can) in the center of the picture.

"This," I wrote to Marty that September, "is one of my proudest accomplishments."

It had taken twenty-one months to accomplish, but this is how it came about:

When I returned from Harare, I wrote to Clean Up the World in Australia, requesting their "How To Do It" kit and literature in French that I might pass along to members of the town government.

My friend and Lastoursville's deputy mayor Antoinette was more than receptive to my Clean Up Lastoursville crusade. As a former pediatric nurse, she needed little convincing that there is a direct link between environmental filth and human disease. And the fact that Clean Up the World was a worldwide, United Nations-backed organization that would provide guidance and support, made the campaign even more appealing. As a fellow-Taurus, Antionette stubbornly took the case to her higher-ups, and she refused to take no for an answer.

My French friend Francine's husband Louis donated four large oil barrels, which he cut in half at the waistline and drilled holes in near the base for rain water drainage. I painted all eight trash receptacles bright red and printed on each in three-inch-high, white capital letters, "*POUBELLE*."

My Friday night English class, spearheaded by one of the brightest students, Martial, took up the cause and spread the word throughout the high school about Lastoursville's involvement in Clean Up the World. "We can make Lastoursville world famous!" they told their teenage peers.

I made posters and a batik banner that boldly proclaimed, *"Pour Faire Lastoursville Plus Belle, Utilisez Les Poubelles!"* (to make Lastoursville more beautiful, use the garbage cans) and posted them all over town. The mayor's office agreed to station the *poubelles* at critical places throughout *centreville* and to collect the trash on a regular basis.

The day of the event was like a *fête*. There was singing and dancing in the streets as people filled the big, heavy-duty, bright blue plastic Clean Up the World-donated trash bags. The happy parade marched along what the organization's annual report grandly described "the grand boulevard of Lastoursville, starting from the *Gare-Routiere* to the small market, passing through the main marketplace, targeting waste in public areas." Martial, head high, led the way, wearing his new, Clean Up the World T-shirt and carrying a large Clean Up the World banner. Youssef snapped photos from every angle, as if he were reporting for *Time* magazine. He knew there was a chance one of his photos would be published in Clean Up the World's annual report. He would be a published photographer at last.

Like the Pied Piper's following, our happy band of trash collectors increased in numbers as we proceeded down the town's main street. Everyone, it seemed, wanted to play a part. Shopkeepers, delighted to see the space in front of their stores cleaned up, donated money to the cause. Antoinette and I, working side-by-side, giggled like little girls over the success of our coup. At the end of the road, over forty large bags filled with trash were counted, and more than a hundred people were rewarded for their efforts with cold soft drinks provided by the town council. "We'll do this again!" a town official told the crowd. "Every year!"

The beautiful thing about getting older, I thought that evening before falling asleep, is that you can look back over your shoulder and see the patterns in your life's path. This led to that, and that led to the next thing, and though you didn't know it at the time, they were all meant to lead you to where you are right now. Did I do the right thing by leaving Rhodesia in April 1972, returning to the States, and then taking this decades-long, circuitous route back to Africa?, I asked myself again. My heart's answer that night was more beautiful — *plus belle* — than I ever could have dreamed.

Sue's Christmas Meringue Cake ("Pavlova")

This delicate and regal-looking dessert, which is said to have originated in Australia, is also a popular party finale in Anglophone Africa.

1½ teaspoons pure vanilla extract
½ teaspoon cream of tartar (or 2 teaspoons white vinegar)
1½ tablespoons cornstarch
1½ cups granulated sugar
¾ cup (about 6) large egg whites, at room temperature
a pinch of salt

2 pints fresh berries, such as hulled, sliced strawberries, tossed
    with ¼ cup sugar, or thawed frozen berries with sauce
Vanilla ice cream
Whipped Cream
Mint sprig (optional)

Place rack in the middle of the oven and preheat the oven to 275 degrees. Line a large baking sheet with parchment paper. Pour the vanilla and vinegar (if using) into a small cup. Stir the cornstarch into the sugar in a small bowl.

In a large bowl of a heavy-duty mixer fitted with whisk attachment, whip egg whites, cream of tartar (if using), and salt, starting on low, increasing incrementally to medium speed until soft peaks begin to form, approximately 2 to 3 minutes.

Increase speed to medium-high, then slowly sprinkle in the sugar-cornstarch mixture. A few minutes after these dry ingredients are added, slowly pour in the vanilla and vinegar (if you didn't use cream of tartar). Increase speed and whip until meringue is glossy and stiff peaks form when the whisk is lifted, 4 to 5 minutes.

Pipe or spoon the meringue into a circle, approximately 8 inches in diameter and approximately 1 inch thick. Pipe around the perimeter of the circle to build up the sides, forming a "nest."

Place baking sheet in the oven. Reduce oven temperature to 250 degrees. Bake for 50-60 minutes (turning the pan around midway through baking), or until the meringue is crisp and dry to the touch on the outside. Gently lift from the baking sheet and cool on a wire rack.

When ready to serve, fill meringue "nest" with scoops of ice cream, topped with berries, topped with whipped cream. Garnish with mint sprig, if desired. Serves 8 to 10.

Come and See

*To become a complete person, we must travel many paths,
and to truly own anything we must first of all give it away.
This is not a riddle. Only those who share their multiple
and varied skills, true friendships, and a sense of community
and knowledge of the earth know they are safe wherever they go.*
— BILL MOLLISON, *Introduction to Permaculture*

With Dr. Djimet (right) and his hospital staff

On the first of September 1998 I began a new journal, this one a small, cloth-covered spiral-bound blank book with good-quality paper, which had been a gift from my friend and neighbor Kathy in New York. I titled it "African Travels" and dedicated it to my young granddaughter, Lauren, with love. I hoped to give it to her one day, when she was much older, so that she might read it to better understand both the Africa of my experience and her Nonnie, me.

"I'll be leaving Lastoursville by express train bound for Libreville on the 24th of this new month," I wrote on this new journal's first page, "but I'm already packing up: some things to give to the next volunteer — books, magazines, puppets, pots, plates, breakables; some things to take to NYC, for a short, I hope, stay; and the rest to take to and leave in Segou, Mali, our ultimate destination. ... I also need to pack memories — the little things I've loved about my life here — like the palm trees outside my windows. I'm not, of course, certain where life will take me next; but wherever it is, I hope there will be palm trees...."

For every daily entry in this journal, I also made a small water-color painting, to preserve my memories with more than just words. Although Youssef took many photographs, I wanted to try my hand at painting, for the lesson in quiet, attentive seeing it might teach me. I painted the biggest palm tree in the front of my house and the ingenious oblong nests I'd watched the weaver birds build in it, "*petit à petit*." I painted the new red rooster who had begun to visit me every morning, boldly crossing the busy road after looking both ways, with his two baby chicks in tow — one black, one white — begging for raw rice the way *Dîner* had once done. I painted the view from my study window of the distant, mist-shrouded mountains at dawn and, on another page, a sunset scene over the Ogooué River, with a timelessly practical *pirogue* in the foreground.

I painted a red hibiscus flower from my front garden and wrote about the lessons I'd learned from my first gardening efforts — how the okra plant, for example, metamorphoses from a pretty, yellow flower to a luscious, long green vegetable, to a dried, dusky seed pod. "I'm in the 'seed pod' stage of my life now," I wrote, "needing to plant my ideas wherever Life sends me."

I painted my view of the thick green forest and the red-brick-color dirt roads that I saw while traveling in the back of Dr. Djimet's pickup truck as Youssef and I, along with most of the hospital staff, took part in a massive national polio vaccination drive. "For three days," I recounted in the journal, "in small teams, we fanned out into every corner of this province, stopping at each village to give two drops of the oral vaccine to every child five years old and under...."

On the third day of our vaccination drive, Friday, September 9, our team traveled the farthest — over 50 kilometers deep into the forest. We took the road toward Bambidie but veered left into Ndangui, one of the two gold-mining regions of Gabon. Augustin, the hospital's ambulance driver, was driving Dr. Djimet's new, four-door

Toyota pickup truck, doing at least 60 mph on the dusty dirt roads. Caroline, head nurse at the PMI and the *directrice* of this vaccination drive, sat in front with Augustin ("Never again," she told me privately at the end of the drive), and three of the young nurses sat in the back seat. Youssef and I, by choice, because we wanted a full view of the lush forest scenery, sat in the bed of the speeding pickup, holding on to both our belongings and to the truck's sides so as not to fly out.

We stopped at various villages along the way, including one called Akieni, a sprawling development of neat little wood houses, where most of the men, I was told, worked for the new forestry company, CFG. There, the wizened, wily old chief called me over and whispered a request for *l'argent*, giving me a sad story about his poor health and heartbreak since he lost his wife six months ago.

"Sorry to disappoint you, chief," I had to tell him in so many words, "but I'm a volunteer with no money." *And*, I wanted to add but didn't, *don't you have gold here?* He shrugged and gave me an "Oh-well-I-tried" expression. Then he smiled as if to say, "No hard feelings."

We drove deeper into the forest, where the villages, with their tiny, rectangular mud-wattle houses with natural grass roofs were the most authentic and traditional I'd yet to see in Gabon. At the end of the line, after whipping up and down winding dirt roads — cut by the forestry companies at great expense, in the hopes of even greater profits — we parked at a charming and friendly village called La Chute and continued the rest of our journey toward villages inaccessible by car or truck or anything else, on foot.

From there we hiked toward our destination ("*pas loin*," we were told — not far), a village ironically called "*Venez Voir*" — Come and See. As we walked — and walked and walked and walked — for over an hour, along a narrow, well-trod pathway, winding through jungly underbrush, over wobbly log foot bridges, past sandy dunes and craters created by the many gold diggers, beside swamps of yellowish, still water, the village's name *Venez Voir* became something of a joke among the members of our team. With our increasing perspiration and thirst, we renamed this Oz-like place, *Venez Boir* — Come and Drink.

But when we finally reached the by-now fabled village, we found the effort worthwhile. The people were warm and welcoming, and the children — unlike the littlest ones in other remote villages we'd visited who had run screaming when they saw me, the first white person they'd obviously ever seen in their young lives — weren't terrified by my whiteness. To the children of *Venez Voir*, I wasn't a frightful ghost. So I happily rewarded them with a puppet show in which Chantal Chanson taught them the wash-your-hands-for-good-health song.

As our vaccination team paraded through *Venez Voir*, with Augustin leading the way, carrying the polio-vaccine-filled cooler on his head, village life went on as usual. People looked up, said *bonjour*, smiled genuinely friendly, unfazed smiles, then went back to whatever they'd been doing: trimming someone's hair, making something out of wood, weaving a reed basket, preparing a meal at an open fire, mashing manioc in a basin-like *mortier.*

The young mothers brought their five-years-old-and-under children to receive their two drops of oral polio vaccine at the town's main meeting hall, where the dapper, middle-aged chief of police and his cronies were already drinking straight whisky at 11 o'clock in the morning. (*Venez Boir*, indeed.)

Evidently, this was a special outing for some of the littlest girls: They were dressed in their prettiest, frilliest little dresses, with matching lacy bonnets; and they marched proudly along with their older siblings in new, clean plastic shoes.

Some of our entourage stayed behind in the town hall (to drink?) after all the eligible little ones were vaccinated. But others of us pressed on: There were more villages deeper still into this for-est-jungle-swamp territory, and we still had the energy and interest to reach them. More long, log footbridges followed; more narrow, well-trod paths.

"This experience," I told my new journal, "turned out to be the best adventure Youssef and I have had here in Gabon. We saw people digging for and panning gold. We saw gold. The whole experience, for me, was pure gold."

In the new journal, I drew a scrawny monkey walking on all fours at the top of the page dated September 16. I painted its face blue, its neck yellow, and its tail red, then told the sad story of one of its kind:

On the second day of last week's vaccination drive, Caroline had the car stop by a roadside stand on the way home so she could buy for her big family's dinner the presumably fresh catch-of-the-day for sale: a very surprised looking, very dead, skinny little monkey. This soon-to-be stew, to be served with manioc and/or plantains to her ten children, was deposited on top of the spare tire that lay flat in the back, near where I happened to be sitting. So I had the time to study my new traveling companion at close range.

In fact, I could hardly take my eyes off the thing: Blue face, yellow-furred cheeks and upper body, rust-red tail, bright red tongue sticking out, pendulous little breasts, utterly human-like hands. And she was still bleeding from the neck where she'd been shot.

Thomas, my ten-year-old grandson and his class, to whom I've been writing for the past two years, always ask me about monkeys — not the people here, but the monkeys. *Have I seen any monkeys yet?* they want to know.

It's as if, to the kids in the U.S., Africa is one big zoo filled only with wild animals. People don't even feature. Yes, I can tell Thomas and his classmates when I see them in November — yes, I've seen a monkey, all right, and close up. Here monkeys aren't caged in zoos; they're hunted, shot, skinned, gutted, and cooked for dinner.

My last painting in Lastoursville, of the train station, was painted on the day of our departure, September 24, 1998, which would have been my mother Lee's 82nd birthday. My mother, who had been an avid amateur painter, had always encouraged me to take up painting. "It's so relaxing, Bon," she'd say, "and you'd be so good at it!" But I'd never even tried until now.

My amateurish artistic attempt at capturing the train station shows a blocky cement structure painted yellow and brown, with a slanted corrugated roof and terra cotta-colored earth in the front, dappled with clumps of tall, wild grass. This painting "is far from a success," I admit to the journal, while waiting for the new express train's arrival to take Youssef and me to Libreville, the first leg of our long journey to Mali. "It's not to scale and the station is not this clean. It's actually littered with garbage, cluttered already with baggage, filling with people. But, like a lot of my efforts here, this painting is better than nothing." *Perhaps all artists paint what they want to see, rather than what is,* I thought.

Dr. Djimet had driven Youssef and me to the train station, helped unload our bags from the back of his pickup, and hugged me goodbye. During the previous week, I'd methodically said my goodbyes to the people I knew and loved in Lastoursville, especially my classes and colleagues at the hospital, the women of *Cité* OCTRA, my students at the Women's Center, my sisterly friend Antoinette and my *maman*, Henriette. I knew I could stay in touch with Bev, Morgan, and Francine by correspondence, so our goodbyes were more like *à bientôt*—til soon. But I also knew it was unlikely I'd ever see or hear from my African women friends again; few of them could write or afford the costly airmail postage. With welling eyes, I assured them they would always be in my heart and in my best memories of Gabon.

"Everything I wanted from this Peace Corps adventure," I wrote to Marty just before my departure, "— a new life in a new land, speaking a new language (well, almost), making new friends, seeing the world from a new point of view, and so on — I've gotten. I'm very thankful. I won't be heartbroken to kiss Lastoursville goodbye, but I'm awfully glad I had the chance to spend these past two years here."

By the last page of this "African Travels" journal, Youssef and I had settled into a rental house in *quartier* Pelangana, Segou, Mali, where we would stay together for another year, and then I would remain alone for an additional year, working with women on an economic development project of my own creation. This last entry in that journal, dated December 23, 1998, which I refer to as my "commencement address for whomever," reads:

Follow your heart; go where it leads.
Be who you are, however odd that might seem to others.
Use your unique talents for good.
There's so much good that needs to be done
in this big, yet small, world.

Martha Cooper

Acknowledgments

There are many people who made this book possible and to whom I owe immense thanks: my sister Heather Wood, who supported my Peace Corps efforts every step of the way and gave me encouraging feedback on early drafts of these chapters; my Antioch–LA mentors — Sharman Apt Russell, Valerie Boyd, and Bernadette Murphy — who helped guide and shape this narrative from the start; my dear friend John Coyne and his partner in Peace Corps publishing endeavors, Marian Haley Beil, who established the Peace Corps Writers imprint, of which my *Crocodile* is proud to be the first; my sisterly friend Barbara Scott, editor and book designer par excellence, whose inspired design has made this *Crocodile* so handsome.

But above all, my deepest appreciation goes to my longtime friend and former next-door neighbor on New York's Upper West Side, photographer Martha Cooper. At a time in my life when I needed to turn the page, get away, start anew (call it a belated midlife crisis if you will), when any other New York buddy would have told me flatly, *"Get a grip,"* Marty said something along these lines: "You're thinking of joining the Peace Corps? GO FOR IT, my dear! I'll take care of everything here for you while you're away."

Marty could say this because she'd been there. She belonged to the not-in-the-least-secret society, the anything-but-elite club of

RPCVs, returned Peace Corps volunteers. She knew what the Peace Corps experience provided. She knew intuitively that it would give me what I was aching for — not an escape from reality but a greater sense of meaning and purpose. Marty's own Peace Corps service in Thailand in the early 1960s, only a few years after the Peace Corps was established by the Kennedy administration, had fostered her innate fearlessness, sparked her curiosity about the world, and had given her an unremitting willingness to go — camera in hand — where most others would never dare to tread.

How to Cook a Crocodile would not exist if my friend Marty Cooper hadn't made it possible for me to join the Peace Corps in the first place. She managed all of my affairs in the years I was away. She remained a touchstone for me, maintaining a lively correspondence across the miles — before e-mailing was an option. She came to visit me in Gabon and took most of the marvelous photos shown in this book. Without her help and support, I would never have lived in Lastoursville, I would never have met all these memorable people, I would never have been able to write these too-true stories and share them in this way. One of these stories, written between the lines, is about Sisterhood — and how indebted I am to such a friend.

Bonnie Lee Black
Taos, New Mexico
August 2010

Left: Thailand, 1964 — Martha Cooper
with Hmong villagers near Chieng Kham,
when she taught English as a Peace Corps
volunteer

Recipe Index

Bibliography

Black, Bonnie Lee. *Somewhere Child*. New York: Viking Press, 1981.

Cisse, Youssouf Tata. Seydou Keita. New York: Scalo Publishers, 1997.

Clarke, Thurston. *Equator: A Journey*. New York: Avon Books, 1988.

Denzer, Kiko. *Build Your Own Earth Oven*. Blodgett, OR: Hand Print Press, 2001.

Dinesen, Isak. *Out of Africa*. New York: Random House, 1938.

Ecott, Tim. *Vanilla: Travels in Search of the Ice Cream Orchid*. New York: Grove Press, 2004.

Fisher, M. F. K. *How to Cook a Wolf*. New York: North Point Press, 1942.

Kingsley, Mary. *Travels in West Africa [1897]*. Washington, DC: National Geographic Society, 2002.

Lawder, Donald. *Fishing in the Sky*. The Permanent Press, Dec. 1997.

Marquez, Gabriel Garcia. *Love in the Time of Cholera*. New York: Penguin, 1989.

Mollison, Bill. *Introduction to Permaculture*. Tyalgum, Australia: Tagari Publications, 1991.

Pollan, Michael. *The Botany of Desire: A Plant's-Eye View of the World*. New York: Random House, 2002.

Russell, Sharman Apt. *Hunger: An Unnatural History*. New York: Basic Books, 2005.

Schell, Jonathan. *The Fate of the Earth*. New York: Avon, 1982.

Schweitzer, Albert. *The Primeval Forest* [1931]. Baltimore: Johns Hopkins University Press, 1998.

Postscript

There are countless ways of doing good in this world and feeling enriched for having done so. You could consider joining the Peace Corps — "the toughest job you'll ever love" — and serving in Africa, for example. But while you're contemplating that extreme step, you might want to give even a small amount to a worthy cause that will help Africa's children. Just $10, for example, to such organizations as Bed Nets for Kids (www.bednetsforkids.org) or Malaria No More (www.malarianomore.org) will provide an at-risk family with a large, long-lasting insecticide-treated bed net to protect against life-threatening, malaria-carrying, nighttime-biting mosquitoes. Every one of us can make a difference and feel richly rewarded in the process.

— Bonnie Lee Black
Taos, New Mexico

Martha Cooper

About the Author

Bonnie Lee Black earned a bachelor of arts degree from Columbia University in New York in 1979 and an MFA in Creative Writing from Antioch University-Los Angeles in 2007. She was a professional writer and editor in New York for twenty years and has been an educator in the U.S. and overseas for over fifteen years.

Black is the author of the memoir *Somewhere Child* (Viking Press, NY, 1981), which was instrumental in the creation of the National Center for Missing and Exploited Children. This second memoir, about her Peace Corps service in Gabon, Central Africa, is the first in a new Peace Corps Writers book imprint. She recently finished writing Patchwork: A Memoir of Mali about her economic development work in Mali, West Africa.

Black's essays have appeared in a number of published anthologies and literary journals, including (most recently) *Under the Sun, Alimentum* and *Persimmon Tree.* She now lives in Taos, New Mexico, and teaches English and Creative Nonfiction Writing at UNM-Taos.

Bike riding along the Couse Pasture in Taos, New Mexico, May 2010

CPSIA information can be obtained at www.ICGtesting.com
Printed in the USA
LVOW011610041211

257771LV00007B/98/P